Visual Alterity

Visual Alterity

Seeing Difference in Cinema

RANDALL HALLE

UNIVERSITY OF
ILLINOIS PRESS
Urbana, Chicago, and Springfield

© 2021 by the Board of Trustees
of the University of Illinois
All rights reserved
1 2 3 4 5 C P 5 4 3 2 1
♾ This book is printed on acid-free paper.

Library of Congress Cataloging-in-Publication Data
Names: Halle, Randall, author.
Title: Visual alterity : seeing difference in cinema / Randall Halle.
Description: Urbana : University of Illinois Press, 2021. | Includes
    bibliographical references and index.
Identifiers: LCCN 2020032136 (print) | LCCN 2020032137 (ebook)
    | ISBN 9780252043703 (cloth) | ISBN 9780252085680
    (paperback) | ISBN 9780252052590 (ebook)
Subjects: LCSH: Visual perception in motion pictures. | Motion
    pictures—Philosophy.
Classification: LCC PN1995.9.V59 H35 2021 (print) | LCC
    PN1995.9.V59 (ebook) | DDC 791.4301—dc23
LC record available at https://lccn.loc.gov/2020032136
LC ebook record available at https://lccn.loc.gov/2020032137

Contents

Acknowledgments   vii

Introduction   1

1   The Image of the Some Thing Other   13

2   Self/Other Image: Hegel   26

3   Phenomenology and Alterity: Seeing Is Always Seeing of Something Else   54

4   Apparatus Theory Now More Than Ever!   66

5   Cine-Cognition: Montage   84

6   Cine-Cognition: Collage, Fragmentation, Integration   98

7   Cine-Cognition: The *Kippbild*, Dis/Ambiguation   113

8   The Apparatus of Difference: Xenophobia/philia   143

9   The Cinematic Face: Interior Recognition, Gay Surface, Queer Multistability   154

10   The Ethics of Visual Alterity: The Face of the Other, the Faceless Other   178

Conclusion   201

Notes   209

Bibliography   221

Index   241

Acknowledgments

Major research for this book was conducted while I was a Fulbright Scholar. I benefited greatly from the generosity of that grant and the time it afforded. As always, the Berlin Program for Advanced German and European Studies, and especially Karin Goihl, have helped make Berlin a place where I am at home to think freely.

Many people have shared ideas, offered reflections, and given much appreciated feedback on various parts of the project along the way. I would especially like to thank Daniela Berghahn, Ljudmila Bilkic, Michael Brynntrup, Francesco Casetti, Paul Cooke, Douglas Crimp, John Davidson, Wolfgang Fuhrmann, Rosalind Galt, David Gramling, Debbie Gould, Thomas Haakenson, Birgit Hein, Aniko Imre, Dina Iordanova, Cilas Kemedjio, Lutz Koepnick, Marius Kuhn, Alice Kuzniar, Venkat Mani, Bjørn Melhus, Barbara Mennel, John Michael, Daniel Morgan, Laura Mulvey, Elizabeth Otto, Katrin Pahl, Brigitte Peucker, Brad Prager, Eric Rentschler, Karl Schoonover, Jörg Schweinitz, Katrin Sieg, David Sofra, Birgit Tautz, Michael Temple, Maria Tortajada, Margrit Tröhler, Katie Trumpener, and Sharon Willis.

The University of Pittsburgh has offered me a great intellectual home, and my colleagues have been a great support and important interlocutors. The programs in German Studies, Film and Media Studies, European Studies, Global Studies, and the Humanities Center have variously offered important venues in which I could benefit from the exchange of ideas. I want to thank Mark Lynn viii · *Acknowledgments*

Anderson, Susan Andrade, Jonathan Arac, Daniel Balderston, Charles Exley, Nancy Condee, Sabine von Dirke, Josh Ellenbogen, Lucy Fischer, Giuseppina Mecchia, Neepa Majumdar, Lina Insana, Marcia Landy, John Lyon, Colin MacCabe, John Markoff, Barbara McCloskey, Clark Muenzer, Volodia Padunov, David Pettersen, Klaus Post, Mina Rajagopalan, and Terry Smith. I am especially grateful to Jedd Hakimi, who generously shared insights into a brave new world of games.

I am grateful to the students in my Visual Alterity, Avant-Garde Film, and Apparatus Theory seminars for the opportunity to develop ideas with them. I especially benefited from the contributions of Emi Finkelstein, Yvonne Franke, Adam Hebert, Paula Kupfer, Daniel Malinowski, Silpa Mukherjee, Meredith North, Ben Ogrodnick, and Nikhil Titus brought to our discussions.

And to my delight, in those conversations Jesse Anderson-Lehman illuminated codec and Steve Sloto introduced YTP.

I always gain insights from Sabine Penack and Rita Bakacs.

I am grateful to Jill R. Hughes for refining the text. It is a privilege to have Danny Nasset as editor. He kept me on track.

Most of all I want to thank Mohammed Bamyeh, with whom I see more and better.

Visual Alterity

Introduction

> We cannot improve the making of our eyes,
> but we can endlessly perfect the camera.
> —Vertov, *Kino-Eye*

An urgency attends to the intersection of visual and alterity studies. The 1990s as a transnational era initiated a reimagining of our communities, a reimagining that took on new dynamics and proportions after 2001. The globalization of capital and the unceasing expansion of the free market, the violent explosions caused by a global network of religious fanatics, the tragic displacements and brutal contact instigated by George W. Bush's perpetual global war on terror, the outbreak of the Great Recession, the escalation of global tensions in the face of global environmental crises, the waves of refugees unleashed by the wars and repressions in the Arab world and the Greater Middle East, a pandemic that sundered global logistics, the xenophobic populism that draws anxious citizens to support demagogues—all of these developments have brought us closer and yet also parceled us into groups even farther apart than geographical distance. All of these developments have intensified what is at stake in the way we imagine our connections to each other and to our others, who we recognize as equal, and who we abject as foreign and threatening.

I have argued extensively elsewhere: if it was print culture that facilitated the imagined community of the era of nationalism, it is visual culture that facilitates the imaginative communities of the transnational era.[1] The narratives of visual culture, their flows and networks, draw us into new connections both global and local. They recreate relations of identity and difference. In this study I add to this observation that our perception of the other, our vision of our world,

2 · *Introduction*

has no "natural" form or "normal" perspective. We always see embodied in a place and from a perspective. We perceive our world not from a position that we have freely chosen but in an environment that is given and in conditions that we have inherited. Moreover, we always perceive through a technology of sight, a *techne* of vision. *Our perception of the other is located not only in a where and when but in a how. And for the last century and a quarter the avant-garde of that how has been called the cinema.*

The study of alterity—that quality or state of being other—presents itself as a central dynamic of contemporary politics, economics, society, and culture. The age of nationalism, the era of essentializing philosophy, and the period of totalizing political systems relied on identity formation. The nation-state in all its forms drew its citizens into totality through the presumed essential unity of the interests of its people. The nation belonged together because of its difference from other nations. Now our communities undergo fundamental transformation and some of the most exciting thinkers of our own post-national, post-structural, post-post-modern moment increasingly vie over the relationship of universalization to totalization, difference to identity, fluid solidarities versus grand conflicting blocks of, for example, clashing civilizations. Lacanian Marxists come to praise the nation and exhort to enclaves while quantitative objectivists praise open borders and free flows of labor. Trans* separates from queer into distinct communities, while Anthropocene climate activists promote worldly interdependence of all species. Whatever form these transformations finally take, it is certain that at the outset of this new era we confront a tension between the recognition of the equality of political subjects and their alterity. Our polities no longer appear as comprised of identical subjects but rather as an amalgam of alterior citizens, who have forgotten how to speak with one another let alone negotiate compromises. Such communal arrangements pose fundamental challenges to notions of political unity and the possibility of democratic consensus. *We have left behind an era of identity and entered into an era of alterity.*

In this era we are made anxious and uncomfortable by difference, by the other, by our perception of the alterior. Yet this book proceeds from the point that *perception is based on perceiving difference.* We could actually say that the phrase "visual alterity" is repetitive, redundant. To see in the world is to see difference, to distinguish, differentiate, discriminate, categorize, individuate. Perception is a discriminating apparatus. The philosophical considerations of alterity have entailed considerations of the emergence of self-consciousness in relation to the other. In 2018 Ohio State University's Wexner Center opened a retrospective of the works of Mickalene Thomas under the title *I Can't See You without Me.* In 1971 Conway Twitty released his country hit "I Can't See Me without You."

In 1964 in his seminars on the Four Fundamental Concepts of Psychoanalysis, Jacques Lacan famously relates the tale of a sardine can: "You see that can? Well, it doesn't see you!" From Lacanian to country and western, from high to popular artists, we understand that perceptions of other and self are inextricable. The investigation of visual alterity describes, then, a certain form of perception out of which the self emerges. This study of visual alterity is not just about seeing difference but about being conscious of *how* one sees difference. We may be anxious to see difference because of dynamics of power and exclusion. To be sure, to see is to discriminate; nevertheless, to see difference is itself not a determination on how we discriminate. Seeing difference and techniques of exclusion are connected but not equivalent. We can see this way or that way. That we see race and gender is not a determination of *how* we see race or gender. To investigate this process of visual discrimination is to move from perception to apperception, conscious perception. We need not fear seeing difference; we need to consider what we make of that difference.

As a study of visual alterity, this project begins phenomenologically by questioning not just how we perceive but how we perceive the other. A phenomenology of visual alterity has extensive ramifications, offering, if not answers, at least insights as response to significant questions. *In a period of changing solidarities, how do we recognize new differences? How do we go beyond the distinctions that determine our ways of knowing, and seeing, in order to arrive at new ways of knowing, new ways of seeing? How do we come to see difference differently?*

Film and Philosophy/Film Philosophy

Film, the moving image, or cinema is a central and privileged place of investigation in this study. The point of this study, however, is not to have a set of films that illustrate the predetermined points of visual alterity per se but to proceed from the understanding that relationships of difference structure all acts of signification, and hence we can investigate any object in this regard with a certain openness and consider in our perception what it reveals to us about the very act of perception itself.

Since the 1990s in particular, the interrelationship of film and philosophy as a direction in film studies has enjoyed a growth of research. Various critics have explored untapped philosophical directions as alternatives to Marxist and feminist film theory. Rather than develop grand theory, film *and* philosophy has been undertaken as a conjugational project. The work has developed primarily through the question, What can philosophy help us reveal about the act of viewing a film? Film phenomenology, for instance, draws on the theoretical method of phenomenology. While Edmund Husserl, Martin Heidegger, Maurice Merleau-Ponty, or Emmanuel Levinas may not have considered film specifically or extensively, they did develop theoretical methods that allow us to develop our appreciation for the knowledge film provides. Yet knowledge and film really are not as stable a difference as proposed by phenomenologists; the love of wisdom, *phila sophia*, and the questions of perception were inextricable for the metaphysicians. Philosophy is a set of principles, a methodology, or concepts, as Gilles Deleuze and Félix Guattari suggested, drawn from perception.[2] Without seeking to belabor the point, we can understand the importance of the term "theory" for the project of film and philosophy if we regard more closely its etymology.

Theory, before it took on its more current meaning as a set of principles or a methodology in the sciences and arts, was much more directly related to visuality. It still contains a denotation of conception or mental scheme. Theory derives from Greek and Latin *theoria*, where the notion of speculation included contemplation and a "looking at things." The Greek verb *theorein*, from which *theoria* stems, meant to consider, speculate, or look at and, broken down further into the parts *thea*, a view, and *horan*, to see. To theorize thus stems from an act of seeing, looking, observing, or even spectating. In Greek *thea* is a view, a seat at the theater, and *theoros* is the spectator or the one who questions the oracle. Aristotelian observation of the material world and Platonic contemplation of the ideal world had a common spectatorial connection.

It is perhaps banal to observe that the Greeks did not have access to film; however, the relationship of philosophy to the Greek stage is well known.[3] I recall this point to underscore the connection between knowledge and ways of seeing. Theory, which provides knowledge, arises from a particular historical perspective determined by the technological possibilities of seeing. Seeing and knowing are not two separate activities. The way we know is determined by the way we see. Friedrich Nietzsche's study of the birth of tragedy revealed the connection between philosophy and the spectator's position in the amphitheater. Following Nietzsche, we understand that the specific geometry of spectating defined by a theater was not just any *thea horan*; it was the site of a birth of a new way of knowing. It was not a matter of theater and philosophy but theater *as* philosophy.

From antiquity to the nineteenth century, the space of theater staged each current episteme. The stage was not a separate world of representations; the theater represented the way we stage our worlds. But then something happened to theater, and we must appreciate that with the advent of film our way of knowing changed fundamentally. Film as invitation to an act of viewing, cinema as a site of the sustained act of spectating, is not simply a special case of human activity, play, or entertainment that can be approached philosophically. Rather, film as an outgrowth of modern industrial production, as the site of ongoing transformations deriving from our technological developments, instantiates modern epistemology. *Cinema is not the site of a particular way of knowing; it is a central and privileged site in which the way of knowing comes most clearly into appearance.*

Dziga Vertov based his manifesto celebration of *Kino-Pravda* in an understanding that *kino*, cinema, offered a whole new truth to humanity.[4] Cinema extended the human eye, making it possible that humans could look at things never before seen. It was not simply that we would be able to see a flower blossom, a bullet shatter a glass window, or any of the other "experiments" recorded by educational documentarists for classroom purposes. Vertov's celebration of the cinematic eye derives from something more fundamental and revolutionary. Taking on a new view, a new *thea*, does not just facilitate; it instantiates new *theorein*. You are what you see, or perhaps better stated, how you see is how you know. Your knowledge is defined by your ways of seeing, and seeing differently means to know differently. It is not just a matter of film *and* philosophy; rather film *is* philosophy, film philosophy.

Cinema and Cognition/Cine-Cognition

But Vertov's notion of *Kino-Eye* was not only a matter of film philosophy. It was based on an idea that the new techniques of cinema could reveal the world anew. Vertov, Sergei Eisenstein, and the avant-garde in general understood that revolutions in the means of cinematic production were joined to the revolution of minds. Vertov's Kino-Pravda, cinema truth, presumed that moving-image recording technologies would change the way we think and how we transform our cognitive capacities. Vertov was not alone. It was a revolutionary moment in which the way early film philosophers celebrated the camera would be as revealing a plenitude to us, a world of truth beyond what the eye could see, the truth of the world through an eye extended by its imaging technologies. Of course, that is not what happened. Instead we had to learn that cinema and Vertov's own Kino-Pravda newsreels made visible to us some aspects of the world while making others invisible. We had to learn that our visual technology does not reveal plenitude of sight; it provides a frame of seeing. The camera is a technology, a framing device, not a mechanism of plenitude. Time and time again we have had the promise of a visual plenitude. But the sensible is always "distributed" as Jacques Rancière asserts. Every era, epoch, and episteme has its way of seeing, its distribution of what can be seen, and what can be seen as self and alterior.

6 · *Introduction*

Most recently the internet and smartphones have offered that promise broadly and with fanfare. On the other hand, surveillance technology and artificial intelligence have reactivated our dreams of plenitude as nightmares. But they are not. Neither smartphone nor surveillance apparatus is a plenitude. They do not see all, they do not know everything, they know a lot of things in a particular way, in a particular frame, certainly in an often dangerous frame of inhumane security and authoritarian anxiety. But it is not everything. It is a frame, a way of seeing, a way of differentiating and only that.

Neuro and cognitive scientists look to the images of functional magnetic resonance imaging (fMRI) or the patterns produced by eye-tracking devices with an expectation that they will find there plenitude, that they will reveal the hidden mysteries of the brain, but they only produce images that do not reproduce the brain. And they are certainly not our mind. Our ways of seeing may be part of technologies of discrimination, but they also are primed to see differently, to see difference differently. If there is any experience of plenitude, it is not in a single moment of omniscience but in the experience of the mind as an apparatus of differentiation, a destabilizing, deterritorializing, dis-integrating antidote to the technologies of discrimination that would stabilize and territorialize our perceptions.

We repeatedly have to learn that technology in all instances is a framework for knowledge, a techne; it creates an enframement by which we know some things but not all things. Technology does not give us to know everything; it sets us to knowing in a particular way. The images produced by our technologies call forth new ways of seeing; they require reading practices that postulate correlations to the world. Cinema, as a techne of knowing, determined knowing itself. Nevertheless, precisely because Kino-Pravda was not all knowledge, it points to a defining moment in cognition. Cinema and cognition do not produce just any type of knowledge; cinema, the camera, presented a new way of knowing the world that emerged in a historic moment and defined our cognitive processes anew. There is not a distinction of cinema and cognition but rather cine-cognition.

Cine-cognition: before Vertov spoke of cine-truth, Hugo Münsterberg spoke of "photoknowledge." It was actually Münsterberg who first turned our attention to the relation of cognition and the moving image, asking not just how we see but how we know what we see: "The means by which the moving picture impress us and appeal to us. . . . What psychological factors are involved when we watch the happenings on the screen?"[5] In his work *The Photoplay*, Münsterberg considered depth and motion, attention, memory and imagination, and emotions, all aspects, as Andreas Baranowski and Heiko Hecht argue, foundational to contemporary cognitive investigations of film.[6] The realism debates of the 1920s and '30s, Walter Benjamin's considerations of technology and reproduction, these works recognized the ability of the image to have an impact on the consciousness of the viewer. Yet after Münsterberg few critics undertook investigations of cinema and cognition with specific attention to the actual cognitive processes of the spectator. Psychoanalysis and behaviorism dominated discussions of consciousness and perception with different concerns.

Importantly, Béla Balázs and Rudolf Arnheim did work with Gestalt psychology. Arnheim in particular explored *Visual Thinking*, taking the insights of Gestalt to considerations of aesthetics.[7] That major project appeared in 1968, right in the midst of the cognitive revolution. In 1967 Ulric Neisser had published *Cognitive Psychology*, offering an antidote to behaviorism.[8] Rather than treat mental processes as unobservable responses to exterior stimuli, cognitive psychology sought to establish models focused on the detection of perception, attention, memory, and emotions. Breaking with behaviorism, it was not the input so much as the mechanisms of processing, storing, and recalling that input that came under consideration. A number of scholars praise David Bordwell's 1985 classic *Narration in the Fiction Film* as the first major return of cognitive studies to the medium of film.[9] Rightly so, as that book did move film studies away from a code-based analysis: semiotic, psychoanalytic, or Marxian. And it refocused our attention on "how does cinematic narration work? What does the spectator do in comprehending a narrative film? What features and structures solicit narrative comprehension?"[10] He set out to treat film viewing as a "dynamic, perceptual-cognitive process."[11] The book was, of course, not a project of clinical psychology. It focused on the formal and stylistic in films. It did not actually break with dominant modes of semiotic and formalist analysis. It even relied on national style distinctions. Yet it placed those in relation to the *story-comprehending cognitive activities of the film viewers*. And it did not give up on the aesthetics of the image—the particulars of the input, as it were—to focus singularly on the cognitive mechanism. *Narration in the Fiction Film* gestured toward a holistic approach of input *and* process, critical film history *and* mechanisms of cognition. Much work has been done on cognitive film theory since then, and much can be said about it, and I will return to do so. But in this introduction I want to underscore that for quite a while cognitive film theory forgot this holism modeled in *Narration*.

Important at this historic juncture is that cognitive research has created a new level of visual scholarship. We have moved more from *technologies of seeing* to *technologies of sight*: telescopes and microscopes versus magnetic resonance imaging and positron-emission tomography scanning. We have moved from

8 · *Introduction*

seeing with the eye to reading the image. And cognitive and neuroscientific research gives us increasingly to see how we see; it represents to us our own mechanisms of sight. This techne might be described as offering us a form of "metavision." As metathinking is the "thinking about thought," we are now in a position of "seeing sight." This study of visual alterity thus also takes up this trajectory from photoknowledge, through visual thinking, into the explorations of visual intelligence and perceptual systems of the cognitive and neuroscientific turns.[12] Whenever cognitive and neuroscientific approaches suggest that there is a divide between our input and our process, our brains and our technologies, between our minds and our technes, however, I approach such claims critically, even skeptically. When Jeffrey Zacks suggests that "our brains didn't evolve to watch movies. Movies evolved to take advantage of the brains we have," he counterproductively returns us to a behaviorist model of stimuli impacting a hardwired but passive perceptual system.[13] Our brains may not have evolved to watch movies, but our minds have evolved because of cinema. Our moving images, our cinemas, our screens have transformed our cognitive capacities.[14] Our cognitive capacities may not have evolved in the sense of improved, but they have changed.

Thus, as with film and theory, it is not cinema and cognition; rather, film is cognition: cine-cognition. Cine-cognition is a form of cognition that arose at a particular time in a particular form. It is not a special form of cognition, nor is it inevitable, nor is it permanent. Cine-cognition is one way of knowing, one way of organizing our perceptual systems; it may be the dominant mode currently, but it is not a permanent, stable, singular way. And indeed cine-cognition in 2025 will not be the same as it was in 1895. Our brains transform as do our technologies; they are not distinct. Our science fiction genres may show us to be afraid that we will become objects of our own technologies. But our technologies are not alterior to our subjects; rather, it is in our techne that our subjects arise. As a work of metavision, this project on visual alterity is interested in our visual intelligence—that capacity to create what we see, to see ourselves and see those selves in our world, in a particular way through a particular means, a particular techne.

Stereo/Alter Knowledge

We must understand alterity as not simply synonymous with simple difference or otherness, nor with typing or racism—terms to which it is too commonly reduced. While I will not advocate for discrimination or stereotyping, those terms do cover phenomenon and experiences that go beyond their popular negative usage. Consider that stereotype arose first in printing as a method of printing from a plate cast from a mold based on a preformed typeset, a "stereo-type." These printing plates were also sometimes called "clichés." Such methods allowed for a faster, more durable printing of the same image. Stereotype is a reproduction of the same, a repetition. In turn, though, each repetition iterates a difference. No two prints are ever the same; however, the stereotype makes such difference appear *solid*. The word "stereo" derives from the Greek *stereós*, meaning solid. Stereo in recording refers to the practice of using two or more mikes so as to develop a sound of the same. It brings the two differences together to make them solidly the same. A stereoscope, for its part, makes two slightly different images appear the same in a different condition: stereoscope, a sameness in 3D. In the stereotype we find a dynamic of sameness and difference.

The term "alterity" derives from Latin as a designation of the instance when two of something appear together. In a sentence both are *aliud*, or *alius alium*, meaning "one of the other," or *alter alterum*, meaning "and the like." A list of alterior objects might include apples, oranges, bananas, grapes, *alter alterum* (and the like). If the stereo is a reproduction that appears the same, the alter here is a unit in a relationship, simultaneously different and mimetic.

Georg Wilhelm Friedrich Hegel's considerations of alterity, this state or quality of being other, began from this point of the interrelated two and then moved the term to the center of definitions of modern subjectivity. It is from Hegel that much of the contemporary understanding of alterity as a subject construction derives. To remind us, though: the Hegelian alterior draws on the Latin understanding of "the two," so the alterior is not an incommensurable existence that stands outside of the subject. It is not one subject excluding or standing in power over another, a subject objectifying or subjugating another subject. Nor is it a matter of an absolute and essential difference; rather, Hegel asserts that without the other, there can be no self. The alterior is not separate from but a part of self-consciousness. Conscious being becomes self-conscious in alterity. The self arises first in a relationship of alterity, through recognition of the other. Self-consciousness arises in perception of the other. For the self to be, the other must appear. And I can only recognize its selfhood in the limits it experiences through a You. Identity requires alterity. It is possible, however, to distinguish a distinctiveness of the dynamics of alterity and identity. Both entail unification; yet identity is a unification of sameness, whereas alterity is one of difference. We can symbolize such dynamics as A = A versus (A ≠ B). Of course, identity as a matter of consciousness is never a matter of the exact same (see the consideration of repetition above): "A rose is a rose is a rose." Rather, identity is a dynamic of repetition of the similar; hence one might better symbolize it as A = A', A", A''' and thereby acknowledge that identity is also a relationship of difference. One can also acknowledge that both are a matter of consciousness, especially of recognition. Self-consciousness, subjectivity, identity—these are not stabilities or integrated singularities but a dynamic of sameness and difference.

We will return to Hegel, but for now I want to introduce a proposition that Hegel did not consider. In addition to the alterity of recognition, there are, we can posit, other forms: an intuitive and a radical alterity. To recognize a difference suggests existing contact and the ability to apprehend the other. There is, however, a difference beyond the immediate relationship of two. There is a relationship of difference beyond immediate recognition that can nevertheless be intuited. This difference exceeds the relationship of the two but has not (yet) appeared to the subject: *intuitive alterity*. Our fantasy is stimulated by old maps on which the territories outside the "known" world were marked with the images of fantastical creatures. What was there was not known, yet that there was something there and that the something compelled the imagination points to the activity of alterity. Differentiation reaches actively into the world, beyond what is known immediately, and anticipates a discovery of difference. The subject exists in an expanded field of differentiation of which it is not (yet) aware. Yet the subject appears prepared to come into awareness. We may also, however, describe a certain alterity that is radical: *radical alterity*, unknown to us, unknowable to us. Higgs boson particles, black holes, gamma rays, electrons, infrared, and physics now provide us with a list of aspects of reality that were once outside thought. This list, however, also suggests a constant reaching out on the horizons of knowledge. We can consider a radical alterity a difference beyond recognition, beyond unification, beyond intuition. Radical alterity presents a certain paradox that arises in this field: such otherness that is so different that it does not appear, how can we can recognize it? I can humbly acknowledge that I know I do not know everything, but there is a place of possibility that goes beyond what I am able even to intuit. It would seem that we recognize in the alterior only an other we already know. Radical alterity designates unknown as yet not even other beyond the horizon of our sight—yet somehow always anticipated. The radical alterior may be feared and it may be welcomed; it depends on us. At least that is what our science fiction genre tells us about ourselves and how our uncanny experiences make us feel.

Considering that visual alterity is a large expanse, I focus this work on the appearance of alterity, how the other for the sake of the self appears—not radical but the alterity that brings recognition, calls for response, drives action. From Hegel to Levinas and Julia Kristeva and beyond, alterity has been understood as a condition of subjectivity, the other as the constitution of the self.[15] However, I am more concerned with the less explored question of how alterity compels "reading," an analysis of the world in the differentiations of signification.[16] I will just state here at the start that, for film, visual alterity compels narrative. It determines the relationship between visibility and invisibility within and outside the frame. It establishes historical logics of difference that infuse a film. And, connectedly, it establishes the dialogic continuum between the typical and the stereotypical, which in turn makes it possible for our eyes to "read" a film.

In antiquity the space of theater, as techne, staged its contemporary episteme. I would suggest that in the Renaissance, theater shared the staging of knowledge with architecture and painting. Printing and photography provided new ways of knowing. And then with the advent of film, our way of knowing changed again fundamentally. Film as an invitation to an act of viewing, cinema as a site of the sustained act of spectating, is not simply a special case of human activity, play, or entertainment that can be approached philosophically. Instead, film as an outgrowth of modern industrial production, as the site of ongoing transformations deriving from our technological developments, instantiates modern epistemology. Cinema is not the site of a particular way of knowing; it is a central and privileged site in which the way of knowing comes most clearly into appearance.

Eleven Principles

Out of this discussion, then, I would like to introduce eleven principles that define this study and are operative in the chapters that follow.

1. *There is no seeing in itself. Seeing is always seeing of something.*
2. *Seeing of something is always seeing from a particular perspective in place and time.*
3. *Seeing is dynamic.* Given time, seeing from the same place does not mean that the seen in our perspective becomes static. To hold something in sight does not fix the seen; rather, it engages an unfolding process of recognition.
4. *Perception actively reaches out in time and across space.* The hand reaches out into the world and draws it into our awareness as touch. Sight, like the apparatus of the hand, is that capacity that reaches out into the world well beyond the reach of our physical body.
5. *Seeing is a reaching out into the world that precedes consciousness.* It can be considered as a matter of what Arthur Schopenhauer, Nietzsche, or Heidegger called "will," Sigmund Freud called "drives," or Silvan Tomkins and Mikkel Borch-Jacobsen called "affect."

12 · *Introduction*

6. *Seeing communicates.* While there is certainly a phenomenal world that precedes seeing, we should not think so much in terms of seer and seen. Seeing communicates, constituting mutually seer and seen.

7. *There is no natural seeing that is distinct from technology.* Theaters, stages, paintings, icons, mirrors, glasses, blinders, filters, microscopes, inks and paints, telescopes, windows and curtains, climbing a tree, squinting, shading, television, and moving-image recordings are all ways in which the perspective of seeing is shifted, changed, transformed, extended, enframed, limited, and enhanced. The devices and apparatuses of human innovation are not counter to a "natural seeing"; they are fundamental to the perspective of sight in any particular place and time.

8. *Seeing is always seeing through a particular apparatus.* Sight is the entire apparatus that allows for the seeing of the world. The apparatus of sight is different in every given moment. The sight of the ancient Egyptians and Classical Greeks took place in an apparatus distinct from that of the great astrologers of the subcontinent and the Renaissance Florentines. The sight of that part of the world with access to the web is different from that part of the world without access.

9. *Certain technologies define the apparatus of sight in given eras.* For over one hundred years, cinema and the moving image have been the avant-garde technology of sight.

10. *The apparatus of sight must be understood as a differentiating apparatus capable of ever increasing distinction.* Contemporary psychology suggests that recognition—that process whereby seeing becomes conscious—is based on the ability to see difference. This raises the question, How does the capacity of sight recognize differences that are not already known?

11. We can refer to this unfolding dynamic process of preconscious differentiation as *visual alterity.*

CHAPTER 1

The Image of the Some Thing Other

ein „Ding" ist eine Summe seiner Wirkungen,
synthetisch gebunden durch einen Begriff, Bild.
A "thing" is the sum of its effects, synthetically
united by a concept, an image.

—Nietzsche, *The Will to Power*

Seeing Is Always Seeing of Some Thing

In this chapter I take up the alterity of the image. I do so by rejecting a common approach in phenomenological and cognitive approaches to the (moving) image that assumes a natural seeing, a simple reality separate from the contrived image, a material reality distinct from artifice.

There is no seeing in itself. Seeing is always seeing of something. This something is an other, an alterior. The face in the mirror is other as much as the face across the table, as much as the face in the film or painting. Seeing my own hand is as much seeing something other as is seeing your hand as some other thing. The world appears to us as image; the appearance of the world is image.

In the history of philosophy and psychology, seeing the image has generally been treated as a special instance of seeing, in opposition to a natural sight, reality, or a non-imagistic world. Renaissance artists, for instance, distinguished between a *prospettiva naturalis* and a *prospettiva artificiale*, yet they debated about how to make the artificial image appear more like that which the eye saw naturally. They aspired to the famous tromp l'oeil, which in effect sublated the difference between a *prospettiva naturalis* and a *prospettiva artificiale*. Nevertheless, this distinction holds through the advent of modern phenomenology. In his various treatments, Maurice Merleau-Ponty, the central twentieth-century philosopher of the phenomenology of perception, treats the image as distinct from an experience of natural viewing. The image is approached as having its own categories. The image is part of art; it is artful, artificial, *artificiale*. The image, for Merleau-Ponty, remains an appearance of a distinct artificial—that is, aesthetic—regime. For its part, Marxism extended this approach to the image, insisting on a material reality behind the imagistic world, "real reality" and an "advertised non-reality," a distinction of the real and the ideological.[1] This approach is a mistake.

There is no seeing in itself. Seeing is always seeing of something. The world appears to us as image, the appearance of the world is image. This proposition could be repeated for all sense perception. The "thing" of perception arises in the perceiving—but how? Immanuel Kant's understanding of categories as an aspect of appearance located them as properties of the mind itself. With that he showed how consciousness allows us to be aware of the existence of things outside ourselves and shifted a long history of approaches to *ratio*, reason (*Verstand*), the mechanism of perception that treated the mind as receptive neutral, universal, and not formative. This shift meant that we must take into account the formative capacity of our perceptual system. However, even as subsequent investigations of perception recognized an a priori formative quality of the mind, the categories were treated as static—eternal, always there. They limited the perceptive capacity to the physical world, cutting off access to the fullness of the metaphysical. In this static quality a passivity returned to the understanding of the mind. Modern psychological investigations, however, started to recognize a greater formative capacity and began to consider perception as not passive, receptive, or a camera obscura projection into the brain. Instead they began to explore the active mechanisms, perception as arising out of a Gestalt quality of the mind. They recognized the mind as reducing cognitive dissonance through the association of different elements into a sum that is itself different from the constitutive parts. The Gestalt quality of the mind recognizes a unity that differs from the phenomena themselves.[2] Questioning how this unifying capacity of perception functioned, emergent neuroscience incited "imagery debates" with cognitive psychologists in the 1970s.[3] Reaching into the 1990s, researchers considered heatedly the "categories" of perception: does the brain function simply according to language-based deep structures or if there is brain-based mental imagery? In such approaches a more plastic formative approach to the brain dominates over passive, static, or hardwired understandings of perception.[4]

To be clear, I am not advocating a solipsistic, dualistic, or radical cognitivist approach that focuses singularly on the mind. The brain is not the cause of perception or origin of "reality." And clearly I am opposing a radical materialism. This study proceeds from the position that the brain has an active formative role in relation to sensory input from the phenomenal world. We perceive and we perceive the alterior, the some-thing-other, not simply because the phenomenal world appears in categories of space and time; the phenomenal world arises through processing in the perceptual systems of the brain. Certainly there is some thing materially "out there," but the appearance of a world in consciousness, the ability to recognize recognition, is not located solely in the object. Not something projecting an impression on a spectator but in the activity of perception some thing arises that is something other than the phenomena of the material world or the spectator. Seeing creates the world.

With visual alterity, though, I am not pursuing the unity of Gestalt. I am more interested in chains of signification and the regimes or apparatuses in which the linkages of the chains are formed. Inherent to the perception of light, sound, smells, or other matters of sense perception are translations into other systems of signification: across light/aural/olfactory waves, to vibrations on receptors, and chemical processes, through synaptic networks and so on. Each translation actively transports one form of input into the information of the next system. These perceptive translations are not total or complete. Perception arises as much through the haze of blind spots and occlusions as it does through glasses and speakers, salts and oils. But the apparatus that brought cave paintings into signification are radically different from those that brought an Edwin S. Porter moving picture to move.

Nietzsche taught us to consider chains of signification but to be skeptical of arguments based on sequences of cause and effect. Following him, Jacques Derrida taught us that meaning is always deferred through endless chains of differing signifiers. He also taught us to be skeptical of arguments based on origins. The thing of appearance, the alterior that appears, is neither caused by the face of the other nor does it have its origins in our brains. The appearance of a world, the categories of recognition, are not located solely in the mental image. Indeed consciousness, the brain, the mind, the visual intelligence that allows for recognition, and so forth exist not in themselves but arise along with the object of perception in dynamic chains of signification within an elaborate apparatus of perception. Our technologies (of seeing) are as much a part of that apparatus as are our eyes, ears, sense organs, objects and hallucinations, and light sources.[5] Seeing is dynamic. Visual alterity is a dynamic—but what kind?

Reality and Image: Jacques Rancière

ALTERITY AND IMAGENESS

In *Le destin des images* (*The Future of the Image*), Rancière began his reflections precisely with a consideration of the alterity of images.[6] Rancière is attending in this project to the image in the film—not the film image as such but the moments in film where a certain quality of image is perceived, and "imageness," which differs from the moving image, a sense of composition that sets it apart. In order to pursue this line of analysis, he suggested that the "images refer to nothing else" not to insist on a radical disconnection from the "realism" of the recorded image but in order to make the leap to the proposition that "alterity enters into the very composition of the images."[7] What makes this "imageness" appear as different or offset in an image? Rancière seeks to explain imageness as a quality in the language of film itself, those moments when the reality of the diegetic film world gives way to a sense of image, a tableau, a photogenic look. Although he focuses his analysis on the work of film, he does suggest somewhat in passing that alterity goes beyond the image and enters into the relationship we have with the image itself. This step is minor but necessary and of great importance, because ultimately the alterity of the image lies in a relation of the image to the spectator. Imageness, or the perception of a distinct quality of image in a film, has to be an operation of the spectator and not a quality of the film as such. The perception of imageness relies on the viewer's capacity to differentiate this image in the film from that, this image in the film as part of a genre of representing reality as opposed to that image that belongs to a different genre of animating images. Thus Rancière is not speaking of the image as simply a simple photograph, an icon, or a single shot but as a "whole regime of 'imageness.'"[8] Images are much more than shots; they are "operations that couple and uncouple the visible and its signification or speech and its effect, which create and frustrate expectations."[9]

I am happy to follow Rancière in his discussion to this point. Alterity, if it is a key act of perception, the perceiving and organizing of difference as fundamental to perception, must occur in an interaction of perceiver and perceived positioned somewhere and somehow in a relation. This positioning in a relation we can call a "regime"; the mechanisms of positioning we can call an "apparatus." It is fine. Rancière, however, runs into problems when he seeks to distinguish sharply the cinematic image and a "simple reality." He does so to lend a complexity to the cinematic image that is not part of what he sets off then as "simple reality": "The image is never a simple reality [*réalité simple*]. Cinematic images are primarily operations, relations between the sayable and the visible, ways of playing with the before and the after, the cause and effect."[10] He makes this distinction clearly to acknowledge something of the produced quality of the cinematic image, the artistic nature of the art image. He wants to distinguish the images of art as "operations that produce a discrepancy, a dissemblance."[11] In other words, he wants to maintain something of a purposiveness to the production of images that is distinctive from a "real" world, a world "innocent" of image. He wants to

The Image of the Some Thing Other • 17

consider the artfulness of the image as a matter of discrepancy or dissemblance. Rancière is interested, as elsewhere, in the aesthetic regime and the distribution of the sensible (*le partage du sensible*).[12] This is key to his distinction of aesthetics and politics, and in insisting on this distinction of simple reality from "operations that produce a discrepancy, a dissemblance," he hopes to open up space for political action. The insistence on a distinction of simple reality and aesthetic, cinematic image approaches the position of Shklovskian or Brechtian defamiliarization—the image is that which takes us out of the everyday world: the *simple* reality. Defamiliarized from reality, the spectator is better positioned to intervene in the everyday. Beyond Viktor Shklovsky and Bertolt Brecht, this distinction derives from a legacy that we could perhaps trace back to the Greeks but certainly to the line of analysis introduced above leading from the Renaissance distinction of *prospettiva naturalis* from *prospettiva artificiale* to the work of Edmund Husserl and Merleau-Ponty. Thus, although the distinction of simple reality and cinema may seem like a small point in Rancière's text, this allusion to simple reality is a distinction that is the foundation for the greater elaborate analysis. And if Derrida taught us anything, it was to attend to the seemingly minor distinctions that prove essential. It is an essential error.

What would simple reality consist of? "The walls of my study," Husserl might have suggested as he performed a reduction on the simple pen and paper at his desk to find their essence.[13] But if the Renaissance painter of skill could paint a wall to appear as a wall of his study, what is this distinction? And we can consider further which homes have a study and how those studies are outfitted. Does the study not signify class, educational status, specific principles of erudition, and even, typically, masculinity? If the white walls and blank pages of the study represent a place of simple reality, how much simple reality changes when we move from Dong Qichang's Ming dynasty study in Huating to Thomas Mann's postwar villa in Zurich? Okay, to find simple reality would we go outside into someplace more neutral—the streetscape around our homes? Is that streetscape not formed by a regime of planning and choices that require reading and comprehension? Is not the built environment primarily operations, relations between the sayable and the visible, ways of playing with the before and the after, the cause and effect? So do we go to nature, the woods, Heidegger's *Schwarzwald*, which turns out to be a landscape tended by foresters and loggers for centuries? So do we go further to search for simple reality in the forest primeval? Do I, an urban dweller, finally confront a simplistic reality by traveling to Brazil or Indonesia? Some tourists may travel to find the primitive and refresh their souls, but a walk in those woods is likely to require a new schooling of my perception. And those woods are simply disappearing as I write. Perhaps simple reality is, after all, to be found in a monochromatic square of Ad Reinhardt.

18 • CHAPTER 1

If we distinguish simple reality from a complex discrepant and dissembling image, we do so by focusing solely on the image as object, which is what ensues. As such, the image becomes an essence, and the discussion that Rancière unfolds does little to account for the condition of production nor for the condition of the spectator. He focuses on the image and the appearance of a quality of imageness in the images of filmmakers like Luc Bresson. In doing so, he actively excludes the difference in the way the images appear: in the cinema, on a DVD on our television, or as a video projection.[14] The condition of reception and its condition of the spectator are set aside in his argument. He thus reduces the actual potential of understanding the whole regime of imageness, the full apparatus that brings image and spectator together.

REALITY IS NEVER SIMPLE

If we begin from a proposition of visual alterity, that perception relies on differentiating difference and assembling some thing other out of the phenomena, then we might ask instead: the image that creates a dissemblance, how does a spectator approach it differently from a "simple reality"? It is certainly the same set of eyes and ears that sits in front of the screen as those that sit in the car, or move down the street, through the forest, or pass over the pages of a Kindle. We could anticipate a response that the dissemblance itself arises in the gap that the moving image produces between itself and the simple reality, indeed what Rancière calls "hyper-resemblance."[15] From the Renaissance debates about *prospettiva artificiale* to Gotthold Ephraim Lessing's *Laokoon* and beyond, the aesthetic counter to a mimetic representation of nature was the purposive formative hand of the artist. Zeuxis's images of grapes were so real that they would whet the appetite of the observer, yet the aesthetic contest was won by Parrhasius's curtains because they produced a special condition of viewing. These aesthetic paradigms always focused on the artistry of the artist to dupe the spectator into seeing grapes or seeing a curtain, seeing a tromp l'oeil that opens a vision of heaven. But what if we focus on the spectator as critic? Ultimately Parrhasius wins because the viewer sees something new in the image, something new in the potential of the image. The viewer recognizes the artist's work and the attempt to convey more than the grape. The imageness of the image comes into appearance. We might counter, then, the suggestion in Rancière's distinction: the difference is not in the image separate from simple reality. Rather, the spectator perceives the filmic image differently; there is a different quality of perception vis-à-vis images than vis-à-vis simple reality.

It might have been more in line with other parts of Rancière's oeuvre if he had written that the image is never simply material. Reality is never simple. Neuroscience has shown us, however, that our cognitive systems seek to simplify

The Image of the Some Thing Other • 19

the mass of data inundating the brain. Perceptive mechanisms like "chunking" (the bundling of input), "priming" (anticipation based on previous experience), "experience recognition" (key to priming), "situational awareness" (environmental scanning), and so on facilitate navigation of complex situations through a reduction of input and response time.[16] At the same time, attentiveness is also a human capacity that restores complexity to input.[17] I will take up the work of cognitive and neuroscience in more detail later, but I draw quickly on it now to underscore that we need to attend more directly to the capacity of the brain and the work of the mind as active forces in the positioning of the subject to interact with the world. I am not interested in rejecting the capacity of art in a gallery to do something different from a commodity in a shop; a photo's location, whether on a museum's gallery wall or on the shelf in its shop, has a major impact on how we interact with that object, regardless of the composition of differences in its frame. The condition of sitting in the darkened cinema can induce a form of attentiveness that would be dangerous while crossing a busy street. However, the same cinema can overwhelm the senses with blockbuster superhero sensory effects. These differences are inherent not to image but to the conditions of perception and the disposition of the spectators in them.

It would be odd to suggest that the aesthetic regime exists to develop a practice of perception singularly limited to the image or the moment of art. Moreover, that defamiliarization is only a property of the art object, performance, or experience. The cinematic or aesthetic regimes may invite a defamiliarized viewing, but the principle of phenomenological reduction advocated by Husserl, like practices of mindfulness currently *en vogue*, show that anyone at any given time in any given situation has the capacity to view intently, consciously, with focus, thus instilling a condition of defamiliarization. Rather, the point of *ostranenie* or *Verfremdung* was precisely to underscore how the work of art has a general effect on the actions of the spectator. After defamiliarization, the point was, we see "simple reality" anew; we could say that rather than a simple reality, we see a complex reality or, better, reality complexly. And in its long history, a great part of (Western) art has been this production of new ways of seeing along with spectators who see anew differently.

THE RADICAL IMAGE AND THE RADICALISM OF REALITY

Rancière is thus not radical enough. There is no appearance separate from dissemblance. When he distinguishes the "unfolding of inscriptions carried by bodies" from "the interruptive function of their naked non-signifying presence," he suggests a reality behind appearance, an invisible world behind the visible.[18] There is no distinction here; bodies are always inscribed, and to perceive them is to be interrupted by their difference. There is not a naked truth underneath the tattoo on the hipster body. Rancière's text echoes the distinction of ideology from material interest, fake news from real news, a distinction that presumes there is a neutral stream of information that bears truth versus the lies of superstructural information: propaganda. Better for us to consider all we perceive as part of some regime of representation and our material world as inseparable from our ideational. What people know is not based on real or fake, truth versus propaganda. During the Cold War, people knew that state media was a vehicle of propaganda, but the citizens read and listened anyway, with a carefully tuned sense of how to find information between the lines. At the same time, in the media of liberal democratic or fascist populist states, people can also consume the reports of the media as if it does not require a critical reading practice.

The analysis of visual alterity here suggests, by contrast, that there is no naked non-signifying presence; rather, to be present is already to signify in complex relations that precede the individual and that "unfold," change, and transform through and by their own activity. Visual alterity unfolds dynamically, it arises relationally, it narrates. We are better political subjects not by seeking the truth but by recognizing that all information is part of a chain of manipulation. There is not a radical image that reveals truth so that we know how to act in reality. The Gestalt of perception is more and other than the input. The image is not a matter of simple reality. There is not a radical image that reveals truth; the radicalism of reality is in the relation we take to the appearance of our world. It is not a matter of materiality, material reality, mater-reality. It is a matter of alterity, the distinction and differentiations of the perceiving subject. Alterity is the composition of the images, the differences of various signifiers, and the condition of appearance. Alterity is the necessary negotiation of differing positions in the world, a vis-à-vis the appearances of the world. This perception arises in relation to the conditions of the environment, "coupling and uncoupling" the visible, reducing and increasing input, relying on and rejecting expectations, distinguishing and differentiating. The subject moves in the regimes of imageness that organize the world—material and immaterial. Perception creates the world and we perceive the world variously. To perceive differently is to change it.

Technology and Image

THE NEW SEEING

It is not just Rancière who falls into this error of analysis. It is a common mistake to distinguish what we see in the cinema from what we see with our "naked eyes." I know, though, from my own experience that this is not the case. My perception of reality outside the cinema has been on many occasions altered by the images of cinema permanently. When I was a student, I witnessed the sublime blue glow around the neon lights in Wim Wenders's *Paris, Texas* (1984). Since then I know that I have never seen neon light the same way again. The "filling stations" that were a ritual of everyday movement in my youth became something oddly beautiful. The irritating buzz of the neon became an aesthetic experience. What was once utilitarian in nature, the lighting of the station's protective canopy, became something else—not because Wenders filmed my particular filling station but because the image of filling stations I saw in *Paris, Texas* affected all the filling stations I see now, into my adult life. The purposiveness is not (only) in the image but in my observation.

The permanent change in my own perceptive apparatus is a result of the interaction with cinematic apparatus. As with recent insights into the mechanisms of memory, we can underscore that it is not the case that the perception of images is "new" in each moment.[19] Each moment of perception is an accretion of experiences of seeing, an accretion that does not differentiate between the experiences of simple reality and artful images. The recorded image, the scan of the horizon, the view through a telescope, the televisual chat on a portable screen—these instances of seeing are not discrete in the perceptive apparatus but build up overall expectations and anticipations, ways of seeing. There is no perceiving a butcher knife in the same way after seeing it raised to strike in Norman Bates's or Jason's hand.

Of course, the technology of cinema, the apparatus of film, establishes a condition of seeing. The cinematographic does not reproduce things as we see them from a study, but that does not mean there is a "naked" eye. How we see in the cinema may be different from how we see in the study but also how we see from a car, or from a plane, or through a photograph, or without our glasses, or from the observation platform of a tall building.[20] Our ways of seeing are technology dependent. *There is no way of seeing independent of technology*. To be sure, though, each technology affords different ways, different techne of seeing. The recording apparatus can capture images the human eye cannot see. Our recording devices can offer images of waves and vibrations, of bodily interiors or stellar exteriors, beyond what can be qualified as intelligible objects, people, or events. Jean-François Coulais, in his *Images Virtuelles et Horizons du Regard*, has provided a larger history of visual technology and its impact on sight and knowledge.[21] I will return to this study later, but for the moment note the particular possibilities of cinema—for instance, montage, collage, or other techniques—to suture images together and invoke imaginative narrative properties beyond what we can and do experience outside the walls of the black box.

In the first half of the twentieth century, the connection between cinema and consciousness came under scrutiny. During World War I the possibilities of newsreel and narrative films to impact mass morale among the troops brought greater attention to the propagandistic possibilities of cinema. However, the avant-garde hoped for a deeper impact on the spectator. Hans Richter hoped to entrain the soul with his abstract films in order to make the film viewer better equipped for the challenges of modernity.[22] Inspired by Richter's work, László Moholy-Nagy's 1922 article "Produktion—Reproduktion [Production—Reproduction]" in *de Stijl* exuded a modernist sense of progress, praising the synthesis of the human and technological and the move to perfection of the perceptive apparatus.[23] We recall the hope for revolution in consciousness that Russian avant-garde filmmakers like Eisenstein placed in cinema. Most pronounced in the hope for a new consciousness was Vertov's concept of Kino-Eye. Cinema was key to providing a new and fuller view of the material world. Slow motion, time-lapse, microscopic recording, and other techniques opened up new possibilities of seeing that went beyond the possibilities of the "naked eye." Vertov derived his notion of Kino-Pravda/cinema truth from this experience. Vertov approached cinema technology as offering something other and more to the human gaze. He believed that technology brought not just a different perception but more perception, and with more perception came science, knowledge, and truth. But this was revealed not to be the case.

The further development of cinema as a medium and medium of mass propaganda made quickly clear that cinema did not reveal "truth." Nevertheless, the 1929 FiFo (Film and Photo) exhibition in Stuttgart brought together an international showcase of over twelve hundred pieces by more than two hundred photographers and filmmakers from the Soviet Union to North America. This celebration of the "New Seeing" was a bit more tempered in its claims.[24] Any form of seeing something new or differently, any altered vision, was not a step toward a higher order of seeing, a telos of vision. Nevertheless, the new technologies had opened up new ways of seeing. Technology does not offer to the eye a fullness of sight, a seeing-more-than. It does offer to sight, however, another way of perceiving. The exhibition thus advocated for a spectator who was aware not only of the possibilities afforded by the new technologies but also the way those possibilities formed our sight.

The shift from a hope in the perfection of perception to a recognition of the formative capacity of technology brought forward concerns with the specificity of various media and their impact on our ways of knowing—that is, the

The Image of the Some Thing Other • 23

connection between techne and episteme. To be sure, looking at a projected image is different from looking through a microscope, is different from styling in front of a mirror, is different from donning reading glasses in a comfy chair and curling up with a good book. All of these viewing instances, however, rely on technology. They each allude to viewing practices that had to be learned in some manner. And listed as such, they invite us to reconsider how the "gaze" is inseparable from technologies of seeing. Seeing is always a matter of techne, seeing through some technology. But any new technology of sight transforms all manners of seeing. And it calls forward a need for new strategies of critical viewing.

HORKHEIMER/ADORNO AND BERNARD STIEGLER

Max Horkheimer and Theodor Adorno famously took to task the culture industry, especially in its advanced form in Hollywood. Visual technology in their analysis bound audiences into capitalism and industrialized consciousness. The fullness of vision offered by the moving pictures proved to be a constriction:

> The ruthless unity in the culture industry is evidence of what will happen in politics. Marked differentiations such as those of A and B films, or of stories in magazines in different price ranges, depend not so much on subject matter as on classifying, organizing, and labeling consumers. Something is provided for all so that none may escape; the distinctions are emphasized and extended. The public is catered for with a hierarchical range of mass-produced products of varying quality, thus advancing the rule of complete quantification.[25]

Bernard Stiegler, in his revolutionary three-volume study *Technics and Time*, extended and reinvigorated Horkheimer and Adorno's critique, especially in volumes 2 and 3.[26] Overall in the study he followed the impact of technology on consciousness (covering terrain similar to this study). Drawing from Marx, he considered how industrialization not only transformed technology but also impacted our ways of knowing itself. He carefully considered the discussions of technology and techne in twentieth-century philosophy, especially Heidegger and Derrida, in order to come to a new relation to the "objective" world. However, his assessment led to an increasingly pessimistic focus on industrial temporal objects and the industrial temporalization of consciousness.[27] Stiegler identifies cinema as the industrial temporal object sine qua non: "*Cinema* occupies a unique place. Its technics of image and sound—now including informatics and telecommunications—re-invent our belief in stories that are now told with remarkable unparalleled power."[28] In Stiegler's analysis cinema thus designates more than film in the black box. It stands for a larger technology of screens and

24 · CHAPTER 1

programming that leads to a *cinematic consciousness*. Television, a development in this technology, Stiegler labels nothing less than a "spiritual catastrophe."[29]

Like Horkheimer and Adorno before him, Stiegler takes a pessimistic view of cinematic consciousness and ascribes to the spectator a deeply passive position: "During the passing ninety minutes or so (fifty-two in the case of the tele-visual 'hour') of this *pastime*, the time of our consciousness will be totally passive within the thrall of those 'moving' images that are linked by noises, sounds, words, voices."[30] Indeed a half century later Stiegler's approach replicates many of the same moves for which Horkheimer and Adorno were rigorously criticized. And certainly Stiegler is as deeply influenced by Heidegger's cultural pessimism as he is by that of the Frankfurt colleagues. If Vertov hoped for a fullness of vision with the new technology, the approach with Stiegler and the cultural pessimists in general rests on the expectation that there is a whole and full critical consciousness possible, and it exists, ontologically, distinct from and above technology.

In these positions there is much to which we will return, but as much as I also consider here a cinematic consciousness, I want to reassert: consciousness is active and formative; consciousness is inextricable from technology; consciousness is plastic and transforming but also enframed and limited by technology. We can consider the dynamic of technology and consciousness as akin to Nietzschean *übersetzen*, translation as a setting over into a new and different form. The filmstrip, or the digital camera, does record light waves and vibrations. However, the eye still perceives those recordings with the same cognitive capacity with which it sees any other thing, or, we might say, as a moment of visual alterity in which it sees any thing other, in which anything becomes other. The waves and vibrations that are recorded and edited nevertheless must be present as waves and vibrations to meet the active eye's grasping into the world. And whether the waves come from simple reality or from cinema's movements, they still need to be translated into electrochemical processes, passed through neural nets, and processed into meaning. Nietzsche refused a simple separation of the material and ideational. Change the name of a thing and you change the thing itself. Nor was the image separate from the material; rather, the image was part of the play of forces. Nietzsche understood the image as an effect.

The visual alterity of the image is not a property of the image; visual alterity attends to all perception. Regardless of source and purposive production, visual alterity is not a particular property of a particular kind of image: any thing is other; every thing is other. The reading of the emotions off the face of the caregiver is not a different act in essence from the act of reading the emotions off the

The Image of the Some Thing Other • 25

face of Lauren Bacall, Penelope Cruz, or Hanna Schygulla. If the latter appears to us inscribed in image functions and regimes of signification, the image of the caregiver nevertheless also appears always already in a regime of images. The face of the caregiver appears to the infant already part of a regime dominated perhaps in one location by Romantic Madonnas, Hallmark cards, and evening news items of queer parents and their "gaybys." In another location images of mothers might be defined by scenes of martyrdom and the movies of Tahiya Karioka. The social order, the regime of images, and the regime of social legibility are inextricable. As I noted from the outset of this discussion, there is no naked non-signifying presence; rather, to be present is already to signify in complex relations that precede the individual and that "unfold," change, transform through and by their own activity. This regime is as much a part of the apparatus of seeing as is the camera or projector. But no part of this apparatus is static. Visual alterity is dynamic, it unfolds, it is narrative.

CHAPTER 2

Self/Other Image

Hegel

Hegel and Alterity

Whatever critiques of him that have arisen, Hegel nevertheless initiated a critical philosophy that transformed epistemology broadly. Hegelian philosophy established the modern social and human sciences. We know differently because of Hegel. In *Queer Social Philosophy* I spent a great deal of time parsing out Hegel's texts, considering the mechanisms by which we could overcome their own (hetero)normative limitations. I do not replicate that approach here. Instead I am interested in returning to the point of emergence of our contemporary approaches to alterity.

In *The Science of Logic*, in his typical maddening string of words, Hegel puts forward certain observations that are foundational to (visual) alterity. There he draws a relationship between consciousness and the differentiations of self and other:

> Otherness . . . appears as a determination alien to the determinate being . . ., or as the other outside the one determinate being; partly because a determinate being is determined as other only through being compared by a Third, and partly because it is only determined as other on account of the other which is outside it, but is not an other on its own account. At the same time, . . . every determinate being . . . determines itself as an other, so that there is no determinate being which is determined only as such, which is not outside a determinate being and therefore is not itself an other.[1]

I do not want to consider the above text closely; instead, I would like to glean four aspects of visual alterity from this quote.

1. Otherness has a quality that appears to be outside of and imposed on the subject, outside its control. Although alterity need not derive from or create conflict, Hegel does not consider difference in the dialectic as inherently benign. Difference may be universal, but differentiation can be fraught. Any conflicts that arise out of alterity initiate dialectic struggles. As an imposition of otherness, power is exercised in the dialectic, establishing a struggle between a dominant and a counter element. This exteriority of otherness relates to the historical logics of alterity, and it is a service of Hegel to put these struggles into history. If the Egyptian Pharaoh stood in absolute freedom over an empire of enslaved subjects, this opposition of lord and bondsman had transformed over time such that by the nineteenth century the bourgeois had recognized that all are free.[2] And the liberal constitutions had enshrined this freedom as a universal right (albeit for white middle-class men). Alterior relations constantly change. Difference has a history. Differentiations change over time. Power is a dynamic.

2. Otherness *appears*, and this appearance demarcates an outside to the subject. As a result, otherness is constitutive to the subject. There is no identity without difference, no unity without division. The subject and alterior are a dis/union. In *The Phenomenology of Spirit* Hegel describes at length how the subject struggles against determination, experiencing first the other as a limit on its universality. If it were to "win" that struggle and annihilate the other, the subject would lose its own being and become indeterminate. The subject must learn to accept the other as a necessity of self.

3. This quality of alterity sets the dynamic of typicality/stereotypicality into play. The other appears as a type of something, and we come to recognize its complexity beyond the typical qualities, or we do not attend to any development, ignore its complexity, continue to recognize it only as "one of those." The quote from Hegel also leads us to recognize that either all subject relations are bound up in power (Michel Foucault), or there is an aspect of alterity distinct from power relations.

4. And finally in this quote, there is this recognition of the role of the third, the viewer who recognizes difference, whose comparisons determine the other. This latter point relates directly to the question of visibility and invisibility. It is important for us if we seek to understand better the distinction of identity/alterity.

These considerations of alterity are central to appearance and recognition in an apparatus of perception. They are not simply a property of visuality. We do not need to see in order to know the alterior. We do not need the face of the

The History of Difference and the Frame of Cinema

Difference has a history and this history transform consciousness. This observation gleaned from Hegel provides a foundation to the approach throughout this book. In contradistinction to Hegel, it requires us to reject any essentialist differentiations like gender, sex, or race. However, along with Hegel, it compels us to understand consciousness *and* the brain as itself altering, modifying, plastic, malleable.

Hegel already described the dynamic of determination/differentiation as a universal principle of consciousness, as universal to the construction of self-consciousness. We may follow this point; indeed, most of contemporary psychology and cognitive theory derives from this proposition. It established consciousness as relational, social, dynamic, changeable, developmental. *The Phenomenology of Spirit* can be read as an investigation of the development of consciousness from infancy to maturity. However, if consciousness develops on the basis of distinctions of alterity, self/other, Hegel's teleological analysis anticipated a moment of future stability in the dynamic of difference. The condition of synthesis denotes an overcoming of conflictual difference, an arrival at a condition of harmony. Importantly, he did not anticipate that moment of future harmony as a sublation of difference into a universal sameness; rather, he described a future moral state of mutual recognition, a condition of interdependence in difference. Out of this anticipation of future harmony, however, he came to consider that certain differences were themselves essential differences, making them into essences of consciousness. For example, Hegel essentialized gender as a natural difference and allocated women to an essentially irrational, passive, emotional, domestic position.[3] And to Africa he ascribed a position simply outside history: "Africa proper, as far as History goes back, has remained—for all purposes of connection with the rest of the World—shut up; it is the Gold-land compressed within itself—the land of childhood, which lying beyond the day of self-conscious history, is enveloped in the dark mantle of Night."[4] And speaking directly about the inhabitants of sub-Saharan Africa, he contends:

> This distinction between himself as an individual and the universality of his essential being, the African in the uniform, undeveloped oneness of his exis-

tence has not yet attained; so that the Knowledge of an absolute Being, an Other and a Higher than his individual self, is entirely wanting. The Negro, as already observed, exhibits the natural man in his completely wild and untamed state.[5]

Whereas he could see women in their difference as having a sociable role, albeit only in the private sphere, Hegel positioned Africa and its inhabitants into a condition of fundamental essential alterity that would never develop into a state of differentiated consciousness, cut off in his assessment from the potential to develop to universality at the end of history. Ultimately Hegel allocates that potential only to white bourgeois males.

I discuss this at length to make clear that out of this gendered and racial essentialism, Hegel limited his own proposition that consciousness develops in relations of alterity. Without abandoning the understanding of consciousness as arising in differentiation, we can radicalize this proposition and consider how all differences emerge out of historical rationales and all differentiations arise out of particular relations in place and time.

Hegel's very proposition is itself a product of its period and indicates the historicity of rationales of gendered and racial othering. The distinction of masculine and feminine/male and female in Berlin of the nineteenth century is by no means the same as in Lahore of the eighth century and is not the same as that on the spice routes of the twelfth, nor in the courts of France in the thirteenth, or among the Algonquin in the sixteenth, and certainly none of these are the same as in the streets of New York, London, Paris, or Munich in the twenty-first century. Likewise "Africa" has proven a vast continent of rich diversity, able to pose limits to "Europe." The continent of Africa, in all its diversity and richness, is quite capable of unfolding autonomously in history. And "Africans" cannot sufficiently describe a vast continent of peoples and in the world African peoples in the diaspora have revealed a considerable resiliency, negating the violent subjugation of European racists. We might add that the amount of time that Europeans have spent discussing the difference of Africa and Africans only attests to how "Europeans" have themselves been determined by Africa. To be sure, though, the racial ordering of the world itself has a history, and the order imposed by nineteenth-century Europe is different from the racial ordering of the world in the twenty-first century.

Key for the analysis here is that relationships of difference and differentiation determine the subject but are themselves not fixed. The paradigms of differentiation schooling perceptions in Hegel's Berlin are not universal; they are historically contingent. Subjectivity may arise in differentiation, but there is no natural necessity of this or that difference to give rise to a subject.

Consciousness arises in differentiation. Yet differentiations change over time in changing dynamics of power. Thus, we may have to abandon the expectation of a period of universal harmony and post-historicity; power is dynamic. Inasmuch as those power dynamics of differentiation challenge our humanity, any end of history would arrive only with the end of humanity. There are, of course, better and worse arrangements of power.

I repeat here a discussion I have previously undertaken at greater length to underscore: the potential of understanding all differentiations as historically contingent opens up new potentials.[6] Granted, even if the conditions of determination are historical and contingent, hence always in flux, we are nevertheless raised in conditions outside our choosing, outside our control. And we enter into a field of already determined differentiations. Our subjectivity is in effect predetermined by the conditions of differentiation, into which we grow. "Otherness appears" but not just any otherness. We are trained to recognize difference and to recognize it in a particular way. However, to consider that there is an end to it or an outside to it, that differentiation is only ideology, that there is some place in which the determinations of difference give way to a—what? A fullness of being? A universality of consciousness? This would be to repeat the Hegelian error. Self-consciousness arises in differentiation. Contingent patterns of differentiation precede us but are not natural. They are not "simple reality." We may be "trained" to see difference in a particular way, but we can "learn" to see difference differently.

Our world appears to us ordered, as image. Of course, there is something already present in the image viewed, but we do not see all things. Consider that if the frame of cinema enacts dynamics of the visual field, something appears in the frame. The visual field presents some things to the perceptive apparatus. The frame presents particular things in relation to one another. Visual alterity, the determinations of difference that arise in a field of given circumstances, transforms any thing into some thing. Nevertheless, we can shift our frames, change our visual fields. We can see an other thing.

This changing unfolding of the visual field is history. It is at the heart of story. If visual alterity describes a propensity of the perceiver to become subject in recognition, to see otherness, detect difference, it is because we enter into the dynamic "narrating" those differentiations, making them to be looked at, making them to be seen. The history of gender or race is a history of seeing something, seeing some people as some thing, in a particular way at a particular time.

For more than a century the frame of cinema has offered us something, some images, as sets of potential differentiations—that is, narratives, specific narratives. And narrative film developed precisely as an elaborated condition of a purposive form of visual communication, drawing our eye here and encouraging us to read this image in a particular way. Rancière's discussion of the imageness of the image actually describes as much the practice within a still image, an icon, as it does the editing together of moving images or the unfolding of images in a static view across time. Yet the frames of all these images lade them with "operations that couple and uncouple the visible and its signification or speech and its effect, which create and frustrate expectations."[7]

THE PHENOMENOLOGICAL HISTORY OF SEEING

Can history offer some order to considering the phenomenon of sight? If Hegel initiated a revolution in the thinking of philosophy when he suggested that philosophy is the history of philosophy, what happens if we consider sight not as a given sense but as the history of sight? How do we do this without becoming encumbered by essentialism, determinism, cognitive hardwiring, or other failures to think this proposition through far enough?

I already pointed to Bernard Stiegler's *Technics and Time* as a project that takes up a history of technological seeing, yet I noted how in that project the direction into pessimism derives from a lingering notion of unencumbered seeing. Friedrich Kittler's work could be seen as the opposite approach. Kittler's media history most famously intensified the focus on technology, arguing for an investigation of the communication apparatus in order to switch our understanding of ontology from the human being in the technological apparatus to the apparatus as producing a "being human."[8] I am enough of a Hegelian to suggest that in the case of such oppositions, the "truth" lies somewhere else. Thus I would point to the brilliant study *Images Virtuelles et Horizons du Regard*, by Jean-François Coulais. In that project Coulais explores a history of "looking"—that is, seeing from a particular place and time and within a particular understanding of perspective. He treats ocular vision not as a natural state but as a relationship with the production of what we can call "the image" as a shorthand here, where the image also includes the built environment (e.g., the cityscape) and the cultivated space (e.g., the landscape). We could say that seeing is always "through and of" a particular technology.

To Coulais's study we might also add other "scapes," like the socially organized environment (e.g., ethnoscape). Ultimately it is the same perceptive apparatus that views the "natural," the figurative, the symbolic, the abstract, or the moving image. Further, Coulais considers that a relationship of ocular vision and the image arises in reading practices that are culturally, socially, and historically specific. The study underscores that we may see in the moment, but we perceive historically. Moreover, it leads us to consider that we are not only what we see but also how we see.

Coulais undertakes to ground his study in a long history; for instance, he describes a connection between the spatial imaginary that generated the modern discourse of architecture, the geographic imaginary that drove the cartographic organizing of the globe, and the virtual imaginary that defined the science of optics. He suggests that it was the planning of the architectural monuments of the Middle Ages, the production of the Gothic cathedrals that established a set of geometric standards and a reproducible process that actually helped break apart the medieval world. Architecture trained the eye to see differently, to see aesthetically *and* scientifically. The move from place to space, from ordering the built environment to organizing the world, was a small step. Likewise, and interconnected, however, was the science of optics. Optics, as a reinvigoration of the work of Ibn Sahl and Ibn Al-Haytham, shifted within the considerations of Renaissance perspective.[9] Coulais notes a breaking apart in the Renaissance of the natural and artificial image, a rupture of medieval referentiality, which allowed for a web or network of relations between and among the visible and invisible, the seen and unseen. Coulais understands the distinction in the new science of optics as sundering this world, negating the unseen into the realm of fantasy and representation, and further generating a separation of a real and a virtual world. The drawn image, like that which rays of light cast on the back of the eye or the wall of the camera obscura, references the natural world yet itself is artificial.[10]

And it leads Coulais ultimately to a claim of the newness of the virtual image and the production of virtual reality. This position is where the project becomes most provocative and compelling: the virtual image is not a fundamental rupture or destruction of the photographic. The dynamics of recording and representing do not disappear one instead of the other. Rather, as with animation, the virtual or digital image simply moves the image toward practices of representation and away from those of recording. However, the presence of frame and ground, of light and shadow, angle and distance, and figuration and abstraction continue to operate.

In providing a history of sight, Coulais in effect reveals that seeing is itself not a natural phenomenon but rather a phenomenology in the Hegelian sense, a phenomenon with history. I am not interested in following Hegel and suggesting that there is a necessary privileged development of this phenomenon toward a telos of fullness and universality. Sight is a thinking sight. And even more generally, perception is the history of thinking perception. Furthermore, what happens if we consider perception as the history of conscious reflection on perception?

Considering historical transitions in the thinking of sight as Coulais does is not unique. In a different mode, Martin Jay's influential study *Downcast Eyes: The Denigration of Vision in Twentieth-Century French Thought* recounts a history of philosophical thinking about sight and perception.[11] Yet Jay's study also reveals to us that that moment of transformation in the phenomenology of sight itself was bound, and to a large extent has remained bound, to a notion of ocular vision as natural and outside of history. I will come back to this point in chapter 3.

Telling versus Showing: Narrative and Alterity in Film

IMAGENESS AND NARRATIVES OF DIFFERENCE

Hegel showed us that imageness appears as otherness determining the subject. Difference *appears*, but how? As such or dynamically? Rancière sought to consider visual alterity as a property in the image, the imageness of images. For his analysis this imageness emerges outside of the narrative. By contrast, the classical theory of alterity treats difference as residing in the dynamic relations of the images. Theories of film narrative put forward by David Bordwell and colleagues closely follow the Hegelian proposition; film narrative is understood as following a pattern of order/disruption/resolution, or in Hegelian terms, thesis/antithesis/synthesis.[12] If we glance over the analyses of film narratives that follow from this perspective, we recognize how alterity as such drives a diegetic chain. An affair, a murder, a move, a striking of an iceberg, or some other event creates a disruption. It creates a condition that is antithetical to the order of the opening sequence. This *difference* drives the rest of the film toward a restoration of harmony, typically a synthesis of a "higher order": the dyad of true love, the reassertion of justice, the global peace after the destruction of the monster, and so on.

Much of film and genre theory has focused on how the narrative of films has been driven by disruption, especially to bourgeois heterosexual norms.[13] For over a decade, the fiancé/fiancée who meets the true love of her/his life and the disruption to wedding plans that it causes drove the successes of such screwball comedies as *It Happened One Night* (Capra 1934), *Bringing up Baby* (Hawks 1938), *The Philadelphia Story* (Cukor 1940), and *The More the Merrier* (Stevens 1943).[14] The generic strategy of the screwball comedy has had long legs, developing further into the present and driving much of the successes of many films by Joel and Ethan Coen, as well as the careers of contemporary actors like Reese

34 · CHAPTER 2

Witherspoon, Jennifer Aniston, Sandra Bullock, and Hugh Grant, and most recently a whole burgeoning industry of gay/camp/drag films.[15] Beyond Hollywood it has had international impact on camp films like Pedro Almodóvar's 1988 breakthrough film, *Women on the Edge of a Nervous Breakdown* (*Mujeres al borde de un ataque de nervios*) (1988), and the German box office hit *Maybe, Maybe Not* (*der bewegte Mann*) (Wortmann 1994). With more than three million viewers, the last-named film kicked off the German comedy wave of the 1990s. It begins with a disruption to a couple: Doro catches her philandering boyfriend, Axel, in flagrante delicto and kicks him out onto the streets and, by chance, into the gay scene. The quest to rebuild *proper* heterosexual relationships drives the rest of the film. In *Women on the Edge* that quest unwinds fully with Pepa in the end refusing Ivan and taking on the role of single mother. By contrast, in *Maybe, Maybe Not* heteronormativity is restored with Axel and Doro coming together in the maternity ward after he has been "straightened up" with some help from gay men.[16] Starting in the 1990s, then, we can note a different differentiation; the alterior to bourgeois heterosexual coupling actually comes to drive the films to their synthesis.

However, the focus on narrative says nothing about the specific of the visuals by which the narrative is given to us to see. What role does the visual play in the alterity of narrative? In *From Plato to Lumière* André Gaudreault sought to offer a new paradigm of narration by relying on the visual quality of film. He focused on "monstration," which he defined as a mechanism of presenting directly.[17] He distinguished monstration sharply from narration, or representing by means of some mediation. Monstration proceeds in film especially by showing and not telling, with moving images and not by means of spoken word. Certainly this analysis has opened up a reconsideration of narratology as much as it has offered new ways of considering the specificity of the moving image. However, if Gaudreault's considerations focused closely on the moving image as separate from the narrative text, we may consider visual alterity as a means to negotiate aspects of story *and* mise-en-scène.

We can understand alterity as propelling narrative. If we glance over the history of narrative film, we will recognize as themes a litany of differences that form conflicts at the heart of the narratives, differences that we are given to see. In his classic study of the screwball comedy, Stanley Cavell noted how difference compels the narrative along: class difference, educational difference, generational difference, ethnic difference, gender, race, and so on.[18] A conflict is established as a result of a protagonist belonging to a distinct group or occupying a position as other: a professor among the upper class, a wealthy person among the poor, an actress among the moralizing middle class, a migrant

Self/Other Image • 35

in a new national/ethnic community, a guest worker Turk, an exiled political figure, an assimilated Jew among the anti-Semites, a homosexual in heteronormative society, a person jobless among the employed, a sex worker among the bourgeois, someone disabled among the enabled, and so on. In this vein we can return to *Bringing up Baby*, *Women on the Edge*, or *Maybe, Maybe Not*, which begin with gender difference but also quickly take up visual representations of class, educational, and sexual difference. The character and quality of Katharine Hepburn's socialite Susan Vance takes on its contours in opposition to Virginia Walker's staid, academic, uptight Alice Swallow. Almodóvar shows us a world of differences coded on the dress and comportment of the women. Axel as heterosexual appears in the midst of a circle of gay men who contrast with him as either fey queens or as a hypermasculine butcher. The imageness of these characters and their spectacular qualities drive the dynamic of the narratives. And although these narratives do find resolution, "resolution" is not necessary in relations of alterity. *Women on the Edge*, although it ends with a revelation of pregnancy, eschews any restoration of the bourgeois nuclear family, and the fate of Pepa is left open.

DIFFERENCE-TO-BE-LOOKED-AT, DIFFERENCE-TO-BE-SEEN

Monstration is not naïve. Whatever we are given to see is not "innocent." The dynamics of difference are also dynamics of power, although seeing difference does not tell us how that power dynamic will play out. For instance, the attempts by Hollywood to attend to US race relations has relied on the representation of racial difference. In mainstream films—that is, films marketed to an audience that sees itself as white—blackness appears as difference. The much celebrated fictional Wakanda appears as an entire location of exception; a moment of visual pleasure arises in the Marvel Universe films whenever the film first arrives in the Afrofuturist megacity, precisely because it is exceptional, fantastical, different from every other place. This is a *difference to be looked at*, a spectacle of difference. Related to that reference to the classic work of Laura Mulvey is a different difference: the *difference to be seen*, a techne of visual alterity. Consider how in the history of Hollywood, in films from *Pinky* (Kazan 1949) to *Imitation of Life* (Sirk 1959), the films' visuals keep the audience in a position of seeing a difference that is not obvious to others. The films produce an extra-diegetic knowledge, a way of seeing difference that must be produced. When in *Imitation of Life* Annie sees her daughter Sarah Jane dancing at the strip joint, we see how the white male audience does not recognize the performer as black. The film backs away from presenting race as (only) performative by insisting on the veracity of Annie's gaze that sees her daughter as black. The film positions us to see Sarah

Jane through her mother's eyes, to see her racial difference. Even though it does actually reveal a difference of differentiation, this treatment of race as an essential difference to be seen continues right to the present. In *BlacKkKlansman* (Lee 2018) the passing is sonic, constructing a joke on the racists in the film's diegesis yet ensuring that the audience sees blackness and sees it as difference. The humor of the film derives from the audience seeing the black Ron Stallworth "speak white." A serious moment in the film arises when Stallworth confronts his partner, Flip Zimmerman, with Zimmerman's Jewishness. A difference that had to that point remained largely uncoded in the film becomes a matter to be seen as passing in a world of violent differentiation. The narratives of these two films are driven by this visualizing of difference, difference to be seen.

The German comedy wave came to a generic end with the film *Everything Will Be Fine* (*Alles wird gut*) (Maccarone 1998). Queer filmmaker Angelina Maccarone made her debut with this film that presents difference differently. It begins with an expulsion out of a relationship but ruptures the heteronormativity of the genre: Katja dumps her girlfriend Nabou for a different lover. Still obsessed with Katja, to be near her Nabou takes a job as a housecleaner for the older, career-oriented, and engaged-to-be-married businesswoman Kim, who lives one floor above Katja. And with this meeting the film enters into the realm of the screwball comedy. An intense interaction begins because Kim and Nabou have radically different ideas about responsibility, career, Afro-German identity, lesbian sexuality, and cleanliness. And these differences compel comedic situations. We are given to see these as differences to be looked at—for example, Kim's business-smart apparel versus Nabou's '90s techno hip. Nabou eventually forgets Katja, and Kim leaves her fiancé at the altar. This is a narrative propelled by monstration of ethnic/racial, generational, sexual, gendered, and class difference. But a different difference also appears in the film, to its credit and what made it stand out at the time. The film includes random scenes of racist interactions in which the difference to be seen is the racist seeing of difference. Nabou in the subway is confronted with a "well-meaning" elderly woman who cannot see Nabou as German, instead seeing her as from a "hot country." And so she inquires about how Nabou deals with the cold. The film positions the audience with Nabou to find the woman ridiculous, but fundamentally to see her seeing a difference that is not there for the audience. Such moments continue in the film at various levels, keeping the viewer on the inside of the joke or the understanding of the wink and nod. The racist appears in the film, and the film positions the viewer to see the racist as different.

Typically the shot angle presents the alterity to be looked at, with high or low angles depicting dynamics of power and otherness. We famously see evil through a low angle, stretching from *Nosferatu* (Murnau 1922) to Darth Vader (*Star Wars*, Lucas 1977), Michael Meyers (*Halloween*, Carpenter 1978), Voldemort (*Harry Potter and the Philosopher's Stone*, Columbus 2001), and beyond. Marion Crane is famously murdered from a slightly high angle (*Psycho*, Hitchcock 1960). More subtly, the young Rose is introduced in *Titanic* (Cameron 1997) repeatedly from a high angle, revealing her helplessness and entrapment in an arranged marriage. *Barbara* (Petzold 2013) opens with a high-angle shot out of a window down onto a woman. Two men discuss her arrival—a doctor at the clinic where she will work and the *Stasi* (state security) officer who is monitoring her. Here the main character, Barbara, arrives at the provincial clinic in the German Democratic Republic to which she's been transferred as a result of her attempt to leave the country. From the opening, under police surveillance and small-town scrutiny, the film positions her as subject to a view of an all-pervading threatening difference.

We could continue endlessly with the investigation of narratives and visual alterity. But to recap the argument thus far: monstration is not a presentation of just anything, of any old thing. Monstration must be a presentation of difference, or there is no story. Visual alterity shows differentiation in action and leads us to make a distinction between seeing difference and seeing otherness. The older woman sees Nabou not just as different but as an other. But let's move a step further and consider differentiating as a constant of perception and key to appearance: difference is not an essence, although otherness must be distinguished.

Otherness That Constitutes the Self

(CRITICAL) COGNITIVE THEORY: APPROACHES TO STEREOTYPING

If, as Hegel indicated, otherness constitutes the self, then the complexity of the self depends on the differentiations of others. The group identity, the sense of self as belonging to a collective of the same, derives from a reduction or even refusal of differentiation. In this self/other dynamic, however, some others appear the same. Some others appear more complexly, some others less. Recall the opening discussion of stereo and alterior: the stereo is a reproduction that appears the same; the alter here is a unit in a relationship, simultaneously different and mimetic. The stereoscope made two slightly different images appear the same in a different condition, whereas in alterity the category made a set of differences appear as same: apples, oranges, bananas, grapes, tomato are all fruit. Here we come to a question: How do we see similarity and how we distinguish different differences? Not all distinctions of self and other are the same. Differentiation distinguishes the self from the other, yet we can fail to differentiate the other finely, distinctly. To fail to see the facets of the other forecloses an experience of the self as complex and multifaceted. What does this mean for the propensity of differentiations to turn the other into something static, a stereotype?

Hegel's assessment of differentiation had little to do with the contemporary approach to stereotyping, especially in the humanities. Thus, it is important to consider that in the field of psychology that emerged after Hegel, scholars have explored the motivations for stereotyping but have done so often from a "value-neutral position." Classic studies like *The Authoritarian Personality* sought to be descriptive of anti-Semitic and racist motivations yet described latent homosexuality as the psychological motivating factor.[19] Gordon Allport, in his classic *The Nature of Prejudice*, approached stereotypes as possibly bearing positive sentiments.[20] More recently cognitive and neuroscientific research has taken up the question of stereotyping as a categorizing mechanism in the perceptive apparatus that contends with the mass of input in the environment. Cognitive research differentiates lower- and higher-level functions with lower/preconscious perception largely consisting of filters to sort out input that does not require higher-level processing. A conundrum of a sort arises in this description of consciousness: too much information would seem to overwhelm the ability of higher consciousness to respond to complexity. What we recognize as complex has already been simplified by our own perceptive capacities. Consciousness, self-consciousness, arises late in the process.

A foundation of current research directions is the notion that we do not recognize everything; rather, that which comes into recognition has already gone through differentiation and categorization deriving from already lived experience. The mass of input becomes simplified, reduced, limited to particular aspects. For example, lower-level functions prime person perception or facial recognition through categorization. Scholars suggest that these priming mechanisms include especially race and gender.[21] Researchers like Carol Martin and Malia Mason have recorded the high efficiency provided by social categorization, especially gender and race. Cognitive scientists like Perry Hinton have used the term "stereotyping" to describe this process.[22] A 2016 issue of the journal *Nature Neuroscience* extended this line of research, describing facial recognition and social categories as a part of stereotyping in perception—treating it as a mechanism of efficiency.[23] In 2017, however, Tiffany Ito and Silvia Tomelleri did seek to distinguish functions of social categorization from stereotyping.[24]

There is much that could be said about this work, not the least is that the terms of race and gender are not approached critically. The scholars noted above

Self/Other Image • 39

discuss blackness and whiteness as social categorizations without a hint of consideration of their constructed quality. This problem extends to the larger field. *The Handbook of Categorization in Cognitive Science* discusses race uncritically and is focused on a US context so that the authors use terms like "Asian" or "black" with no critical reflection.[25] "Racial categorization is a ubiquitous phenomenon in our judgments and perceptions of ourselves and others."[26] The terms "white," "black," and "Asian" are treated as if they are globally consistent racial categories and not describing very different social constructions—even if one remains only in the English language but shifts to Canada, England, Nigeria, or South Africa. Within the field, social categorization has not yet developed a reflection on differences in constructions of blackness or gender from one place to another. And although biologists and geneticists have long underscored that there is no biological basis to race, the term finds its way into the research as a given category. Certainly there is recognition of a need to attend to such questions. "At any rate, future research on racial categorization should be adaptive and continually probe for the emergence of new racial constructions."[27] And because the field relies on feedback loops and the influence of top-down/bottom-up processes, there is clearly room for future research to investigate the social construction of categories as such.

CRITICAL FILM STUDIES AND VISUAL CATEGORIZATION

I am not interested here in rejecting the significant research under way, and certainly not out of hand; we can draw a long arch from philosophical considerations through nascent psychology into contemporary cognitive and neuroscientific studies, a long trajectory of considerations of differentiation, distinction, and categorization as core to self, other, and group perception. The identification of efficiency as a fundamental cognitive function is itself interesting and important to the considerations of cinema and regimes of representation. But for cognitive and neuroscientific research, it should also be important to recognize that film studies has developed a long trajectory of investigation of social categorization. Discussions of the representation of difference, their social, cultural, and class specificities, have actually hallmarked film studies. In the early period of the discipline, film scholars like Donald Bogle, with his classic study *Toms, Coons, Mulattoes, Mammies, and Bucks*, developed elaborate critiques of categories of representation.[28] The new social movements, decolonization, fostered the attention to image regimes' paradigms as vehicles of power and oppression.

In the 1990s, however, significant voices emerged to critique the analysis of stereotyping as it had developed; at the time, Stephen Neale even suggested that the term "stereotype" may be so problematic as to be useless.[29] Neale argued against an approach to stereotypes that compiled catalogs of stereotypes or that led back to a treatment of the category as essential empirical difference. What good does it do to show historic representations of African Americans, Latinx, women, and so on, if the presumptions of essential difference that foster exclusion and oppression do not also come into focus, if the study does not give way to a critical race study that puts constructions of whiteness alongside blackness, heterosexuality alongside homosexuality, "masculinity" and "femininity" as operative terms in systems of differentiation? Catalogs of the stereotypes of yesteryear risk allowing them to appear as humorous or out of step with the current moment, but that sensibility may mask how the powers of objectification have changed; focus on the old stereotype cannot ignore how new stereotypes arise in the present to perpetuate those exclusions of the past. Neale advocated for an approach that treated stereotypes as dynamic differentiations in a field of power. The focus on the image as stereotype must expand to include the conditions that produce that image. Indeed, moving from the cataloging of images, subsequent engagements with stereotyping led film studies scholars to focus on the mechanisms of exclusion that make the production of stereotypes possible.[30]

A return to Hegel, however, helps us consider that the "in-group" does not simply stereotype the other as "out-group"; rather, the act of stereotyping creates the group. In- and out-groups are not essences or determinate social necessities. They are contingent. Differentiation, however, distinction of the other from self, is a necessity for the self. The refusal to differentiate the other is itself a refusal to distinguish the self. Stereotyping is not simply a superior gazing subject retaining a privilege of seeing the other as non-differentiated. Such an assessment assumes a coherence of the self that can determine the differentiations of the other rather than recognizing how the formation of self derives from a condition of distinction and not from an experience of wholeness. Indeed, Hegel already noted, "every determinate being determines itself as an other."

The self is not whole; rather, self takes shape in the contours of distinctions. The self is part of a whole inasmuch as it fails to distinguish the other. However, this process of determining self as other does not address the impact of those determinations on the other. While forms of difference arise in the formation of the subject as such, race, ethnicity, class, gender—the typical categories of the stereotypical—are always contingent and never a necessity. If we consider the stereotype as a form of differentiation that limits or even damages the other subject—in effect, reduces the other to object—the question then becomes, By what mechanisms do we move from the alterity that restricts, limits, and prevents an unfolding of subjectivity to a form of otherness that sustains the

Self/Other Image · 41

subjects mutually? How do we rid our visual field of categories that lead to static otherness? Let us consider how this may transpire in cinema, as a technology of seeing. As a technology of seeing difference, a film can model ways of seeing and can form and transform intersubjective relations.

STEREO/TYPIFICATION AND NON/DIFFERENTIATION

Throughout his impressive career, Richard Dyer has offered profound considerations of stereotyping in cinema, a hallmark of which has been a distinction between the stereotype and the type. When considering these terms, Dyer treats the type and stereotype not as stable catalogs of distinctions but as active processes. He thus goes on to consider not a category but a dynamic of typicality and stereotypicality, typification and stereotypification.[31] In line with the long history of psychological and cognitive research, he discusses typicality as an easy and efficient way to quickly render otherness visible, to demarcate both identity and alterity. Typicality allows us to read each other and thereby proves important in the process of subject construction. Dyer thus aligns his analysis with Georg Simmel, who described a need in modernity to present oneself as legible in mass society. The racial, ethnic, gendered, or classed type is not an essence or category in this approach as it is in the work of some contemporary cognitive and neuroscience. Typicality, for that matter, does not appear as a negation of the character of the individual; rather, it is the beginning of an appearance, a legibility, a visual shorthand to start an interaction. Social categorization in this approach is as much a mechanism whereby the subject produces a self as the way subjects perceive others. Indeed, for Simmel, significant for modernity was the ability of the individual to negotiate the means of appearing as a "type."[32] For both Simmel and Dyer, to appear as type need not be the end but can mark the beginning of this process of legibility. To appear as a shop girl or secretary is not the end of the story but the beginning of the romance.

Dyer's work brings us to consider the interface of cinema and perception, underscoring the principles of efficiency in cognition. Typicality is a necessary and key aspect of efficient perception in that most modern of technologies of representation: cinema. The visual medium does not operate with the same descriptive tools of the written medium. An author can take time describing surroundings and others over pages and pages. Certainly in films like *My Dinner with Andre* (Malle 1981), *Stranger Than Paradise* (Jarmusch 1984), *Night on Earth* (Jarmusch 1991), or most films by Eric Rohmer, dialogue can build up information much like a written text, yet in films their description is largely visual. We see a plenitude instead of hearing description. Visual description relies on both an immediate plenitude of setting and the transitoriness of that plenitude from

42 · CHAPTER 2

scene to scene, shot to shot. In a written work, readers become aware of setting and characterization through a process over time that builds on increasing descriptive elements, but they also rely on the imagination to fill in the "missing pieces." In a film, especially those that rely on establishing shots, everything is there all at once. Our eyes scan in seconds an image that contains information and description that would take pages to describe in the literary form. Thus, to convey meaning a film must rely on typicality as a visual shorthand. Typicality in effect addresses the viewer. Our eye searches for visual cues as to how to read this scene, and here the use of typicality allows the eye to read with speed. Cognitive studies of perception that verify the mechanism of categorization as a means to increase the speed of perception measure the experience of the perceiver and not how the perceived makes itself legible. While a few studies have sought to assess the experience of first-time viewers or childhood viewing practices, no contemporary researchers can go back to study the perceptive mechanisms before cinema to see how and in what way cinema may have schooled this capacity and developed the patterns of legibility that underlie social categorization.[33]

Dyer consistently points out that typicality easily becomes stereotypicality. Whereas typicality conveys information as a visual shorthand, thereby allowing the subject to develop in the unfolding of the narrative, stereotypicality reduces and stymies any unfolding process. In Dyer's analysis we begin from the expectation that all characters appear as legible types; however, those who unfold into a complexity resist the reduction to stereotype. It is when characters become encumbered and restricted by visual cues that we move to stereotypical representations. This dynamic could be applied to entire categories of supporting, secondary, and stock characters, background figures for whom the narrow focus on the main figures constricts them from further unfolding. They serve as a distinction to highlight qualities of the main figures and nothing more.

However, in the history of cinema, there are indeed films that have strategically refused differentiation to figures who play significant roles, and in them we can discover certain practices of social category construction. The American racist classic *Birth of a Nation* (Griffith 1915) set up an opposition between white and black not simply on the basis of the difference between the whiteface and blackface of the actors. The lascivious, base static state of the blackface actors contrasted with the whiteface characters, whose stories unfold with complexity of motivations. Blackness appears here as always a threat to the unfolding of white subjects. I want to underscore that neither blackness nor whiteness (here as blackface and whiteface) are natural, and nor are any attributes attached to the imageness of blackened and whitened faces; rather, a technology of viewing

Self/Other Image · 43

prepares its audience, the perceiving subjects in this apparatus, to see an other and see this other in a particular way.

SEEING RACISM, ANTI-SEMITISM, HOMOPHOBIA

Learning from the gross flat representations in *Birth of a Nation*, the infamous Nazi-era film *Jud Süß* (*Jew Süss*) (Harlan 1940) advanced the deployment of typicality and stereotypicality with a scientific deftness. The film has been the object of much scholarly research and a recent set of feature and documentary films about its production.[34] With this film we have an entire state cultural apparatus deployed to draw out an anti-Semitic response in the spectator. It developed practices of legibility and categorization to meet not the anti-Semitic viewer but rather the "unconvinced." In the move to the Final Solution, Himmler had discussed the predicament that every German has a "decent Jew" in his social circle.[35] In order to unleash a general anti-Semitic sentiment among the Germans, the category "Jew" had to replace the local knowledge of Jewish friends and acquaintances. All Jewish Germans had to become equivalent to *the Jew*, an essentially non-German category of difference.

Thus, in *Jud Süß* the famous Weimar-era actor Werner Krauss plays multiple characters, all of them Jewish. He plays them in such a way, however, that through makeup and mannerism it is difficult to notice that he is the actor under the makeup: the servant character has on his livery, the butcher has on a stained apron, the rabbi character wears long dark robes, and so on. In one single scene he actually appears as three different characters who interact with each other and who, through clever editing, carry on a conversation. By relying on Krauss to play all of these roles, the film trains the eye of the viewer in an anti-Semitic viewing practice that Valerie Weinstein has discussed productively through the term "Allosemitism."[36] Here the viewer is provided a sense visually that all Jews are the same. The difference to be seen is a static difference, a reduction to otherness, a robbing of subjectivity. It is in its assertion of essential otherness a refusal of differentiation. However—and this cannot be stressed enough—that refusal of differentiation has as much an impact on the subject as it does on the object. The refusal of differentiation creates the possibility of the subject being in a group, being grouped with the anti-Semites.

At the same time, the cleverness and danger of the film does not end there. The film deploys another strategy to foster anti-Semitic viewing. If the Werner Krauss characters suggest that "they are all the same," the title character, Süß Oppenheimer, appears in a different strategy. With him the film worked with blends to show the transition of the main character from a "ghetto Jew" to a courtier. In his opening appearance, he is visited in the Frankfurt ghetto by a

The blend of Süß Oppenheimer's transformation into courtier. *Jud Süß* (Harlan 1940) Dissolve 1. Courtesy of Friedrich Wilhelm Murnau Foundation

representative of the Duke of Württemberg. Oppenheimer appears in a caftan, a fantastical representation of orthodoxy, speaking accented broken German. To get his financial support, the representative has to agree to allow Oppenheimer to appear in person at court, something impossible given the ban on Jews in Württemberg. How can he hope to travel to Stuttgart, given his appearance?

Through the dialogue of the film, Süß Oppenheimer makes it initially clear that he is able and ready to assimilate his appearance—but not his behavior. Thus, two very important blends at the beginning and closing of the film allow the audience to see Süß Oppenheimer's transformation from a caftaned resident of the Frankfurt ghetto into a dandy courtier and back. The camera works to portray how this assimilation takes place.

The blend seeks to convince the spectator of the existence of a difference that is not immediately apparent to the eye. If Werner Krauss suggests to the eye that "they are all alike," Oppenheimer suggests that "they could be anywhere." Any dandy could be a Jew and Jews could be anywhere, it seeks to show. In spite of the visual difference the character assumes, then, the film deploys this technique again to refuse differentiation.

The blend of Süß Oppenheimer's transformation back from courtier. *Jud Süß* (Harlan 1940) Dissolve 2. Courtesy of Friedrich Wilhelm Murnau Foundation

Farber recognizes Süß Oppenheimer's difference at a distance. *Jud Süß* (Harlan 1940) Moment of Recognition. Courtesy of Friedrich Wilhelm Murnau Foundation

46 · CHAPTER 2

As if this were not enough, the film also contains at least one figure who, in spite of Süß Oppenheimer's bourgeois appearance, is able to recognize him "for what he is." Here the technology of the film, not just to present a difference "to be looked at" but to create a technique of seeing difference, "a difference to be seen," becomes clear. We are asked to align ourselves with the viewing practice of Karl Faber, who is not fooled, who is able to see "the Jew." For the sake of narrative, Faber's view is not the dominant perspective in the film. Only we can see the transitions; only the viewer has all the visual information and sees all the visual difference and differentiation. And the viewer is invited to fever along as the hapless Germans fall victim to the machinations of the duke's new adviser.

The film was released in conjunction with the introduction of the death camps of the Holocaust and sought to rupture the relationship of the masses of occupied Europe with the European Jews, insisting on making visible an invisible essence, to break the hold of knowledge of the friend down the street or next door and accomplish the triumph of a category over a varied different and complex humanity. It was released at the same time as Fritz Hippler's rabidly anti-Semitic "documentary" *Der ewige Jude* (*The Eternal Jew*) (1940), which had the same goal. The documentary proved a flop. An aggressive voice-over narrator accompanies equally antagonistic images. *The Eternal Jew* could only work as propagandistic point of view. It insists—it demands—see here, look this way, recognize these facts. The costume drama *Jud Süß*, on the other hand, belonged to larger genre traditions; dubbed into nine languages, its subtle camerawork meant it could attract a record audience of 20 million, only a small portion of whom may have been anti-Semites, all of whom left the cinema with a new technology of seeing the visual field.

The techniques developed in *Jud Süß* can be deployed to radically other ends. Viewers may operate according to social categorization, predisposing them to certain readings or certain images to be received as other. And while that recognition could be considered at the heart of the techniques of *Jud Süß*, Wolfgang Petersen in his classic *Das Boot* (1981) deployed it explicitly to overcome certain forms of differentiation. He sought in the film to reduce social categorization that derived from an understanding of German soldiers as Nazis, as enemies. It sought to make visible its protagonists as regular guys, humans, common people in a desperate situation.[37] British and American sailors who had no fondness for the Third Reich nevertheless reported watching the film with great engagement. That film's location on a submarine, distant from explicit Nazi images, created an emphasis on the common soldier that allowed non-German audiences to cathect with characters who had primarily appeared as enemy or conflictual other. The viewers were drawn away from conflictual national identity to see submariners as a shared *alter alterum* and a commonality of those others recognized as like.

If a film can school us to see difference, then of course a film can work against given patterns of social categorization, seeking in its diegesis to change social and historical patterns of differentiation. Rosa von Praunheim's film *It Is Not the Homosexual Who Is Perverse, but the Society in Which He Lives* (1971) set off the gay rights movement in Germany, deploying a not dissimilar representational technique. In that film von Praunheim relied on visual stereotypes as a form of progressive confrontation, displaying the homosexual subculture as consisting of "leather queens, bourgeois aesthetes, toilet fags," and so on. This salacious anthropological portrayal sets up as foil to all of these stereotypes a character, Daniel, who passes through all of these phases like Christian in John Bunyan's *Pilgrim's Progress* until he arrives at a final position of becoming a self-conscious and self-determining type of gay activist. The film actively and strategically deploys the opposition of static stereotype versus the type who unfolds into the fullness of character. Out of the rather heated discussion that ensued and the desire to resist the stereotype, fifty gay rights organizations formed. By contrast, over the course of the next two decades, films sought to present a positive image of gays and lesbians, like the classic coming-out film *Desert Hearts* (Dietch 1986) or the slice-of-gay-life film *Torch Song Trilogy* (Beckoff 1988). In doing so, however, gayness became the defining element to the characters, ultimately entrapping them in the very strategy designed to bring them into visibility: they appeared as gay men and women. The openings of typicality never gave way, restricting them to being seen as only the type. By contrast, in the film *Everything Will Be Fine* we find strategies to rupture stereotyping and restore complexity to the characters. There are numerous diegetic direct displays of stereotyping discussed above as the difference to be seen; in this case, we could describe it as the difference to be seen differently. Moreover, we find other film techniques to confront stereotypical viewing practices. In a particularly well filmed scene, Nabou is at work in a kiosk, awkwardly dressed in apron and a lace cap that perches awkwardly on her natural African hair. A series of customers appear at the window and make comments that derive from misreading Nabou. Point-of-view shots and reaction shots position the viewer to take up Nabou's perspective, but rather than reduce her to the stereotype of the customer, we experience her growing anger and reread Nabou with a greater complexity. The film creates this emotional awareness as a result of our having followed the diegesis. The viewer is led into viewing practices that work precisely against stereotypicality.

A film can thus establish extra-diegetic alterity, an alterity that does not adhere to the images of the film. In the unfolding of the narrative, a film can provide

48 · CHAPTER 2

a superabundance of knowledge, positioning the viewer as third-person omniscient, often to heighten tension, often to display a failure of visible alterity.
We can consider as active counter to *Jud Süß* the scene of passing that appears
in *Europa Europa* (*Hitlerjunge Salomon*) (Holland 1990). The viewer knows that
the main character, Salomon Perel, is Jewish and hiding from persecution in, of
all places, an elite Nazi school. A poignant scene emerges when a teacher who
professes the ability to differentiate Jews and Aryans turns to Salomon as an
example. The viewer experiences a tension, fearful of the power of this third to
recognize difference. The teacher inspects "Josef Peters," and tension mounts
over the anticipation of discovery. However, the teacher fails and the tension
dissipates. We know that Salomon is different, but the teacher cannot see it. The
teacher is the inverse of the Faber character, and with it the film seeks to rupture
the spectacularity of anti-Semitism. This trope now returns frequently. It is
present in the celebrated *Aimee & Jaguar* (Färberböck 1998), where the character
Lily Wust claims that she can smell a Jew. Wust is similarly put to the test. In this
trope visual alterity fails, yet in doing so, difference is reinforced in the awareness
of the viewer, relegated to the nonvisual. We could then pursue if this inversion
of the technique of *Jud Süß* undermines the category of essential difference.

There are numerous mechanisms whereby a film draws its viewers into
a recognition of difference within its diegesis. Visual codes and framing are
the most immediate: appearance of the body, dress, techniques of intercutting, the camera lingering on the body in long takes, lighting for difference, a
frame that transforms difference into the exotic. Of course, comparisons are
not passively undertaken in the relationship of the viewer to the film. The viewers are not subject solely to the visual text playing out in front of them. *Suture*
(McGehee and Siegel 1993) presents a rarity in that the film's images exist in
a compelling conflict with its diegesis. In this neo-noir thriller of mistaken
identities, Vincent Towers convinces his almost identical half brother, Clay, to
switch identities with him. It is part of an elaborate plot to hide the fact that
Vincent has murdered their father. He stages an accident with Clay, blowing
up the car he is driving, in an attempt to stage his own death. However, Clay
survives with memory loss and massive facial trauma. The reconstruction of
his face takes place according to pictures of Vincent. Clay then becomes the
object of the police investigation into the death of his father. Believing himself
to be Vincent, he is nevertheless haunted by memories of Clay. The actors in
the film playing Vincent and Clay, however, do not look alike. Vincent is played
by Michael Harris and Clay by Dennis Haysbert. The initial sequence of the two
brothers describing how uncanny their resemblance is jars with the image of
Harris, who is thin with a receding hairline and white, looking into the face of

Haysbert, who is taller, muscular, and black. The visual difference of the two actors plays no role in the film, where their appearance is identical. To enter this filmic world, the spectator has to overcome a certain dissonance between the received black/white racialized patterns of perceiving difference and the film's logic that refuses to see that difference. The film does not undo received patters of racial differentiation; however, the dissonance it establishes opens up possibilities for the viewer to experience such differentiations differently.

In *Transformation Scenario* (2018) Clemens von Wedemeyer brought our attention to a new form of the refusal of difference. Increasingly filmmakers are turning to crowds generated by algorithms rather than relying on expensive human extras. Blockbuster films like *Lord of the Rings* (Jackson 2001–2003) moved the process out of clearly animated figures into live-action appearance. The Wembley Stadium sequence in *Bohemian Rhapsody* (Singer 2018) is the most recent film to seek a seamless appearance of animated crowd with live-action actors. Von Wedemeyer's project, a single-channel projection with multiple inset screens, explores the artificial mass, taking them from the background and bringing them into focus. A central point of the exploration is how the figures are made to appear to be engaged in believable group behaviors. The project considers how those images of the undifferentiated mass can be deployed to present an appearance of power. Demonstrations, electoral victory celebrations, rallies—what happens when their impact becomes expanded visually through the addition of algorithmic crowds?

Cinema as a mass medium draws in a mass audience, not simply one viewer but viewers, and in its ability to construct viewing practices lies its power. Differentiation, the refusal to differentiate, the expansion of complex subjectivity or expansion of group coherency, is a dynamic of sociohistorical and cultural context. In portraying difference, films can rely on differentiation to speak to, or on behalf of, in effect alterior positions in conflict, to transform power dynamics. Responsively, critically, we must ask, How may we see difference differently?

Alterity: The Other and the Third

The point is not to blind ourselves to difference. Difference must be seen. Differentiation is not simply any activity; through difference/differentiation the conscious subject comes into being, becomes aware of the world beyond the self. Self-conscious being in the world arises in the appearance of the world as outside the self. The subject experiences limits that distinguish the world and all the brave new others in it. The Hegelian model of subjectivity is not one of a preformed subject. It is not a monad lost in spectating, isolated. It is not a

50 • CHAPTER 2

subject viewing preformed otherness, objective. The Hegelian subject arises in the moment of apprehension, the act of viewing. Perceiving, an act of differentiating, does not overwhelm the subject; the subject exists in awareness of its own alterity. The subject arises in a condition of estrangement from itself, and Hegel postulates the first response as one of aggression to the other. To sense the other is to fall from the grace of universality; to destroy the other is to return to the lost paradise of universal consciousness, but it is then also to lose the experience of the self, of self-consciousness. Consciousness must come to the conclusion that it cannot have it both ways. It exists because of that which is foreign to itself. This "foreignness," as Georg Simmel would later suggest, does not overwhelm; rather, it constitutes the subject as a sociable being.[38]

Hegel, however, mentions in the relation of alterity a third. Already hinted at above, we want to consider this third more precisely, to consider that there are patterns of alterity in a film that are not ours. We may enter into the narrative in some form, but we are not the narrative. If there is a third in the film, we are also the third, watching, weighing, engaging in the narrative. Our viewing the film produces the narration. Hegel's third must look and weigh, must draw into comparison. Difference is not simply any activity; through difference/differentiation the conscious subject comes into being. Hegel's project is multifaceted, but describing consciousness, self-conscious being in the world, is central to the project. And the activity of Hegel's third intrigues us because it sets up a dynamic of spectatorship that is radically different from the Lacanian/Althusserian–inspired model of suture that dominated film studies for decades. The third's engagement in spectatorship does not result in a loss of subjectivity, as posited in suture theory.[39] The spectators do not transfer self-consciousness onto the images and characters of the film. The model of suture, once important for apparatus theory, implies an ideological "duping" effect. The anti-Semitic technology of *Jud Süß* was not a duping. Suture posits the spectator's loss of self, compensated for by becoming a subject in the film. Even though Lacanian psychoanalysis emerged in part through an engagement with Hegel, Hegel's third offers a model of subjectivity that is not lost in spectating; rather, the subject arrives as its self precisely in spectating. Rather than the loss of self posited in suture, visual alterity suggests that spectating determines subjectivity.

In con films from *Ocean's Eleven* (Milestone 1960) to *The Sting* (Hill 1973) through to the reloaded *Ocean's* series of films, the spectator is buffeted between a position of being the third viewing the film and the narrative that holds a figure who knows more than the spectator. Inside and outside the narrative the con film relies on the pleasure of "Did you see it coming?" By contrast, the detective film often rests on the knowledge that a third did see it. Sherlock sees more, and the pleasure of the spectator is to see like Sherlock. Columbo sees more, but his pleasure is that his bumbling, disheveled quality makes it hard for the guilty to believe he sees their guilt; we, the spectator, know to trust him, though, and he becomes our avenging third in the narrative. Playing with the quality of the spectating third, *Der plötzliche Reichtum der armen Leute von Krombach* (*The Sudden Wealth of the Poor People of Krombach*) (Schlöndorff 1971) is based on a documented case from the early nineteenth century. In this film a group of people agree to rob the post coach that passes by their town. These are poor plebians with little about them that is remarkable. They are covered in the muck of Krombach. They dream of a better future as a result of the robbery, but because they are inept they have to try multiple times. We follow their bumbling in numerous attempts and gain a bit of sympathy for them. After finally having succeeded at robbing the coach, however, the group is almost immediately caught. Their robbery sets into motion the surveillance of the police. We go from being the third to an outsider who appears, a third drawn in to make comparisons, predisposed to recognize difference. From out of their poverty they cannot refrain from spending their money, and as soon as they do, they become obvious. What was once identical, plebian, and unremarkable becomes different. Their wealth marks them as different to the comparisons of the police, the third searching for them.

In this film the third as surveilling detective becomes positioned in the narrative of the film and directly thematized. This third is positioned to surveil, to compare, and thereby exercises power. The third sees the villagers as an alterity. They are put under suspicion collectively as *alius alium*. They are apprehended *alter alterum*. We learn to see like the policing force of the state. Here the character of the state appears as the policing force taking on the quality of the third, yet a suture of the spectator to the interests of the state does not occur. Even if the third is a representative, the apprehension of the "robbers" in the end does not serve to make us align our subjectivity with the agents of the state; more likely, it secures our horror at the measures of retribution to which the peasants are exposed. Volker Schlöndorff has specialized in these observing characters with varying relations to power. In his award-winning *Der junge Törless* (*Young Torless*) (1966), Schlöndorff drew on the power of the observing third to investigate the authoritarian conditions and willingness to collaborate that marked the Third Reich. And again, even though the film appears to us largely aligned with Torless's point of view, we are not sutured into a position of desiring to be agents of proto-fascism. One can take this as an indication that the spectators are to be left to their own critical devices. These films thematize the third.

In the film apparatus, regardless of the narrative, there is always another third present. This third is outside the narrative: the viewer. And in opposition

52 · CHAPTER 2

to a third within the diegesis of the narrative, the film narrative offers comparisons to the viewer, guiding, leading the viewer to recognize difference, making particular forms of difference visible in its images—state/peasants, poor/rich.

Harun Farocki's 2007 *Vergleich über ein Drittes* (*Comparisons via a Third*) takes up the question of the third in cinema in its two-channel installation form.[40] The same work also appeared two years later in a sixty-two-minute essay film version by the name *Zum Vergleich* (*By Comparison*). In the installation form, the film plays on two monitors for a loop length of twenty-four minutes. The installation itself becomes the third, making the comparison of the images on the two channels possible. The installation breaks up the serial nature of the montage of images and brings them into a new form of collage. They play side by side, allowing for a comparison of radically different images. It is the position outside the two that brings them into a relation of alterity, *alius alium*.

The installation can consist of two channels. These can be on monitors or projected onto walls or separate screens. They can invite a spectator to sit in a darkened gallery space and watch in a quasi-kino, or they can stand in space as monitors on pedestals, allowing the spectator more freedom to move in space. The images are timed in relation to each other. The two channels do not loop at an independent pace of their own. It was this structured quality to the two channels that facilitated the reworking of the images into a single-channel "film."

As an installation the two channels project images of brick makers in various global locations at work. Bricks, because of their weight, prove resistant to globalization, tending to be produced locally within local systems of production. The images come from India, Burkina Faso, France, Switzerland, and Germany. They range from handmade sundried bricks to highly industrialized practices. In France the bricks are made in a factory that has not changed since the nineteenth century. In Burkina Faso the construction of a community center is undertaken as a community project. In India the process is backbreakingly intensive. In Switzerland the workers are individualized and isolated observers in a robot and assembly line work environment. Physical labor is gone but so is sociality. The installation does not present one method of brick production as better than the other. It presents differences in production, in labor conditions, commented on only by twenty intertitles.

The spectator, through the technology of a two-channel installation, takes up literally a third position in relation to the images. The connections, distinctions, differentiations, as well as the commonalities and identities are up to the spectator to recognize. Farocki's project was not one of narrative; however, I bring it into the considerations of alterity and narrative here because it points to the otherwise unreflected quality of the technology of cinema itself to act as an apparatus of alterity, a techne of knowing in a particular way, through a particular condition of perspective and differentiation.

* * *

Narrative cinema engages the differentiating subject via the image in the relations within the moving image but also through the fundamental position of the spectator as a third to the action on the screen. Visual alterity in narrative cinema arises in the image through mise-en-scène, via characters and the figures they cut, but also via the technology of cinema and the way it positions the spectator.

CHAPTER 3

Phenomenology and Alterity

Seeing Is Always Seeing of Something Else

"Idea"—the most "abstract" immaterial term of phenomenology, the heart of its quest for universality—"idea" itself derives from the Greek word *idein*, to see. How do we move toward a film phenomenology, not a phenomenology of film? How do we develop an approach that accounts for film philosophy—not film and philosophy, nor simply film as philosophy, but film philosophy, film bringing forward knowledge, wisdom?

Thinking Seeing

As discussed in chapter 2, Jean-François Coulais offered us a history of sight and social-technical organization: seeing as social technology. Foucault's *Discipline and Punish*, with its attention to the panopticon as a social technology of seeing, follows a similar analysis with a focus on prisons and other surveillance institutions. I also pointed to Martin Jay as attending to the history of philosophy, especially the emergence of modern phenomenology. Jay's history of philosophy shows the link of ocular vision and philosophical thought.[1] Nevertheless, and in spite of the rise of an active movement of film philosophy, the history of philosophy as a history of thinking-seeing/sight-thought has not had a broad impact on the work of philosophical critical theoretical reflective thought as such.

To think.

To think freely, without determination, openly, attentive and focused: desires of modern thought.

To experience freedom in thinking, we may at best be aware of thinking as thinking.

And thinking awarely, being aware of consciousness, is the first step in the phenomenological reduction—not Cartesian doubt but awareness of thinking. *Consciousness is always consciousness of something.*[2] Consciousness sets the phenomenological world in motion. Consciousness is different from thinking. To be aware of thinking, to think consciously, is to make thinking into a thing, an object, a *Gegenstand*, a standing against or perhaps a leaning on.

The Greek word θεωρεῖν (*theorein*) meant to consider, speculate, or look at. It broke down further into the parts *thea*, a view, and *horan*, to see. To theorize and theater are acts of seeing, looking, observing, or even spectating.

Thinking sight and theorizing seeing.

Sight is a form of perception, not perception itself. It is a part of perception, an important part. Sight is, of course, not the only form of perception, and perception is not the only activity of consciousness. In fact it is quite clearly possible to do without seeing and still perceive just as it is possible to do without perception and still be conscious.[3] However, *if* sight is present, or "at hand," then it does act as the primary mode of perception, not the only but the primary.

We would be dissatisfied if having sight meant giving up on our other senses, if our only interface with the world was accomplished through sight, if we were forced to choose sight alone among all the modes of perception. But sight does subordinate the senses, giving a certain order to perception.

Sight makes the world present in a particular and profound way. In sight we perceive the world from a particular place. Sight positions, coordinates, locates, and localizes the world. Sight makes the world present in a particular way, and it makes us present in the world in a particular place and time. Sight is a form of presence in the world. Heidegger speaks of presence through the German word *Vorhandensein*, a being at hand, being graspable to the hand. The world is at hand, the hand reaches into the world. But he did not think this position through far enough. The hand may follow vision as it reaches out into the world. To see is to reach into the world beyond the stretch of the hand, beyond the extent of the body. To see is to grasp the world in sight. Sight makes presence in the world into a *Voraugensein*, a being in front of the eyes, a *Für-das-Auge-Sein*, a being for the eye. Sight, insomuch as it functions as a synonym for perception, is a reaching into the world. The first act of will is perception and after that movement of the hand or body. Seeing is active; it is an action. Heidegger could have known this, but he famously abandoned

56 · CHAPTER 3

Nietzschean becoming for essentialist being, being in the world (*Dasein*) instead of the play of force in time.[4]

It was Nietzsche's considerations of *The Birth of Tragedy* that at heart recognized the link between theory, *thea horan*, and theater, or *thea* (a view, a seeing) *-tron* (a suffix denoting place). Nietzsche recognized a relation between philosophy and sight, thinking and seeing. For Nietzsche, though, the masses of powers at work in the world exert force on each other, and perception helps the subject become aware of these exertions. Perception, according to Nietzsche, is reactive, reacting and responding to external stimuli. Nietzsche's notion of active and reactive imagined the senses as being slow and hence inherently reactive. We retreat from the burning only after the damage has begun, not actively but reactively. Light that hits our retinas sets in motion a chemical reaction that takes a bit of time, a delay. This is a response, and if we run or set ourselves in motion to meet a charging rhino, our reaction is not transformed into an action by simply making reactive a pejorative value of active. Thus, in this model Nietzsche critically treats a notion of vision akin to the camera obscura. For Nietzsche, perception gave consciousness the illusion of being active; Nietzsche wanted to rupture that illusion and liberate consciousness to become a real active force, a "will to power." Modern phenomenology emerged largely naïve to thinking seeing.

Phenomenologists Seeing Film

EDMUND HUSSERL

Edmund Husserl considered perception like Galen thought of sight: as a form of ray, broadcasting out, illuminating the horizon. Consciousness in the action of perceiving is thus simultaneously like spotlight and camera; it illuminates the object, bringing it into focus, and then it frames it and develops it like a piece of film rolling in a camera. In this approach to perception, Husserl infused phenomenology with an intentionality of approach to the world.[5] In effect unlike Nietzsche, Husserl recognized senses and perception as fundamentally active. Sight, sense perception, moved out into the world like an illuminating ray.

In his *Ideas for a Pure Phenomenology* Husserl observed that the world precedes us, it "is there for us all, and to which we ourselves none the less belong."[6] We take up a relation to this world in *natürlicher Einstellung*, translated as a natural attitude, but we can also understand *Einstellung* as a positioning—a taking up of position—in the world. *Einstellung* is also the word for a shot, the positioning of a camera as it enframes the world for a period in time. For Husserl, the natural positioning takes place through the senses: sight, touch, hearing, and so on. Husserl's subjects are like a recording camera with additional senses, positioned in the world. The camera and its lighting equipment shine out into a world in order to record it. Although this comparison is worth considering, it is an awkward one. Husserl was not thinking of the camera, although his thinking parallels developments in recording and projection in his moment.

Husserl's natural world is at hand, and the subject takes up a position in it. It is a given, but transforming world and the thinking, reflecting subject, or *cogito*, arises in this world in the natural positioning. The world is always there and our being is always in the world. It is in this positioning that the world gains meaning. That world that is at hand gains meaning in the activity of the hand. Sight brings the world into position, giving it depth, locating it to the right or left. Sight localizes the world and imbues it with *fakta*, or facticity.[7] That Husserl posits simply a natural position in the world, however, means that the fakta of perception are not actually the facts of the world—just like the frame of the camera defines a field of perception that differs from the entire visual world. On the one hand, Husserl's perceiving subject arises in a particular world, a particular space and time. Yet on the other, his observation about the world being "for me simply there" allows him to think about another world, a universal world that exceeds the localized world of the particular consciousness. Husserl's essences were the opposite of Hegel's essentialisms. The subject he considers arises in space and time, yet he is interested in understanding a universal subject in a universal world, a consciousness and world in any-space at any-time or in the phenomenology at a higher level of all-space and at all-times. It is a general subject in a general condition. The specific determination of the world cuts the subject off from the universal world of any-space and any-time.

For Husserl, the project of phenomenology is to move the intentionality to higher orders, away from the local individual determinations. And according to Husserl, the subject can accomplish this task by suspending natural perception. The subject in cognition is always able to engage in a phenomenological reduction, an *epoché*, a bracketing out of the locations of sight, a moving away from the specific meaning given to the object when taken to hand. The principle of phenomenology, Husserl's phenomenological reduction, requires the intentionally experiencing subject to bracket out of all that is present in this specific world and place and time. And radicalizing his understanding of intentionality, he describes consciousness as in effect a relation of intentionality in this world: "Jedes Bewußtsein ist Bewußtsein von etwas," "every conscious-being is always conscious-being of something."[8]

58 · CHAPTER 3

Something, a state of affairs, a value, a wish—all arise in explicit relation to cognition; they take on "being" because of the consciousness of cognition, by cause of "conscious being." Of course the camera is not aware of itself and has no conscious being. Thus here the awkward comparison can no longer obtain. It is the cinematographer, the editor, or the spectator who may be well aware of the camera and the limitations of its frame. They are the conscious being in the cinematic world.

Husserl then goes on to pursue a method described by the term *epoché*. The epoché designates a means to overcome the actual cogito and arrive at pure ego, whose radiating focus is directed at the "pure object."[9] He may as well have pursued an all-recording camera. Husserl's project drifted in this way toward mysticism, a charge against which he became very engaged.[10] For subsequent phenomenological investigation, this proposition had a profound impact, driving it away from the actual world, the *noema*, or the world as perceived, and into the universal. Husserl's student and former assistant Martin Heidegger thus turned phenomenological investigation away from cognition toward ontology. Pursuing this history further does not interest me here. The move away from the actual world and the localized cogito to pure ego travels a path out of practicality that I am not interested in following.

"Consciousness is always consciousness of something."[11] That statement, however, still seems profound and compelling. What happens if we do not move with it into universality and ontology but remain with the local and contingent? And what about that special instance of consciousness, that special contingent form of perception: sight? What if we do accept with Husserl that sight is not reactive, not simply a wire or conduit, a tube that directs information into consciousness? What do we experience if we observe that sight is always perception of something? With that I do not mean simply that consciousness through sight sees things; this observation would flatten out into a common and commonsensical tautology. Consider that single and contingent forms of consciousness, seeing/sight in a particular place and a particular time, are not simply a matter of consciousness establishing a relationship to the world. Sight, the perception of something, brings the world into place and time, into meaning and space. Sight is an activity of consciousness. We may not always be aware of how we perceive, but perception is an awareness of the world. Consciousness enters into the world in this awareness. If we focus on this general activity of consciousness, then the seeing-seen, perceiver-perceived, *noetic-noema* relationship calls forth a world, sets our world in motion. Sight is active, constitutive, and meaningful for world and subject.

Consciousness is active in the world, and sight is a means, a mechanism, whereby consciousness reaches out into the lush materiality of the world. Thinking makes of four dots in space a square and five dots a circle or so. Thinking makes a circle shaded lightly on "top" appear concave and lightly on "bottom" convex. Thinking visually recognizes "gaps" in "patterns" and fills them in. Henri Bergson and Gilles Deleuze observed how the movement image appears nowhere except in the mind. Consciousness acts upon a flickering image through the chemical burn of the retina, the networking of synaptic bundles, the phi phenomenon and beta movements that arise, into the sense-making functions of the brain, all to produce out of the flicker an image that moves and delights and entertains. We are more than cats staring at shiny objects. Staring at the screen brings a world into existence that is unavailable to those without the special and contingent form of perception, *sight*, unavailable to those whose consciousness is based on extrasensory perception or whose consciousness has no perceptive faculty at all.

Sight reaches out into the world and skims its surfaces. What if we bring back the earlier comparison and do think of the camera and its lighting as holding insight here? What if we think of the night vision lenses that rely on infrared, or the very current advances in laser robotic "eyes," as deriving from the fundamental way that perception actively illuminates a world into being, allowing for human engagement? Human sight is extended by technology so that we can see more than is given by the eye alone, so that we can see in the dark, see through walls and clothing, and bags and suitcases, beneath flesh and into the vibrating rave of the muons and into the vibrating rave of stars clustered at the center of the galaxy, into people's apartments, and bathrooms and bedrooms, and right into the hair on their head. Such seeing precedes reaching and touching but is every bit as much an act of will, an action of willing.

Certainly sight does not reach out into the world and chisel away at marble with the heat of vision. We are not Superman. Let that task fall to the other parts of will and consciousness and body. The hands can get dirty sticking into muck, while the eye can discover unaided that pile ahead into which we now need not fall. Sight keeps us from becoming the mouse in Franz Kafka's one-paragraph anecdote "A Little Fable."[12] The mouse fearing the sight of the broad world allowed its path to be the safe one. The path became dangerous with the mousetrap ahead in the corner, and the mouse is stalled. Worse yet, the mouse seems to have timidly closed its eyes to the approach of the wise cat, who sagely advises that the mouse need "only turn around" right before she eats it. The cat sees open-eyed other options "at hand" and enjoys a nice dinner.

60 · CHAPTER 3

MAURICE MERLEAU-PONTY

Maurice Merleau-Ponty is perhaps still to be described as the philosopher of sight. Certainly he is the phenomenologist who turned the project of phenomenology to considerations of sight. Taking up the approach that consciousness is always consciousness of something, Merleau-Ponty began from the question of how that something became an object to the conscious subject. He considered more intensely not just *that* the object was perceived but began to ask *how* it was perceived. And in these considerations he focused on sight as the primary means of perception in the world. In sight the world becomes visible. Hence with Merleau-Ponty we undergo a shift from consciousness to sight: sight is always seeing something.

It might be expected that a discussion about the phenomenology of sight by a film scholar would have immediately turned to Merleau-Ponty. Certainly we are all indebted to the extensive work of Vivian Sobchack for adapting Merleau-Ponty to discussions of cinema. And that is, for me, the central critical problem. Merleau-Ponty, the phenomenologist of sight, needs to be adapted to cinema. Daniel Yacavone recently surveyed the burgeoning field of phenomenologically based film studies and revealed that in all their various directions, scholars continue to contend with Merleau-Ponty's treatment of film as a special form of perception, like painting, an aesthetic form.[13]

In all of Merleau-Ponty's discussions of sight and seeing, he devoted only one lecture, "The Film and the New Psychology," to questions of cinema. This lecture, held in 1945 and collected in the volume *Sense and Non-Sense*, proves surprisingly oblivious to the object of discussion. He did return to cinema briefly in essays on art, especially in his celebrated essay on Cézanne, yet in these essays he discusses the medium without indicating much familiarity with the state of cinema in his contemporary moment. In "The Film and the New Psychology" the actual discussion of film takes up only a third of the essay, otherwise devoted to the insights Gestalt psychology provided for analyses of seeing. Although written fifteen years after the triumph of sound, in the essay Merleau-Ponty was still thinking of visual films as separate from sound films. Of course, it is possible to make profound observations by discussing a historical object; that he is considering a historical mode of film production is in itself not a problem. The difficulty lies in the fact that he treats cinema and the perception of film as a special case, a special instance of viewing. Film is a perceptual object distinct from the world and the natural seeing of ocular vision. In this essay his exploration of film is undertaken only as a particular application of general principles of perception:

This is why the movies can be so gripping in their presentation of man: they do not give us his thoughts, as novels have done for so long, but his conduct or behavior. They directly present to us that special way of being in the world, of dealing with things and other people, which we can see in the sign language of gesture and gaze and which clearly defines each person we know.[14]

"The film" here is a form of cinematographic language that parallels other forms of intentional communication: writing, sign language, style, and fashion. It shows behaviors, it shows actions, it shows gestures, which Merleau-Ponty treats as a special way of being in the world. The practice of viewing people, their gestures, and behaviors is approached not as a behavior that defines perception in the modern world but as a special act. Cinema is not a place where the moving image and the reading practices it elicits from ocular vision define a new form of seeing, a new phenomenon of perception, a new moment in the phenomenology of consciousness. In effect, Merleau-Ponty treats film as he does painting or the other arts; these are forms distinct from the moment of the "natural attitude" that Husserl described. They are objects that pose an aesthetic question, a moment of defamiliarized seeing, as it were. Merleau-Ponty thus continues the gesture of phenomenology to orient the analysis to a universal decontextualized and contentless practice. Where via Husserl we can consider that sight is always seeing of something, Merleau-Ponty inherits from Husserl the goal of the phenomenological approach to abstract the "thing" into an any-thing located in any-space and any-time. Cinema, and its significance for a general consideration of perception, is thus dismissed because it is understood as a specific and particular form of seeing and not recognized as, say, *an avant-garde of sight*.

To be sure, Merleau-Ponty considers the defamiliarized seeing of the aesthetic experience as relating back to the general acts of perception. In this essay he distinguishes what happens in the frame of the painting, "art," from what happens in the frame of the film, "drama." The joy of art lies in its showing how something takes on meaning not by referring to already established and acquired ideas but by the temporal or spatial arrangement of elements. As we saw above, a movie has meaning in the same way that a thing does: neither of them speaks to an isolated understanding; rather, both appeal to our power to tacitly decipher the world of "men" and to coexist with them. It is true that in our ordinary lives we lose sight of this aesthetic value of the tiniest perceived thing. It is also true that the perceived form is never perfect in real life, that it always has blurs, smudges, and superfluous matter. Cinematographic drama is finer grained than real-life dramas; it takes place in a world that is more exact

62 · CHAPTER 3

than the real world. But in the last analysis, perception permits us to understand the meaning of the cinema. A movie is not thought; it is perceived.[15]

Both art and cinematographic drama, according to Merleau-Ponty, take the viewer out of the "real world." Merleau-Ponty may be thinking here of the ability of the aesthetic condition to instill a certain *ostranenie*. The movie, like the work of art in general, defers from the quotidian genres in order to show us bits and pieces of how we see. Art defamiliarizes in order to help us reflect on and recognize how the quotidian familiar functions. Merleau-Ponty's transformation of the epoché was to treat it like art and its *ostranenie*. The epoché, however, is thought, and *ostranenie* is perceived.

By placing emphasis on the cinematographic drama—in other words, narrative film—Merleau-Ponty can treat cinema as a special instance of perception, and this distinction continues largely to obtain in phenomenological approaches to cinema. In Merleau-Ponty's case, he is, however, confusing editing and narrative. There are certainly many moving images without drama. Merleau-Ponty does not consider what it would mean to show a film of the Empire State Building that unfolds in real time or a film of a Yule log as it burns. Likewise, there are many plays with intense drama that transpire in real life. I would emphasize that it is the same perceptive apparatus that views the "real world" and the cinematic. There is no difference between the eyes that view movement in the cinema and those that view it in the lobby. The apparatus of perception does not change in the moment the house lights dim and the projector's light begins. It does not change if it is in the cinema, the theater, the home, or the battlefield.

Cinema is not a special instance of seeing; it is a technology that transforms perception. Sobchack and others consider cinema's technology in its impact on the perceptive apparatus as if these were separate. However, our technology of seeing, cinematic or otherwise, is a part of the perceptive apparatus, which itself has a long dynamic history of transformation. There are not bodies equipped with ocular vision that perceive naturally at one time and in an unnatural estranged fashion at others. It may be the case that the cinema is a particular place distinct from the sidewalk or the forest clearing, but the technologies of sight transform the apparatus of perception. The forest clearing is perceived differently in the cinematic age than it was in the painterly era, than it was in the era of spectacles, than it was in the era of burnished bronze. Sight is always seeing of something at some time and in some place and in some way.

SARA AHMED

In the phenomenological approach as Husserl introduced it, vision, seeing, sight, and perception are to be freed of the particular and contingent; they are to be disembodied. (This aspiration has been taken up positively by many disciplines as an orientation toward value-free science and knowledge unencumbered by the limitations of the situated observer.) Husserl's position was possible only because he ignored the body, took ocular vision to be natural, considered perception distinct from actual sight, and in bracketing out all of these matters sought to treat perception as a universal essence, one that was key to a transcendent experience of the world. However, in his last work, *The Visible and the Invisible*, Merleau-Ponty took up this point and treated perception as "in my body as a thing of the world."[16] But the goal he set for phenomenology, the arriving at a "gaze of the mind, *intuitus mentis*," focused on ideality in any time and any place. Merleau-Ponty's consideration of the body and perception becomes a conundrum of a disembodied embodiment, which can only take place through "an almost carnal existence of the idea, as well as by a sublimation of the flesh."[17] In this, his last, unfinished work, he began to develop an almost ascetical mysticism: a chastening and denial of the body that remained a paper proposition.

In a most radical inversion, Sara Ahmed has argued recently and convincingly that the value freedom promised by phenomenological bracketing has been an illusion, masking the situatedness of the observer in conditions of race, class, sex, gender, north/south, orient/occident, and developed/developing world disparities.[18] She has highlighted that sexual, raced, and global-economic orientation are a "matter" of beings; "'being' itself becomes (sexually) oriented."[19] Ahmed's analysis seeks to reveal how the universalism of the value-free subject actually masks a normativity of the oriented, situated, embodied analyst, undoing the Husserlian intention of the project. The potential that Husserl recognized in phenomenology lies not in excluding the situatedness of the body but precisely in the exploration of its orientation in space and time. Bodies, beings, are always in place and time.

In our exploration of sight, however, we can push this embodied phenomenology even further. Although she has discussed films, Ahmed has not considered cinema, sight, nor the perceptive apparatus as such.[20] Certainly bodies are located and perceived in particular social, cultural, and economic perspectives. But this approach considers how bodies are perceived and not how the body itself perceives. To consider that the body is perceived as gendered without considering how the gendered body perceives is a limitation. The world that appears to our vision is a world matched to the potentials for knowledge of our bodies. The perception afforded by sight is determined by a body generally equipped with two eyes in a relation to each other that does not produce just any possibility of seeing but a particular form of binocular sight. What appears to one eye is not the same as what is perceived with two. Binocular sight is of another

64 · CHAPTER 3

order than monocular images, a point that Merleau-Ponty recognized.[21] Vision results from the a priori of the body and its apparatus for seeing; such vision is typically binocular, color-receptive, spatially antagonistic, contextual, and comparative. Ahmed's considerations might actually be described as a further determination of vision, deriving from the specific body's social significance, historical emergence, and economic position—in effect, an a priori of social psychology. But the sight of a body that is trained to play soccer differs from that of a body that is not even allowed into a soccer stadium because its engendering forecloses its being bodily in that space. We see how we can see and what we are trained to see.

Sight is seeing of some thing in some time and some place from some position. Sight is seeing within a particular apparatus of perception. Sight, vision, and the activity of seeing are affected by and effected in a particular structure, arrangement, or organization. Perception, of course, is not fully encompassed by seeing. Yet let us add to these observations a deep suspicion of any continued notion of natural vision. Ocular vision cannot be separated from technology. Consider the impact of polished surfaces, ground glass, mirrors and lenses, eyeglasses and telescopes. Technologies are part of the apparatus of perception: the production of the image. The mechanisms of film recording and projection, the airplane that affords a view at fifty thousand feet, the space capsule that affords a view at 100 million feet—these shape the perceptive capacity of ocular vision as much as Renaissance copying tools or fires in Neolithic caves did.

The body actively engages in the reception of appearance not simply as a matter of apperception versus perception, not only as a matter of comparison to past experiences, but as an active engagement of a sight system with the perceived. Thus, rather than approach cinema as a particular of perception, we can recognize it as constitutive of certain basic principles of sight that are not reserved solely to bodies at the cinema.

*   *   *

There is no natural seeing. If the same perceptive apparatus apprehends the streetscape and the moving image of the streetscape, it is the art of seeing, the strategy of reading, that distinguishes those scenes. Taking a seat in the cinema, standing in a gallery, and walking out onto the street or down a forest path actualize different forms of attention. These different actions prime different memory systems. Face recognition at a family reunion engages different mechanisms of visual discrimination than those engaged while viewing a Katharine Hepburn film retrospective. During a walk across an open field on a sunny day, the retina may scan broadly and the fovea may leap in mini-saccades

Phenomenology and Alterity • 65

millisecond by millisecond without centering on a target object. Standing in front of an installation, a scanning process will begin, during which the fovea may center on a target object and pause. The focus of the gaze allows for conscious awareness to activate, naming mechanisms to start, associative memories to engage, and emotions to arise. But let us be clear, the walk in the field may also contain moments when the gaze focuses on an object—say, a flower or a cloud—and in the cinema the eye may leap in mini-saccades as images whirl across the screen without specific information. One location does not result in one type of seeing.

However, because one takes place in a field and one in a cinema, why would one be natural seeing and the other "unnatural"? Of course, the "natural seeing" proposed by Husserl, Merleau-Ponty, Sobchack, and other phenomenologists is a notion that the field is seeing without technology. *There is no seeing that is distinct from technology.* While someone is seated in a cinema, their gaze may be sutured to specific fields of an image, mid-screen background; their attention may be held through specific mechanisms, such as spotlighting on the gun; their conscious awareness may be prolonged by the activity of the receptive fields, such as the conversing couple in the middle of the tracking shot. We pay attention for ninety minutes, but is that attention consistently the same? Is the way we pay attention during a ninety-minute walk in a meadow consistent and unvarying? What happens to perception during a ninety-minute drive through rolling meadows? Different contexts do entail different mechanisms, neural pathways, and behavior psychologies to process the information and perceptions that are entailed. But inasmuch as there is not a form of seeing that is specific to one locale, we must also take into account transformations in practices of perception. Having seen a meadow in the cinema, the perception of a meadow in the open from a car has changed indelibly. With the visual technology of cinema emerged a new way of seeing, a new techne of knowing, just as had emerged with the techniques of photography, or proscenium theater, or the grinding of ochre to make paint. *Seeing is always seeing through a particular apparatus. Certain technologies define the apparatus of sight in given eras.*

CHAPTER 4

Apparatus Theory Now More Than Ever!

After long years of critique of classic apparatus theory, I would like to begin this chapter by recalling a passage from one of the foundational texts:

> The cinema—the historically constitutable cinematic statements—functions with and in the set of apparatuses of representation at work in a society. There are not only the representations produced by the representative apparatuses as such (painting, theatre, cinema, etc.); there are also participating in the movement of the whole, the systems of the delegating of power (political representation), the ceaseless working-up of social imaginaries (historical, ideological representations) and a large part, even, of the modes of relational behaviour (balances of power, confrontations, manoeuvres of seduction, strategies of defense, marking of differences or affiliations). On the other hand, but at the same time, the hypothesis would be that a society is only such in that it is *driven by representation*. If the social machine manufactures representations, it also manufactures *itself* from representations—the latter operative at once as means, matter and condition of sociality.
>
> Thus the historical variation of cinematic techniques, their appearance-disappearance, their phases of convergence, their periods of dominance and decline seem to me to depend not on a rational-linear order of technological perfectibility nor on an autonomous instance of scientific "progress," but much rather in the offsettings, adjustments, arrangements carried out by a social configuration in order to represent itself, that is, at once to grasp itself, identify itself and itself produce itself in its representations.[1]

We benefited greatly from this endeavor to consider not only the image on the screen, not only the moving-image technology that records that image, not only the people behind the camera or in the audience, but the entire apparatus of cinema as a collective endeavor, the sum of its many parts. I want in this chapter to return us to the questions of this apparatus and to ask us to consider not just how we see difference but how difference comes to appear within our technologies of seeing.

Seeing is always seeing of something. We do not see the other any way but in a given way. We do not see this way and that; we see the other in a particular way in a particular time, through a particular apparatus of perception. From the start this study has insisted that *there is no natural seeing that is distinct from technology.* Stages, paintings, icons, mirrors, glasses, blinders, filters, microscopes, inks and paints, telescopes, windows and curtains, climbing a tree, squinting, shading, television, moving-image recordings, are all ways in which the perspective of seeing is shifted, changed, transformed, extended, enframed, limited, and enhanced. The devices and apparatuses of human innovation are not counter to a natural seeing; they are fundamental to the perspective of sight in any particular place and time. *Seeing is always seeing through a particular apparatus.* Sight is the entire apparatus that allows for the seeing of the world.

However, sight is not the same as perception. The famous "Gorilla Experiment" suggests that seeing and perceiving may actually diverge at times. Subjects in this cognitive experiment are given instructions to watch a basketball game and count the number of times the ball is passed from player to player. Upon completion they are asked what the number was and what they thought about the gorilla that passed through the game. Although they can provide a number, repeatedly half the subjects respond with confusion about the gorilla. Shown a video of the game they watched, they now recognize that during the play, a person in a gorilla costume came out, walked across the court performing antics, and walked off.[2]

This experiment shakes the faith, hope, or simple expectation we may have that if we look at something—really look at it—we will see it, even see through it. Attending to something, it seems, can actually result in our ability to see, to perceive something else. To focus on some thing may make us blind to the something other. This experiment, often described as an example of "change blindness," points to various cognitive processes in the brain's perceptive apparatus. Often distinguished as higher and lower brain functions by cognitive and neuroscientific research, attention as a higher function requires a great deal of "processing capacity," and as a result, focused attention actually results in a form of blindness to other details. Even when a person in a gorilla suit passes right past the fovea—the central focal point of the eyes—when all the input

68 · CHAPTER 4

necessary for seeing enters into the apparatus of sight, the gorilla may not be perceived. Clearly, seeing is happening but is not passed on into "higher-level" processes. Nietzsche already criticized the propensity to treat consciousness as a higher order. He described consciousness as secondary, arising later in evolution and coming into function only after stimuli had already been processed by the logics of the body. Perception follows stimulus; if directed to focus on one thing, it will not recognize the other until that other rises to a certain level of stimulus, until it overcomes a certain perceptual threshold. This insight into inattentional blindness has a significant impact on what we might describe as conscious perception, critical seeing, or mindfulness in recognition.

While these aspects of the limitations of consciousness may be a long-term constant in the current stage of humanoid brain development, the apparatus of perception is different in every given moment. The perception of Babylonian astrologers differs from the Renaissance Florentines and from the astrophysicists of the Hubble telescope. It is not simply a matter of what they see but how they are positioned to perceive. The capacity to perceive and the technologies of sight come together in particular configurations, *apparatuses*, changing and shifting from era to era, technology to technology. These shifts and changes are not innocent. The anti-Semitic visual apparatus of Nazi Germany and fascist Europe, the racialized optics of the US police apparatus, the representational potentials of livestreaming climate activists on Twitch—all point to the impacts of such shifts and technological changes. *For over one hundred years, moving images have been the avant-garde of our technologies of sight.* To pursue this point, the intersection of cognitive capacities, technology, and "image," requires a theory of apparatus.

Cognitive Film Studies and the End/s
of Classic Apparatus Theory

For decades apparatus theory designated the primary approach by which film scholars explored not simply the moving images on the screen but the technology that brought them there as well. The initial discussions of apparatus theory were explicitly oriented toward a history of moving-image technology.[3] They countered a technological determinism that had come to dominate historical work of the period, and they instigated an important consideration of the social, economic, and political rationales propelling transformations in cinema. Moreover, they considered the experience of the spectator vis-à-vis the moving image. In the earliest Anglophone debates, for instance, Barbara and Joseph Anderson argued against a dominant cognitive explanation for cinematic perception: the persistence of vision thesis.[4] They pointed to phi phenomena and shifted the site of the mental production of images from the retina to the cognitive neuroscientific processes of the brain.

During the 1980s David Bordwell and Noël Carroll began something of a vendetta against apparatus theory, screen theory, and everything they considered "Grand Theory," culminating in 1996 in their edited collection *Post-Theory*. It is a volume of quite varied work and motivations, although the editors introduced it as a general rejection of the Grand Theory that Bordwell and Carroll described as dominating film studies. Unfortunately, the tone of that work, especially its introduction, caused a great deal of controversy and cast a shadow on the work of more collegial and temperate investigators precisely like Joseph and Barbara Anderson.[5]

There was no need to grandstand as advocates for a post-theoretical rupture with apparatus theory; it was already possible at that time to consider how new work in cognitive and neuroscience had opened up potentials for understanding the viewer's perception vis-à-vis the moving image and the cognitive apprehension of the world as such. Even at the time of the publication of *Post-Theory*, Warren Buckland put forward an excellent attempt at a synthesis of cognitive and semiotic approaches and Per Persson has attempted to develop a "psychological theory of moving imagery."[6] And although the Society for Cognitive Studies of the Moving Image has struggled with the perception that it opposes "Grand Theory" or that it is a partisan in a debate, nevertheless in 2007 *Projections: The Journals for Movies and Mind* emerged as the premier platform for cognitive film studies, becoming a more tempered platform in which to think about cinema and cognition in an orientation of more open debate and testing. The journal's editors at the time introduced its mission with an "intent to open, not close, the discourse."[7]

The turn to the perceiving spectator in cognitive work is important and beneficial. Cognitive work sets *the viewer* against a backdrop of expanding insights into how the brain functions, how the perceptive system—might we even say the perceptive *apparatus*—works, how it intersects with the (moving) image, and how these insights impact human artistic activity. A goal to balance analysis of images with the technological conditions of production and the cognitive capacities we bring as viewers to the conditions of viewing drives this study of visual alterity. Such an approach was not contradictory to the initial discussions of *dispositif*. If we return to the early contributions of the 1970s before the focus narrowed, we see that the initial impulse was to take the full extent of the apparatus into account. The French term *dispositif*, was deployed in place of the more restrictive term *appareil*, the term preferred in historical studies of

70 · CHAPTER 4

film technology. *Dispositif* shifted attention away from the narrow discussion of the camera to the larger technological apparatus of which the camera was only one part. In the discussions of apparatus that emerged, *dispositif* designated the projected image and its relationship to the viewer as well as the process that produces that image to be projected.

What we might now designate as classic apparatus theory helped our understanding of not simply the moving images on the screen but also the mechanisms that brought them there, and in this context cognitive work has added to those insights by grounding knowledge about viewers—how they recognize, apprehend, and perceive the objects and codes moving on the screens. These are not distinct directions unless forced to be. Consider that *Projections* as a journal was published first by the Forum for Movies and Mind, which had begun in 1985 as the Forum for the Psychoanalytic Study of Film.[8] From its point of emergence, cognitive inquiry and the "Grand Theory" that Bordwell and Carroll rejected proved not to be incompatible by any means.

It was actually an odd gesture on the part of Bordwell and Carroll, and it was a strange vendetta to take up at a time when significant debates about "Grand Theory" were behind us and the general directions of screen and apparatus theory had struck out in new directions. Indeed in the Anglophone world the specific considerations of apparatus had already gone quiescent. For decades, apparatus theory had fostered the considerations of mind and spectatorship, understanding the larger film apparatus as intersecting with the consciousness of the spectator. Bordwell and Carroll were right that the discussions of apparatus theory in the Anglophone world had worked into constricting deployment of Lacanian-Althusserian theory, but as a result, that narrow focus had already been subjected to important debates about such issues as the status of the spectator.[9] By the 1990s new directions inspired by cultural studies had questioned the Marxian approach to cinema as an ideological and illusory machine. Laura Mulvey had published important cautions about the reduction of cinematic pleasure to scopophilia. Few scholars continued to approach cinema as a mechanism of subjective entrapment in an oppressive culture industry. It was always an odd proposition to negate the object one studies, to resist the passions that motivate our viewing and deny the pleasures of looking. Asceticism typically requires ideology to mask its rigidity; rather than inquiry, it fosters inquisition. So when Bordwell and Carrol held up the scientific clinical work on the viewer of cognitive science as an antidote to apparatus theory's subjective suppositions, it was its own bit of reactionary vendetta against a "foe" already in retreat, and it stultified the necessary discussion of how our moving images get to the screens we view. In the face of their critique, it should be underscored that classic apparatus theory revealed a great deal about the configuration of the conditions of production as well as the technologies of the moving image and their historical developments.

Unfortunately, in the contemporary moment, apparatus theory in the Anglophone world has fallen out of the center of film studies, leaving behind a lacuna. Where once the connections of the moving image to the technologies of its production and the consciousness of its spectators in reception motivated lively debates, those complexities have devolved into distinct fields, including studies of industry, affect, cognition, production, and reception.

Apparatus Theory Redo

In this chapter I am not interested in defending or restoring the classic apparatus theory. I am, however, interested in considering the various facets of the work just outlined as incitement to an apparatus theory for the contemporary period. I might quip that each era gets the apparatus theory it deserves. There have been a few attempts in the Anglo-American context to retain classic apparatus theory by either maintaining the general outline or modifying on the basis of the critiques. Paul Anthony Vaughn extended the Althusserian paradigm of "repressive state apparatus," coining the descriptor "transnational repressive apparatus."[10] Chris Robé and his colleagues simply updated the Marxism of the 1970s with an infusion of slogans from Michael Hardt and Antonio Negri.[11] James Snead returned to the Freudian psychoanalytic paradigm to counter Laura Mulvey's critiques, finding a "polymorphically perverse oscillation between possible roles, creating a radically broadened freedom of identification."[12] A recent collection of essays in *Film Criticism* took up a reconsideration of apparatus by turning away from Freud and Lacan toward object relations theory. In doing so the contributors still maintain that cinematic identification is the spectator's primary point of entry into the cinematic apparatus. They suggest that while retaining identification, their critique "undoes Metzian (Freudian, Lacanian) teleology and reminds us that identification always occurs incompletely, non-, anti-, or a-linearly, and oftentimes as much through misrecognition as recognition."[13] Oddly, one can consider that if identification occurs incompletely or as "non-identification" or "anti-identification," then they are saying that it can sometimes not occur at all. Which leaves me to wonder, How do we take as a central process to apparatus theory something that may not occur at all?

Thinking about the complex connectivity of technology, production, and spectatorship has not ceased. Work especially in French, Italian, Dutch, and German on *dispositif/apparat* has continued to provide productive impulses

72 · CHAPTER 4

to thinking about apparatus. Martin Lefebvre and Annie van den Oever have led the way in undertaking reconsiderations of classic texts, especially that of Christian Metz.[14] Already during the debates of classic apparatus theory, both Vilém Flusser and Peter Weibel variously expanded the considerations of apparatus to technologies beyond the cinema.[15] Siegfried Zielinski, Hartmut Winkler, and Friedrich Kittler extended such investigations.[16] And Kittler in his work most famously intensified the focus on technology, arguing for an investigation of apparatus in order to switch our understanding of ontology: from the human being in the apparatus to the apparatus as producing a being human. By contrast to Kittler's *apparat* as ontology, Francesco Casetti, Maria Tortajada, and François Albéra have turned to epistemology; they approach the apparatus as a way of knowing and inspired by Foucault, and they advocate for a deployment of the term "dispositive" in English, suggesting that the translation of the French *dispositif* is a better starting-off point.[17] André Gaudreault, Viva Paci, and Vinzenz Hediger have brought a new focus on film history and film industry.[18] Using the term *apparat*, scholars like Philippe Ortel and Marijke de Valck have brought forward new discussions of spectatorship.[19] And a further group of scholars, including Gilles Delavaud, Eva Tinsobin, and Juliane Rebentisch, have followed the moving image as it moves on to new screens.[20] They attend to the apparatus of new media, new moving-image technologies, and new screening spaces—in effect joining in a chorus of those arguing variously for not just a cinematic form but multiple forms of apparatus, a history of transforming dispositives.

Perhaps worth mentioning distinctly is Giorgio Agamben's essay "Che cos'è un dispositivo?," which drew great interest with its considerations of cell phone technologies and power/*potenza*.[21] And indeed Agamben's considerations of power and apparatus remain fairly unique in the revisions of apparatus, perhaps as too strong a response to the Marxism of classic apparatus theory. Unfortunately, in Agamben's approach, power is only coercive and the state is oppressive. However, technology is not only a vector of negative power and control. Agamben, those inspired by him, and engagements with the apparatus in general need to consider various state forms and various market forms; neither is there one capitalism, nor is it the case that market economy is immediately equivalent to capitalism. And although it is grammatically a semi-uncountable noun, it would help Agamben to consider apparatus as more than a singular system. If Agamben is as disturbed by the ubiquitous cell phone as he claims to be in his essay, labeling it as oppressive power, he needs to recognize that precisely the cell phone with its camera has been central to the formation of opposition in the Arab Spring, Occupy, Black Lives Matter movements, and the new Arab Uprisings, among others.

Although it may have fallen into quiescence, new translations into English and recent original work suggests that even in the Anglophone world a new reception and reconsideration is also under way. And it is not a moment too soon. In the classic period of apparatus theory, the questions posed focused critically on the depiction of reality. Now, however, we may agree that this period of fake news and alternative fact debates, a moment of both tracking apps contracting movement and virtual reality expanding it, calls us to focus on the reality of depiction. It is a worn observation that our media technologies have taken on new forms of surveillance. Our dispositives of control unleashed new forms of state power but also of private power, expression, and creativity. And I would suggest that apparatus theory, the approach that aspired to an integrated understanding of image, technology, material relations, and psyche, offers resources that are urgently needed: apparatus theory now more than ever.

Attentive to the work outside of the Anglophone world, I want to consider for this study three areas of general concentration in contemporary apparatus theory: base:techne, power/techne, and psyche.

BASE:TECHNE VERSUS DISPOSITIVE

Classic apparatus theory emerged out of attempts to go beyond simplistic histories of technology. It sought to think in a complicated fashion the interconnections of production, distribution, screening, and reception: of image *and* technology. Peter Wollen, Jeanne Thomas Allen, Douglas Gomery, and Barry Salt, among others, argued for a heterogeneity of economic and cultural determinants in the development of cinema technologies.[22] They undertook histories that worked against a primacy of camera or recording, pointing to the role of exhibition, editing, film stock, color, and sound. In her essay on standardization in early US cinema, Allen linked technology with the goals of business; Thomas Edison was an entrepreneur and that drove his inventiveness. Rather than approach standardization as driven by a need to make various recording and projecting technology work together, Allen showed that the move to compatibility was driven by other considerations. Rereading the essay it is still a shock to learn how the "American System" she detailed arose "within the firearms industry and as a response to the demands of government contracts for armaments."[23] The approaches of Allen and her colleagues and their insights still motivate good film historiography.

74 · CHAPTER 4

Simultaneously, the discussions countered remnant notions of realism as an aesthetic of political action. Leftist demands for a political cinema trending in that period expected tendentious content for political action, and contributors to classic apparatus theory not only countered this leveling of cinema with appreciation for an avant-garde practice but also defended an open aesthetic field of experimentation. Realism was not a property of the image but the conditions in the apparatus in which it is produced. Technology and practice, aesthetics and politics, theory and practice—while a project of the left, classic apparatus theory tread a path between base and superstructure. The location of apparatus theory within Marxism produced this goal of a unified field of investigation. But within the field of Marxian analysis it also became entangled in the many problems around the period's approaches to politics and ideology. And it was not exempt from considering the proper political deployment of cinema. By the 1980s it had reached its nadir and contributors had moved on to other approaches. Looking back on the debates of the period, Charles Musser paraphrased Lenin to form his pointed dismissal of the classical approach, describing it as "infantile leftism."[24]

Although the idea is pointedly reductive, I suggest critical development of apparatus theory continued in Germany dominated by Friedrich Kittler's work.[25] Famously, he began his best-known book, *Gramophone, Film, Typewriter* (1986), with the line "Media determine our situation."[26] And in doing so, he countered the positions of his Marxian-inspired colleagues. Kittler is often described as pursuing a technological determinism, an accusation that may be accurate given his support for an expulsion of the human from the humanities.[27] Kittler's approach distinguished itself from classic apparatus theory in this sentiment, where central to this theory was a basic interest in human emancipation if not liberation. It was not that he rejected an approach like Allen's but that his approach to technology was of a different order. Kittler positioned his work in line with Foucault's *Archeology of Knowledge*, considering media as the technological base of knowledge that is operative in a given society. Media are not extensions of humans; they are the cultural technologies through which knowledge is produced—by humans. In this equation Kittler focused less on knowledge and more on technology, garnering the moniker of "technodeterminist." As a result, we can note that Kittler moved away from the orientation in Foucault's work that sought to consider better and worse organizations of knowledge/power for life.[28]

The critique of classic apparatus theory that emerged in France was also foundationally influenced by Foucault. We can say that in effect it sought to replace Marx with Foucault, to overcome impasses of Althusserian ideology

Apparatus Theory Now More Than Ever! • 75

with Foucauldian episteme. But if Kittler's work focused on a base of media as producing knowledge as superstructure, colleagues in France sought to overcome impasses arising out of base/superstructure distinctions with a more flexible understanding of *dispositif.* Tortajada, and Albéra's excellent fostering of discussions of dispositive, most recently in the collection *Cine-Dispositives*, has indeed followed this direction, advocating a turn to epistemology/episteme.[29] They take from Foucault the dispositive as a way of knowing—not an ideological determination. This approach opens up a potential to consider the apparatus as more than or other than a device of ideological determination; I caution that this path can err too much in one direction. Such an approach may in its own way also respond to Kittler's technological determinism, but to approach dispositive as an ideational dynamic may unreflectedly also position dispositive as a matter of superstructure.

While there are significant reasons to continue developing the left critique of classic apparatus theory, even to aspire to Foucauldian Marxism, if we follow the French model toward episteme, we might critically consider what it means to take the term "episteme" in too much isolation. Recall that Aristotle placed episteme in a dynamic relation to techne and phronesis: theoretical knowledge, art and skill, practical wisdom. Techne, in particular, related to technology but was not reducible to objects; rather, techne is the knowledge in arts and crafts that arises out of the deployment of tools and technology. Techne leads us to consider knowing derived from relations of material practice. Certainly such an approach is in line with the original impetus of apparatus theory.

To consider apparatus is to consider not only a device but also a way of knowing. A focus on the material device of a typewriter or camera might lead us to err. In considering the entire apparatus that produces moving images, techne designating the material and immaterial, the art and the practice, asks us to recognize those images as not distinct from the material world. Nor is the apparatus of sound technology that produces cellular connections, which Agamben analyzed. These are not representations of the material world; rather, the images and sounds are the practice of the material world as such. In an iteration of classic apparatus theory, Jean-Louis Comolli suggested that apparatus designates nothing less than the means and the modes by which a particular society or social configuration produces and perpetuates its order.[30] Technology is not a determining base: techne is the apparatus of knowledge.

Certainly productive at core remains the exploration under the term "apparatus" of how moving images, spoken word, and communication in general consist of technology, technique, and representation. The exploration of apparatus not as a relation to image but as connection, as communication, as a

76 · CHAPTER 4

technique to realize community, allows us to better address the transformations of moving-image economies resulting from the digital revolution, the emergence of prosumers and content providers, and so on.

POWER/TECHNE

The turn from Marxism in considerations of apparatus may better be described as a turn from Althusser and a narrow focus on ideology. However, in seeking to overcome this impasse, we do not need to swing too far away from "the political." For instance, in spite of his describing classic apparatus theory as infantile leftism, Musser's investigation in *Cine-Dispositives* considers quite explicitly the connection between apparatus and political organizing. In that collection he investigates the pre-cinematic stereopticon as a tool of political mobilization, exploring a new dynamic of politics through image-making, which dominates our political formation to the present; Musser observes that the stereopticon, with its penchant for showing world leaders and marching troops, was involved in a move from "political oratory to political pageantry."[31] Nevertheless, he does not undertake his analysis to consider new political formations but reformulations of "media forms." And in general, although Albéra and Tortajada discuss power at length in the introduction to their collection, they suggest that "the notion of power should be kept separate from the questioning of viewing and listening dispositives."[32] They follow an approach to power that treats it too much as domination.

Indeed, unfortunately, Agamben's considerations of *dispositivo* and his particular approach to Foucault seem to offer the stronger frame to the understanding of power in contemporary reconsiderations of apparatus. Yet in the work of Agamben, the apparatus is reduced to a question of capture and the struggle of living beings. This position is more reductive than classic apparatus theory. If Marxist notions treated apparatus as reproducing bourgeois society, Agamben assesses apparatus in a more negative way, as existentially entrapping. Where Marxist analysis may have held out a hope in class revolution, the apparatus Agamben describes as a coherence of heterogeneous elements presents the universe as full of painful persecutory machines, like the cell phone. Agamben's understanding of the apparatus is more akin to Kafka's machine of torture he described in "In the Penal Colony" than Foucault's considerations of governmentality and subjectivation.[33] In the fight against the apparatus or in the state of being captured, Agamben recognizes that the living being becomes a subject: "I call a subject that which results from the relation and, so to speak, from the relentless fight between living beings and apparatuses."[34] But gone are Foucault's considerations of the positive potentials of power: empowerment, incitement, inspiration, resistance. We may be incited to treat our media apparatus negatively in an era of fake news, alternative facts, permanent accessibility, and loss of anonymity. But it is also a period of positive mobilization and disruptions.

Without reinstating a hierarchy of struggles among empowered and disempowered classes of people, I would insist that there is neither innocent technology nor powerless networks; the apparatus, a techne of power, directs flows of power in communication. The apparatus, techne/power, is expressed in the art of production and reproduction. Apparatus has complex potential, not explicitly positive or negative. To say that our media apparatuses are technologies of power is not the same as saying they are techniques of domination. An apparatus of subjectivization is not automatically one of subjugation. The deployment of camera phones in the Black Lives Matter movement may position people as particular subjects, but the use of the technology counters police brutality and other forms of racial subjugation.

Drawing from the previous chapters, we can state emphatically that images are materially constitutive. The ideational and material are not distinct: *images effect social relations*. And as the moving image has ruptured the narrow confines of the theatrical black box and moved out into the quotidian small screens we carry in our pockets, as it is projected onto the walls and sidewalks of public space, as it materializes virtual reality spaces, the cinematic apparatus adds more complexity to this understanding of the relationship of the ideational to the material. The relationships in the cinematic apparatus are not simply relationships of human to image but rather human to human, machine to image, machine to machine, and image to image—in other words, they are relations of individual subjects, technology, technique, and signification. Changes in signification entail changes in spectators and in material relations of production as much as changes in spectators or in technology affect the other factors.

PSYCHE: COGNITIVE FILM STUDIES AND NEUROCINEMATICS

The question of psyche was perhaps the central point of contention in the Anglophone world and not a matter that can be resolved easily. It remains one of the more difficult matters here and the least explored in all the work of revising apparatus theory. We have to overcome the rupture of cognitive film scholarship and the psychoanalytic model. These are not diremptions, not even necessarily competing models. We must resist a tendency simply to replace the Freudian/Lacanian models of consciousness with cognitive theory and neuroscientific research.

Cognitive research is not a unified terrain. It can include a focus on perceptual and neural processing, on emotion systems and affective responses, or on

78 · CHAPTER 4

recognition and comprehension. It can entail a specific attention to the working of mirror neurons, or it can include an expansive postulation on evolutionary hardwiring and bioculturalism. Clinical work and empirical findings for conceptual analysis are important and, for many engaged in cognitive research, must act as a foundation for theoretical and philosophical inquiry. In thinking about apparatus theory, it is important, however, to note that cognitive work goes hand in hand with technological development. The cognitive turn of the 1960s emerged along with new cybernetic models so that we find a direct relation between the advancement of computers and cognitive theories. But we also find the emergence of new video-recording technologies in the 1970s as compelling techniques of clinical psychological research. In the 1980s eye-tracking devices emerged that allowed for studies of focus and attention to take place. In the 1990s functional magnetic resonance imaging (fMRI) came on the scene and allowed for new mappings of the active brain. The clinical cognitive setting became increasingly beholden to technology. Technology, research, and theorizing consciousness became interconnected.

In the new millennium the technology could be deployed to record activity of a brain perceiving motion, and the investigation of moving images became a project of cognitive psychologists and neuroscientists.[35] By the first decade of these technologies, optical eye tracking, fMRI, and statistical tools like intersubject correlation analysis (ISC) allowed for new forms of mapping out the active viewer of moving images. And they made possible projects like that led by Pia Tikka, who created an interactive cinematic environment allowing for measurements of complex real-time social interactions.[36]

Carl Plantinga suggests that what joins cognitive theorists is a commitment to "clarity of exposition and argument and to the relevance of empirical evidence and the standards of science (where appropriate)."[37] Be that as it may, cognitive research is not the same as research in film studies inspired by cognitive research; we need to be cautious about the truth claims and scientific aspirations of cognitive film studies.

Consider first that there is a disconnect in practitioners of cognitive psychology and cognitive film studies. Consider how in their programmatic essay "Neurocinematics: The Neuroscience of Film," cognitive psychologists Uri Hasson and his colleagues make some large claims about the possibilities of a new film studies embedded in fMRI and ISC:

> ISC may be useful to film studies by providing a quantitative neuroscientific assessment of the impact of different styles of filmmaking on viewers' brains, and a valuable method for the film industry to better assess its products. Finally,

we suggest that this method brings together two separate and largely unrelated disciplines, cognitive neuroscience and film studies, and may open the way for a new interdisciplinary field of "neurocinematic" studies.[38]

This programmatic promise of neurocinematic studies is motivated by psychology and psychological methods of investigation. Its approach, however, is oblivious to a long history of debates in film and media studies around the nature of the creative and culture industries and their impact on spectators. It is made without a sense of the history of film aesthetic politics. What it proposes naïvely aspires to a condition in which cinema/viewership, research, and brain activity become more tightly bound into an apparatus of industrial-commercial image production. Of course, not all cognitive or neurocinematic projects aspire to providing insight into the brain activity for the benefit of Hollywood's blockbuster production. Nevertheless, I approach with alarm claims that fMRI can "penetrate a viewer's mind and record his or her mental states while watching a movie."[39] Movies may be able to evoke similar brain activity across viewers, but do similar images of brain activity equal similar experiences? Within this assessment of the potentials of imaging technology is a lack of necessary critical reflection on the status of the image in a research method that relies on the image.

In the experiment at the heart of the article by Hasson and his coauthors, the researchers compared responses to a static camera recording activity in Washington Square Park in New York City and a clip from *The Good, the Bad, and the Ugly* (Leone 1966). The relationship between the two is described as an "unstructured versus structured movie."[40] And the structured Leone film is found to have a more positive impact on cognition. From this experiment with narrative versus non-narrative film, the researchers conclude that structured film (i.e., edited film) holds attention better. That under these parameters the structured film is found to be better is oddly oblivious to practices of editing. What about the edited films that aspire aesthetically not to be a coherent whole? Are they bad movies? Are they only bad because they don't provide the kind of data wanted or because they do not belong to the genre expectations of entertainment film? Outside of the goals of neurocinematics to serve the industry better, does this research not show us something about the propaganda/ideological potential of a common effect on audiences that might compel moving-image makers to aspire to exactly the opposite? Does it not set up warning signs about the deployment of technology and potential uses for industry, profit, and propaganda? Does it not make us think that there was something to the classic apparatus theory assessment of the culture industry?

80 · CHAPTER 4

The assessments in the article of cognitive responses to the two types of film thus derive from no knowledge of genre and aesthetics, no consideration that there may be movies in which the static camera one-shot is the experience sought after, no consideration of narrative. I could continue here with a discussion of this one article and its shortcomings of analysis, but these lay a decade back. Nevertheless and unfortunately its shortcomings continue to be evidenced in more current work.[41] Thus, as a second point I want to underscore that as neurocinematics develops, it is important that the neurocinematicians know something respectfully of the history of film and critical studies of the medium. Our understanding of cinema and cognition thus needs to develop with an awareness of aesthetic industrial technological histories.

But this has a corollary I want to make as a third point: as the neuroscientist has to appreciate the film scholar's work, likewise, the film scholar needs to understand the developmental experimental quality of the cognitive and neuroscientific work. David Bordwell, as a central advocate for a recognized field of cognitive film studies, has a deep and real knowledge of cognitive research and its broad transformations. He is able to deploy it well in a critique of other film scholars and a denunciation of their Grand Theoretical undertakings. Yet Bordwell's work is not engaged in a similar critical intervention in the paradigms of cognitive psychology. Rather, Bordwell, as with other colleagues, applies cognitive studies. Distancing himself from that role, Bordwell, for example, describes his as a "cognitive perspective rather than a cognitive science."[42] Similarly, Carl Plantinga describes cognitive film scholars as a bit of an eclectic bunch: "One might say that cognitive film theorists tend to be committed to the study of human psychology using the methods of contemporary psychology and analytic philosophy. This can be an amalgam of cognitive, evolutionary, empirical, and/or ecological psychology, with perhaps a bit of neuroscience and dynamical systems theory thrown in the mix."[43] While this is both true and a responsible position that protects against accusations of dilettantish cognitivism, what worries me in this modulation of the relation to cognitive psychology is that it can misrecognize the practice of clinical science.

Bordwell sought to take on the charge that his work is scientistic.[44] He indicted his colleagues who felt comfortable in the scientific claims of structuralism but not cognitivism. But he misunderstood the difference: semiotic film scholars advance the discourse of semiotics whereas cognitive film scholars apply cognitive science. Furthermore, contrary to Bordwell's and Plantinga's praise for the empiricism and clarity of science, clinical or natural scientific research is a method of ordering knowledge. It is not a matter of clarity or empirical facts. Cognitive science, like all natural scientific investigation, is based on postulation and testing. There are competing paradigms and heated debates. Most

Apparatus Theory Now More Than Ever! • 81

experiments in the natural sciences result in "failure"—in other words, they produce a need for further postulation. If the discovery of the general theory of relativity did not explain everything but has led to further and new postulations, would it not be a mistake to assume that the discovery of mirror neurons offers a full and sufficient explanation for what happens when we see a crying face in a movie? A documentable phenomenon like inattentional blindness has multiple cognitive, psychological, neuroscientific, and philosophical implications that have led to further testing and hypothesis building—all in a form of competition with one another. If an evolutionary biological school in neuroscientific research focuses on hardwired responses, scholars of cognitive films should apply them while ignoring work on brain plasticity. Colleagues in the cognitive sciences are constantly developing their thinking, moving their discipline in new directions. Unfortunately, film scholars who reach to their research to apply it can only lose track of the place it holds in debates. An understanding of cinema and cognition thus develops not by applying the postulations of cognitive science but by critically engaging them.

A fourth point to make here is that film scholars can and should look to engage fundamentally in cognitive science as critical participants in the debates. We have much to contribute. Consider the technologism that has marked cognitive psychology from the start. Cognitive work with its reliance on technology would do well to engage reflectedly with its equipment. The cybernetic modeling that dominated cognitive science for decades led to false assumptions about the brain. Memory was treated like a computer hard drive, or rather computer hard drives with their file system archives were thought to mimic human memory systems. We have learned that the brain's memory systems are not like computer archives. The models of recognition that cognitive psychology pursued for years led to reasonable systems for computer facial-recognition technology but not for understanding human-recognition systems, as was long assumed.[45] Or consider that eye-tracking patterns and fMRI have revealed a great deal of the function of the brain and its perceptive systems. But these are not insights into the mind as such and have yet to be exposed to a critical engagement.

As I repeatedly suggested in the introduction, we have to learn that technology in all instances is a framework for knowledge. As a techne, it creates an enframement by which we know some things but not all things. Technology does not lead us to know everything; it sets us to knowing in a particular way. The images produced by fMRI or eye tracking may call forth new ways of seeing, but they establish only correlations to a part of the whole. The whole is always outside our gaze.

Which leads me to a fifth concern: a focus on the brain, the neurons, the mirroring cells of the viewers may offer novel insights, yet we should consider if

82 • CHAPTER 4

cognitive film studies have not replaced *the* spectator with *the* viewer as a result. If brains in a clinical setting produce a uniform image in response to certain uniform stimuli, does that reveal something to us about all viewers? Even if all viewers positioned in front of certain moving images respond in a certain way, does that indicate to us something essential about all viewers? If the limbic and paralimbic regions light up in all brains while viewers are watching a sad movie, does that automatically mean that all viewers are experiencing the emotion of sadness the same way? Do cinematic effects tested in specific clinical settings have a consistent impact on all viewers in nonclinical settings? Is cross-cultural consistency of responses to moving images a sign of hardwiring of the brain, or is it a sign that moving images have offered a culture of watching that is trans-regional? Is it that all brains perceive the same way, or that moving image perception has created a new condition of cinematic cognition? Is the brain that has a smartphone in the pocket the same as the brain that relied on velum to record its images?[46] If we are seeking to go beyond the impasses of apparatus theory, we do not want simply to replace the once overused word "ideology" with a notion of "cinematic effects on neurological processes," do we? Does cinema have control of neurological processes, or is there a moment when the perceptive system and the moving image produce something? There is no perceptive system in itself, and there is no cognitive capacity as such; there is always only a perception of something, a cognition in some way from some perspective, somehow, from some techne.

So, finally, if we reject *the* viewer generalizations in order to develop an understanding of cinema and cognition, it is also important to treat critically assumptions about *the* brain. A suggestion in cognitive approaches is that our emotions along with the frontal cortex evolved in order to give us a fitness advantage. An argument is put forward that cognitive processes are fundamentally bound up with evolution. Visual cognition offered survival or reproduction fitness. David Bordwell expressed such notions in his foundational "A Case for Cognitivism," but certainly Torben Grodal has taken the lead in such approaches.[47] In the face of such approaches, I ask, Do evolutionary or fitness approaches really suggest that we evolved a cognitive apparatus that remains constant and consistent in spite of the world? Even if our cognitive apparatus were indeed hardwired and permanently so, is the wiring we bring into a perceptive condition more determining of our response than the condition itself?

I have lived a life being told that homosexuality is hardwired, and I cannot help myself because I am part of some evolutionary genetic anomaly. Once again the question of my genes as anomalies to the normal straight genes was in the news. It is tiresome. Even if it were the case that a gene makes some males attracted to other males, would it be the case that that attraction is the same across time? Would the genetically determined look I give at men be the same in 1970s New York City, 1930s Berlin, thirteenth-century Beijing, and fifth-century BCE Athens? Would the gaze of a nineteenth-century dandy eroticize the same as a sixteenth-century Ojibwa *ikwekaazo*? It is difficult to accept that we would consider our perception of the Avengers the same as the perception of an antelope on the savannah by our Paleolithic ancestors. Are all our perceptions of the world today derived from wiring that emerged in a past era? Do we recognize cars coming down the street because in our pasts we had to perceive a herd of buffalo headed our way? The biocultural model might explain why all cultures can recognize line drawings, but it does not explain how line drawings have developed specific forms and codes in specific places.[48] And when we experience a difficulty in perception, does that reveal an inability to deal with our world as a result of a reactive consistency? Because our hardwiring emerged while running from buffalos, can we understand why we do not run as well from drones? That there has always been same-sex desire, that we have always looked at lines and curves, and that we have always run does not mean that desiring, looking, or running is always the same in all times and places. I would rather not be incited to follow a Social Darwinist presumption that some earlier state is more determining on contemporary conditions because man in a state of nature was more bound to evolution. It leads quickly to a proposition that because society has rent man from evolution, our determining structures are deployed in an "inappropriate" apparatus and we should aspire to a return to the Paleolithicum. We should certainly not seek to reinstitute evolutionary pressures as did Social Darwinism.

So, while I am not wedded to psychoanalytic models of psyche, I would caution us to consider that current cognitive approaches to moving-image studies may undermine one of the central insights of classic apparatus theory. The outcomes of the debates on the subject were a recognition that psyche is not distinct from material relations; apparatus designated the material technological mediations in which psyche *and* the social configuration are produced and reproduced. Perception, cognition, and vision have always arisen in an apparatus. Any (cognitive) approach that re-ontologizes consciousness, turns the brain into the essence of the mind, and overlooks the imagistic or technological frames of its methods should be dismissed or at least exposed to critical investigation. I am not prepared to commit to one model of the psyche or the other; I remain agnostic. But I do think that for film studies as a field of investigation, it is important that we not simply apply cognitive research; instead, we must offer our own critical interventions.

CHAPTER 5

Cine-Cognition: Montage

The projection of the dialectic system of objects into the brain
—into abstract creation
—into thought
produces dialectic modes of thought—dialectical materialism—
—Eisenstein, "The Dramaturgy of Film Form
(The Dialectical Approach to Film Form)"

There is no natural seeing. There is no seeing that is distinct from technology. Seeing is always seeing through a particular apparatus. Certain technologies define the apparatus of sight in given eras. Film emerged as a revolution in perception. Scientific photography, the work of Alphonse Bertillon, Francis Galton, Etienne Marey, and Eadweard Muybridge, transformed our apprehension of the world, revealing aspects unavailable to the "naked eye." Josh Ellenbogen showed us, however, that these new ways of seeing the world asserted their own aesthetics, an aesthetic of truth and completeness.[1] To understand this work as aesthetic reframes their claims on scientific knowledge. To approach their truth claims critically does not mean to suggest that their work did not provide new insights into the world. They certainly offered a new way of picturing our world. In popular culture Muybridge's chronophotography has gone into the records as revealing to us the legs of the horse in motion.[2] Hugo Münsterberg is one of the first to attend analytically to the revolution in perception offered by film. Lev Kuleshov was one of the first to critically research the mechanisms of moving-image perception. Going beyond descriptive, Kuleshov's research was at the core of questioning how to extend the revolution in perception.

Following Kuleshov's experiments with perception, the Soviet avant-garde settled into montage as essential to cinema. Dziga Vertov, Esfir Shub, Vsevolod

Pudovkin, and Eisenstein focused on montage as a form of dialectic, thereby bringing cinema into a discourse on the mind that traces a line from Hegel and the discussions of chapter 4. Theirs is, of course, a line that runs through Marx and Lenin away from Hegel's idealism toward dialectical materialism. The film avant-garde in general treated cinema not just as a matter of perception, images moving in time, but as a technology of consciousness. The consideration of the connection between image and consciousness infused all the modernist movements in various ways: Impressionists, Dadaists, Surrealists, Objectivists, and so on. But the Soviet colleagues especially set out to deploy film in the service of the revolution. They hoped that moving images could provide a revolution in consciousness even to those far from the immediate centers of revolutionary activity. Although the Soviet avant-gardists may have deployed the term "dialectic" to prove that their work aligned with the new state's goals, they nevertheless participated in that moment when dialectical materialism and Pavlovian behaviorism contributed to the emergence of a Soviet psychology. Thus, well before the contemporary cognitive turn started to pay attention to the moving image, the Soviet avant-garde developed elaborate propositions on the relation between perception, montage, and material actions.

In their considerations of dialectic, filmmakers and theorists like Eisenstein and Vertov focused on the alterity of images. They posited the editing together of two images as the specificity of the medium film; they further advanced that this montage of the images was at core dialectical because it brought two images into various dynamic relations of perception that could actually revolutionize consciousness. At that moment they were at the cutting edge of the cognitive approach to film. Eisenstein's discussion of cine-consciousness, like Vertov's approach to *Kino-Eye*, linked perception of film to behaviors after the projection of the moving image. The Soviet film avant-garde put forward an understanding of the spectator as having a dynamic relationship not simply with an "imagistic" world; they considered as connected the movement of the image and action in the material world as well. Some colleagues in clinical cognitive psychology and neuroscience might not share the Soviet ideals of their forerunners, but they do pursue research that connects the perception of images to behaviors and states of consciousness.

This chapter returns us to the question of montage. As discussed in chapter 2, film, one image in juxtaposition to the other, one after another, is a medium of alterity. Of course, long-take and single-take films slow cinema and lack the editing of images, but the artful deployment of camera movement in extreme long-take films like *Satanstango* (Tarr 1994) or single-take works like *Victoria* (Schipper 2015) still present us with shifting scenes. Maybe more importantly

86 · CHAPTER 5

they point to the dominant mode of narration through editing. We return to this question of montage as a matter of perception, considering how it became once again a point of research for contemporary cognitive and neuroscientific research.

Montage: Kuleshov Reexamined

Montage, the art of editing images together to tell a story in order to induce an affective state in the spectator is key to *narrative* cinema. Film studies as a field almost takes for granted this principle that montage is central to the ability of cinema to narrate. We know, of course, that in the early 1910s Lev Kuleshov began his famous film experiment, intercutting the same image of the actor Ivan Ilyich Mozzhukhin with three different "counter-shots." One analysis of the experiment is that Kuleshov's subjects read different emotions on the face of the actor even though the shot was the same. Fundamentally, Lev Kuleshov recognized that the juxtaposition of two images elicits a shift in the assessment of the image: a bowl of soup and a man's face = he's hungry; a coffin and the same man's face = he's sad. Two images next to each other, or shown in succession, incite a human potential to project emotion. But they also incite a potential to see a relationship between disparate images. This led Kuleshov to identify the core of cinema: its ability to produce meaning—not in the shot itself but in the relationship of shots to each other. The montage of images unleashes an emotional cognitive response in the audience. However, what we know about the experiment is actually secondary, no direct report of the results or the actual conditions of the experiment, nothing that conforms to general standards of the scientific method for reproducibility and testing exists. For a half century we took the Kuleshov effect for granted.

Kuleshov's research received renewed attention as part of the cognitive turn in film studies. In 1992 Stephen Prince and Wayne Hensley sought to test the Kuleshov effect by replicating the experiment exactly.[3] They faced a challenge because the actual experiment itself was lost, making it difficult to replicate Kuleshov's procedure. Nevertheless, based on the descriptions of the process, they reconstructed an experiment and achieved unsatisfactory results. They could not reproduce Kuleshov's findings. They found instead that participants did not consistently project the same emotions, or even any emotions, onto the face of the spectator. In their analysis of their undertaking, asking why it did not succeed, they concentrated on questions of the neutrality of the face in the test. They sought for ways to find a neutral face but could not guarantee that any facial expression was itself neutral as such. In addition to speculating on the impossibility of a neutral facial expression, they considered another possible reason for their inability to replicate the results. Perhaps, they surmised, the results of Kuleshov's experiment derived from test subjects wanting to please Lev Kuleshov. The famous effect was nothing more than a lack of scientific impartiality in the experimental setting, a common beginner's error in clinical psychology.

Prince and Hensley's lack of success in the replication of the experiment and their subsequent blanket rejection of the Kuleshov effect seems to run up against precisely a simple commonsense experience of cinema. Their proof of the error of the experiment, their focus on its faultiness, runs counter to numerous experiences of narrative film. Film audiences have experienced time and time again how splicing two pictures from two different times and locations (actor Raymond Burr shot in the US looking into the camera spliced with a shot of Godzilla on a rampage shot in Japan) brings the two shots together into a relationship (Raymond Burr is a reporter in Japan viewing Godzilla ravage Tokyo). There is meaning in cinema; the experience of montage elicits a response. The bringing-together creates a perception of common space and time, it places one shot into the condition of being a response to another, it cues emotions, and it drives narrative understanding.

Thus it seems more reassuring for cognitive studies that in contrast to Prince and Hensley, more recently Pietra Bruni, while at the University of Pittsburgh, was able to replicate Kuleshov's finding. She did undertake modifications to Kuleshov's experiment, updating the images and technology.[4] As a result, she not only replicated its findings but also identified a broader spectrum of nuance that was read into the face. Further, and around the same time and in a much more technologically sophisticated experimental setting, a research group of neuroscientists led by Dean Mobbs at the University College London, relying on the same kind of strategy Bruni deployed, undertook an fMRI to measure blood oxygen levels in the brain in order to identify the neurological basis for the Kuleshov effect.[5] With more elaborate abilities to measure responses, their research identified specific activity in the bilateral temporal pole, anterior cingulate cortices, amygdala, and bilateral superior temporal sulcus. Their fMRI essentially recorded the Kuleshov effect at work in the brain. However, in their assessment of the experiment, the team redefined the Kuleshov effect, identifying it as a matter of contextual framing—the larger approach to cognition they study. Their theory simply stated, "Context influences social attribution."[6] Thus, the context that the coffin establishes creates a predisposition to see the figure differently than the context that the bowl of soup establishes. Mobbs and his fellow researchers may actually reconcile some of Prince and Hensley's

88 · CHAPTER 5

hesitation by noting precisely that "context acts to alter our perceptions through expectations."[7] Prince and Hensley focused vary narrowly on one dynamic of cognition, describing a failure to see a change in the face. For Mobbs and his colleagues, it was not a question of if the face changed per se but how the face signified change: "Contextual framing relies on the integration of extrinsic contextual cues and the retrieval of stored knowledge about the likely emotional disposition of an actor in this context."[8] In short, we take experienced conditions and project them onto the world around us as a form of priming ourselves to action. The context of the woods at night primes us to be wary, the context of popcorn and a big screen primes us to be ready to be entertained, the presence of a coffin primes us to respond to the grief of the people around us.

Montage: Bioculturalist Cognition or Revolutionary Perception

Contextual framing suggests that a reanalysis of information continually happens and not just in the context of cinema. Framing provides a cognitive condition of efficiency in decision making by positioning the subject into preparation for action—that is, priming. Because it is about speed, however, the framing effect also results in biases in decision making.[9] Furthermore, framing allows for an exclusion, disregard, or even active forgetting of input that is, based on experience, not important for a pending decision or assessment. Other researchers have connected this condition of "forgetting" or disregard to the experience of continuity editing and the lack of recognition of cuts in a work of narrative cinema.[10] Montage is as much about disregard as it is about recognition.

In developing their research within the paradigm of contextual framing, Mobbs and his colleagues connected the Kuleshov effect to an evolutionary condition that gave primates an increased capacity to respond to threats. Further work by Lili Sahakyan, Peter Delaney, and others extended this line of supposition.[11] This tracing back to an evolutionary precondition, or surmising about an origin to a capacity in the contemporary brain, is a typical approach among cognitive and neuroscientific research: "man" in a state of nature, such as hominids in a savannah, must have done X, and this established the wiring of the brain that obtains to this day. Starting a decade ago, this approach has also been at the heart of much research in cognitive film studies. A central work to cognitive film studies like Torben Grodal's *Embodied Visions* pursued a "bioculturalist" approach, in which the movements of information and emotion in the act of film perception derive from capacities that arose in earlier evolutionary states.[12] Beginning from the proposition that cognition and emotional systems

Cine-Cognition: Montage • 89

developed in an evolutionary history to give us survival advantages, Grodal has connected dominant film genres to biological neurological conditions: "a group of reptilian emotions central to action and adventure; a group of *mammalian* emotions related to offspring of care; and separation panic/grief."[13] Thus, tribal hierarchies depicted in sci-fi or war films appeal to hunter-gatherer sensibilities.[14]

Although Grodal's work, as with cognitive film studies in general, has been exposed to extensive criticism, it serves as an important correction to approaches that focus singularly on the image or even its cultural context.[15] Grodal and cognitive scholarship remind us that the body and its perceptive apparatus have not been part of those conversations. Cognitive theory, disability studies, and feminist scholarship in various ways have sought to remind us of the importance of embodiment. And likewise in this study, I encourage thinking through how perception arises out of complex conditions in which the body and its perceptive apparatus play a limiting role. *Seeing of something is always seeing from a particular embodied perspective in a particular place and at a particular time.*

However, in these discussions cognitive scholars often treat the brain as hardwired and our behaviors as somehow innate. I offered an extensive critique of this approach in the preceding chapter and I want to extend that critique here. Scholars may have described a portion of the human brain under the attribution "reptilian brain" based on a particular anatomical biological evolutionary reasoning. Yet it would be a mistake to take the simile too far. The functions we can chart in that portion of the brain are located in the here and now. To deny them a coequality with the rest of the body, to describe the perceptive apparatus as determined by evolution—that is, as anachronistic to the current conditions—is both a descent into errors of logic and rhetoric and a rewarming of determination arguments.

1. "Hardwired" in cognitive and neuroscientific research often means innate. Machines, computers, and electronic devices may be developed for a set task or a set of tasks, and they may be innately hardwired to perform a single function, but the human body and its capacities exceed a fixed structure-function relationship.

2. Evolution-based arguments about behaviors typically erroneously ascribe unreflectedly to a normative model. Words like "evolution," "innate," "hardwired," and so on are often used to describe gender, race, or other culturally determined differences.[16] And such words have come under considerable critical scrutiny for how they fundamentally confuse difference and differentiation in cognition.[17]

3. Whereas evolutionary biology focuses on the diversity of the gene pool,

90 · CHAPTER 5

evolutionary biologists standardize behaviors under a false understanding of Darwin and the concept of "survival of the fittest." Contemporary evolutionary biologists approach the topic as one of biodiversity, ecosystems, and rapid adaptation.[18] Evolution does not hardwire us to one response and one response for all times; evolution expands species diversity and compels difference that undermines standardized behaviors and normative expectations.

4. Cognitive and neuroscientific research relying on a concept of hardwired treats the brain as a static organ, not one that changes. Cognitive and neuroscientists have revised their approaches to the brain and cognition, proposing that perception is not resistant to change, not fixed, not determined in its responses to specific stimuli, not developmentally constrained, nor limited to single functions.[19] Neural fibers bundle and rebundle depending on environmental and cultural factors. The childhood, adult, and elderly brain are constantly transforming.

Rather than understand evolution as hardwiring us to a past static condition, we can approach it as a radical coevality. Evolution is a matter of the present. Evolution means an ability to function in the moment. Evolution is still happening, and the viewing subject is causing it. We are not determined objects in evolutionary processes. We are factors in our own evolution.

Thus it is a significant problem when cognitive film scholars like Grodal repeatedly return to "innate dispositions": "Even if genres are influenced by cultural elements there must be strong influences from innate dispositions."[20] We cannot ignore the basic role of visual feedback and "reading" practices in cognitive formation. Although normative and standardized explanations are seductive, there is something willfully damaging in their assertion in humanistic methodologies. Even at the point of publication of *Embodied Visions*, much natural scientific research had already developed to understand the brain as a plastic, not static, organ. And in the subsequent decade a lively rejection of biological determinism has emerged.

It would be counter to the spirit of this study to suggest that cognition is not a limiting determining factor. We do not see everything and anything. We perceive in conditions that are not freely determined by ourselves. Perception is a process of distinction and differentiation within the limits of the body, the technologies, the cultural reading practices, and the environment of any given moment. Michael Grabowski's edited volume *Neuroscience and the Media* did a great deal to move the discussion from a rigidly embodied approach to an ecological model of brain and media.[21] It likewise follows extensive research in cognitive and neuroscience that attends to the plasticity of the brain.[22] For those cognitive film scholars who insist on asserting bio-evolutionary approaches as justifications for their analyses, certainly the environmental changes the millennia have brought mean that humans do not continue to approach each situation with the brain developed in the Pleistocene, or with the mind asking the same latent question: Is there a saber-toothed tiger on the horizon?

Hardwired approaches that treat cognitive development as static and unidirectional vis-à-vis the environment and culture run into limits and return us to a reductive nature-versus-nurture, hardwiring-versus-culture debate falling on the side of nature and a static brain. (Wherever this approach relies on a unidirectional understanding of perception, it falls into an analytic trap that is uncannily similar to the one that Hegel and the German idealists could not escape but fell into from the other direction, emphasizing the mind as formed too much by culture.) Indeed the proposition of contextual framing and the hardwired approach in general leaves us with a significant question: If we are primed in situations to respond by the conditions we already know, how do we interact with the difference we do not already know? How do we respond differently? How do we recognize other others, other differences? Our perception of the world must have an equal and elaborate mechanism for perceiving differing differences, for seeing difference differently.

If the work of the Soviet avant-garde focused on anything, it was on the newness of perception and the revolutionary capacity of the brain. Montage, cine-cognition, and the cinematic technologization of perception—these are new. They are other forms of cognition, and our ability to perceive through these technologies indicates the plasticity of our cognitive capacities. These are not appendages to innate forms of viewing. They are different, not better.

Montage Reloaded: Dynamic Seeing

But what about this research on Kuleshov? The reading of emotions off a face was not all that was at stake in the Kuleshov effect. Kuleshov established a group of researchers and headed the National Film School. They explored the building blocks of film, the importance of shot succession, and other elements of filmmaking.[23] Certainly the elaborated theory of montage that arose around the subsequent discussions and debates did not revolve around the emotional face. Distinctions of forms of montage, such as rhythmic, vertical, intellectual, associational, and so on, considered much more and quite other than emotional faces. Indeed, if emotions were a concern in the discussions, they concerned more so the emotional affective response of the spectator: what

92 · CHAPTER 5

activated their passions, what activated their reason, what brought them to rally for the revolution.

In 1927 Oskar Fischinger produced a short film that could be approached as already offering an experimental alternative, if not counter, to the notions of montage developed by his Soviet colleagues. He chronicled his three-week journey from Munich to Berlin in a condensed rapid three-and-one-half-minute succession of images recorded in camera. While Fischinger was not engaged in a clinical experiment, he was exploring the possibilities of film being deployed for purposes other than narration. Working on the edges of the avant-garde in Frankfurt, Fischinger had already developed elaborate methods of abstraction relying on melting wax. Thus, the film *München-Berlin Wanderung* (*Walking from Munich to Berlin*) is notionally about a journey from point to point. But the in-camera recording and the rapid speed of the cuts seem to confound the construction of space, place, emotion, reason, even basic recognition, as hallmarks of montage. Certainly they do not elicit a Kuleshov effect in the strictest sense. The string of images recorded in camera do not call forth the emotional cognitive response of the Odessa Steps sequence or the relational montage sequences of Pudovkin's *Mat* (*Mother*) (1926). Even though those films rely on rapid cutting in sequences, Fischinger's sequence is to a great extent almost unrecognizable.[24] The experience of watching that film is one of leaps from image to image. Images may appear as individually recognizable, but overall it lacks immediate structure that makes it legible. It seems to be important that there are no shot/counter-shot, no symbolic or dynamic oppositions that arise in viewing the film. It is idiosyncratic, a particular mingling of images deriving from random encounters on the road.

Repeated viewing of *Munich-Berlin* does allow for an increase of recognition. Faces of a peasant woman; a farmer, frontal profile, left right; a shepherd in his flock, seated, frontal profile, left right come to form a kind of pattern offering some inkling of the conditions in which a traveler with a camera asks, "Do you mind if I take your picture?" The film does not tell a story based on the linking of images; rather, it gestures to a relation of filmmaker to recorded subjects. But attention, focus, and memory struggle to bring clarity to the leaps from shot to shot. For the spectator, the shot sequences evince a logic of the road: literally shots of the road, of natural landscapes, sunsets, a person met along the way, a spot of rest, and so forth. But beyond the knowledge that this film is quite literally a road movie, the sequencing contains only an idiosyncratic string. Its quick cuts connect one shot along the way with another, capturing the randomness but not ordering them in any other particular way.

This technique later became the heart of Jonas Mekas's diary films, inspiring further generations of experimental filmmakers. Mekas added title cards at times to add legibility to the images, but the cards aim for a poetic rather than emphatic quality. In both instances, the in-camera editing of these films seems to defy the logic of montage. Two shots may be connected to each other, yet there is no story and little affect. Cinema seems to have more and other cognitive potentials than narrative and affect.

The speed of images alone cannot be the issue. The scanning eye jumps from image to image, the mini-saccades of our scanning brain, more quickly than the cuts of Fischinger or Mekas's films. However, in that condition of scanning a setting, the perceptive apparatus can bring into conscious awareness a sense of space and a recognition of place. Given the speed by which mini-saccades leap from object to object, the principle of in-camera edits in Fischinger's film cannot be the reason for the lack of recognition.[25] Some other function of perception comes into play here. The string of images of the film diary without emotional connection may actually be revealing what Prince and Hensley surmised: that there is no Kuleshov effect. Nevertheless relying heavily on in-camera editing Hitchcock in *Rope* (1948) and Godard with *À bout de souffle* (*Breathless*) (1960) did create two narrative films that hold viewer attention, even build suspense.

If we approach cognition as one of a dynamic of perception that develops out of the ever changing conditions of the world, if we approach the brain as plastic and transforming over lifetimes and generations, and if we accept that there are no more saber-toothed tigers on the horizon and hence any propensity developed in the last ice age has taken on new qualities in the age of global warming, then we might approach the question of montage differently. Returning to the observations on *Munich-Berlin*, we find there a means to consider the linking functions of montage—when they do not work or work differently. We can ask, What do such conditions tell us about montage? In the case of Fischinger's film diary, something else was at work, something that prevents the action from being understood as anything more than a continuous string of images. As I already noted, it cannot be the rapid succession alone. Fischinger's sequence has cut rates no faster than an action sequence from a contemporary superhero blockbuster. *Inception* (Nolan 2010) and *Dr. Strange* (Derrickson 2016) relied on VFX modeling and fractal and kaleidoscopic animation to create such a rapid stringing of images. The speed of the images may mask some of the awkwardness of mixing live and animated images, but overall it provides a sense of action in a trippy dream world and magical universe. They are certainly more "complex" than the straightforward technique of Fischinger, but the action sequences in *Inception* were legible. Perhaps contemporary audiences have assimilated a highly complex language of montage allowing them to read rapidly a sequence of images. Perhaps in their time, Dr. Strange or Batman sequences would actually have appeared like the experimental blur of Fischinger's in-camera edits. Regardless, at least this contemporary viewer used to superhero films still finds it hard to recognize the images of the journey from Munich to Berlin.

In focusing on the attribution of emotions onto a face, the cognitive research into the Kuleshov effect seems to overlook further and more significant aspects of the work of montage and the relation of the spectator to strings of images. The spectators in Kuleshov's experiment placed the images recorded in radically different places and times into a single ideational space and time frame. They took an image of a bowl of soup and a picture of a man, ideationally placed them in the same room, and made the bowl into an object of the man's gaze. Further, they began to describe a new situation. The subjects took the juxtaposition of two images as incitement to narrate. Although Mobbs and his colleagues show increased blood levels, it is possible that this data proves more than that contextual framing is taking place. It could perhaps also indicate something other than contextual framing. The blood oxygen level–dependent data may not be at all about a matter of emotional projection based on context but rather the activation of a propensity to narrate. In setting up their experiment, Mobbs and his fellow researchers assume a largely one-directional process in which images flow into the cognitive system, they activate stored memories as higher processes, and that leads to suppressed action response. Perhaps rather than a simple input and forward-flow loop, what the fMRI is indicating is a complex multidirectional relationship of perception, recognition, and meaning production.

Clearly some brain activity is being recorded, and a subsequent experiment might investigate if the blood oxygen levels represent a propensity to narrate the world around us. It certainly seems that is what is happening; in the retelling of the Kuleshov experiment, the subjects engaged in an act of narration. Reflecting on Kuleshov, Eisenstein suggested that he and other filmmakers "regarded montage as a means of producing something by describing it."[26] In that observation Eisenstein was concerned with what he considered Kuleshov's "outmoded" principles of editing that treated shots sequentially, as if the shots were a set of building blocks establishing an artifice of narration, or in their sequencing simply unrolling ideas. At the same time, Eisenstein also set his project apart from that of Hollywood, especially the principles of continuity editing that emerged out of Edwin S. Porter's and D. W. Griffith's work. According to Eisenstein, the focus on the face as the emotional melodramatic center and the dualism of parallel editing were limits on the potentials of cinema. The

Cine-Cognition: Montage • 95

entire apparatus of modern cinema could not be limited to showing another train robbery or another car chase.[27] While beginning from the experimental practice of Kuleshov, Eisenstein moved his understanding of montage into new directions. The experiment comes to be about narration and not a matter of reading emotion from the face. Eisenstein is more interested in the propensity to read the world, to find meaning. "Look, he's hungry" may not be a reference at all to an actual reading of hunger from the face of the actor. Rather, it seems to point clearly to a practice of sense making. Montage aligns, then, with this propensity to actively narrate into a recognized reality the chaotic input of the world we inhabit.

Cognitive and neuroscientific research began in the first decade of the new millennium to focus on the broader questions of narration. Advances in fMRI allowed for measurements of the moving, not just still, image in new ways. Event segmentation seemed to align easily with the experience of film viewing. The segmentation of narrative film into discrete units of shots aligned with the understanding that our perceptive apparatus continuously breaks down experiences into segments for processing, selecting which segments go into higher-level cognition, what passes into longer-term memory, and others. The research focused especially on how the perceptive apparatus interacts with those segments. Jeffrey Zacks particularly explored the similarities and differences of behavioral event boundaries and shots.[28] He also researched the attention-driven regulation as a means of overcoming discontinuity in film—in other words, What happens when an edit cuts a scene and places the viewer in a different locale and time? The experiments he conducted resulted in the recognition of neural mechanisms to bridge discontinuities.

A year later Tim J. Smith, Daniel Levin, and James E. Cutting went a step further in conclusions to their experiments. They saw a direct connection between the techniques of continuity editing and "the natural dynamics of attention and humans' assumptions about continuity of space, time, and action."[29] Sermin Ildirar and Stephan Schwan explored the learning process entailed in reading cinema.[30] Separating their population into first-time viewers, low-experienced, and high-experienced adult viewers, they discovered that first-time viewers easily understood the basic elements of shots but not the coherency of the narrative, while experienced viewers understood that a narrative implied a form of coherence that led to the formation of connections even across discontinuous shots. Going beyond a naïve understanding of editing, the groups around Arthur Shimamura and around Katrin Heimann started to focus on techniques—that is, they started to come closer to considerations of montage.[31]

96 · CHAPTER 5

When Eisenstein described an outmoded principle of editing, we recall that for him montage was a clash, collision, harmonization, interaction of moving images, the relationship of shot to shot. This was the essence of the cinema and of apprehension of the world in general. Montage is "an idea that DERIVES from the collision between two shots that are independent of one another."[32] These two shots stand alone, independently, and in their being edited together they produce an idea in the consciousness of the spectator. This dialectic he describes is key to cine-consciousness. The two shots act as quasi self and other, mutually constituting meaning in a Hegelian/Marxian supersession. Film is a relationship of alterity. Maybe the Soviet citizens did not become revolutionary subjects because of viewing *Bronenosets Potyomkin* (*Battleship Potemkin*) (Eisenstein 1925). However, certainly the image has an impact on thought and modes of thought: cine-consciousness. But cinema is capable of more than the production of ideas. Eisenstein aspired to develop a "film syntax," because he largely set out to deploy the cinema as a vehicle of storytelling, the organization of the viewer through organized visual material. Yet the strategy of montage, understood here as narrative editing, the connecting of shots to tell a story, is only one of many other possibilities of cinema.

In no relation to Kuleshov's experiment, Andrew Coward observes simply that the focus on an image (a key to Kuleshov's experimental setting) activates various kinds of processes in cognitive attention: naming, memory, and the establishment of a vivid sensory experience.[33] His summary work underscores that cognition is dynamic. *Seeing is dynamic. Perception actively reaches out in time and across space. Seeing is a reaching out into the world that precedes consciousness.* We begin to see long before we are aware of seeing. The scanning of our environment is a preconscious activity that takes up conscious brain capacities only after time and attention have primed it to start working. We tend to think that reason is the motivation for our actions and that consciousness directs our behaviors, but cognitive research has long shown us a whole set of operations that take place before the complex cognitive capacities become activated. The architecture of our brains provides reserves for a small set of tasks, the work of memory, experiential organization, problem-solving, and so on—all the attributes that Kant praised as being core to reason and the rationality of perception and judgment. Even at the "higher" levels, in these cognitive aspects of explicit conscious perception, a preconscious constitutive process takes place. And for our Kuleshov effect, it is interesting to note that, again completely unrelatedly, Yvonne and Dermot Barnes-Holmes, deploying a relational frame model to describe the brain's higher cognitive processing, draw a link from naming, to storytelling, to problem solving.[34] The subject of the Kuleshov experiment to whom the images are shown can be understood more complexly as evidencing core aspects of this process. The subject focuses attention on the images, activates capacities like naming, begins storytelling, and in doing so sees the world of those images differently. Narration is an aspect of many receptive fields of the brain and key to complex dynamics of self-consciousness. Narration of what one sees, sense making—these are key to cine-cognition.

Fischinger's film seems to elicit a component of this process. It draws the spectator's attention to the images and locates them in a common space, the road, and a single time frame, three weeks. However, the relationship of the images does not incite the kind of storytelling response found in montage. Thus, we might want to describe *Munich-Berlin* as pointing to some other actions of perception active in spectatorship. We could consider it a form of some other juxtaposition—for example, collage.

CHAPTER 6

Cine-Cognition: Collage, Fragmentation, Integration

Although recently artists like Laurie Frick and Michele Banks have been using artistic collage strategies to represent neuroscientific data, collage has received little attention from cognitive scientists.[1] Certainly collage has been discussed as a therapeutic treatment for cognitive traumas and impairments, but this therapeutic approach is an applied aspect of the exploration of cognitive systems.[2] It is not in line with the investigations of montage as an aspect of cognition as such. Closer to what interests me about this subject is Barbara Stafford's work. Stafford has sought for years to bridge the humanities and cognitive science and has researched how "the compound formats of emblems, symbols, collage, and electronic media reveal the brain's grappling to construct mental objects that are redoubled by prior associations."[3] In effect following the questioning of the montage theorists of the 1920s, she has undertaken general studies that explore other cognitive effects unleashed by the juxtaposition of two or more images, of which collage is one. While the juxtaposition and even imposition of one image or more onto or next to other images relies on principles similar to the classic understanding of montage, collage seems to incite not the narration of montage but some other mechanisms of symbolic recognition. It is certainly a meaning-producing activity but of a different form of visual intelligence. For instance, collage seems to subtract the process of emotional project and empathy. For this reason, therapeutic settings prove able to use collage work as opposed to associating and storytelling in order to help trauma patients bring

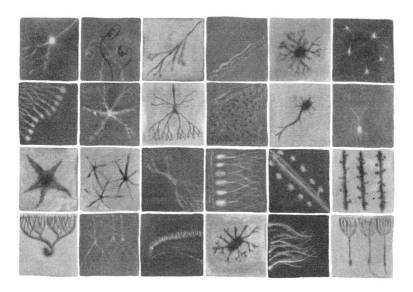

Blue and Lavender Brain Cells (Michele Banks 2014). Courtesy of Michele Banks

order into their experiences. The minimization of emotionality proves helpful in keeping the cognitive systems from being overwhelmed.

By contrast, what we describe as montage seems to rely heavily on emotional responses. Central but not exclusive to montage is the engagement with facial cues. Of course, faces alone do not lead to montage, but they are deployed to elicit maximum emotional effects in narrative film. Interestingly, in Fischinger's 1927 project *München-Berlin Wanderung* (*Walking from Munich to Berlin*), discussed in chapter 5, there are a few shots of faces, young women in particular, during which the camera seems to linger, time slows down, recognition sets in, but neither the preceding or subsequent cut cues up an emotional state as a response to seeing the face. Collage seems to develop meaning without empathy or less emotion and more symbolic processing. It does not seem so connected to facial recognition.

Fischinger, of course, is not the only moving-image artist of his period to explore other strategies of visual intelligence. His colleagues in the art film movements of the European avant-garde experimented with alternatives to the rapidly codifying conventions of narrative film. For example, Hans Richter also famously used what we can identify as collage techniques to produce his classic of Dada film, *Vormittagsspuk* (*Ghosts before Breakfast*) (1928). Here the principle of editing progresses in an order intended *not* to narrate a story, *not* to produce emotional effects, but to produce a sense of non-sense, play, and radical disruption of the expected narrative order. Similar strategies infused works such as *Le Retour à la Raison* (*Return to Reason*) (Ray 1923), *Ballet mécanique* (Léger 1924), *Entr'acte* (Clair 1924), and *Emak Bakia* (Ray 1926). In his classic collection *Dada and Surrealist Film*, Rudolf Kuenzli offered a working definition of Dada film that focused precisely on this aspect:

> Dada-related films have several characteristics in common: they disrupt the viewers' expectations of conventional narrative, their belief in film as presenting reality, and their desire to identify with characters in the film. Dada films are radically non-narrative, non-psychological; they are highly self-referential by constantly pointing to the film apparatus as an illusion-producing machine. Through their cinematic defamiliarization of social reality, they attempt to undermine the norms and codes of social conventions, and thus of conventional filmmaking, which has as its goal to reproduce that conventionality.[4]

We could consider the easy ability to replace the word Dada with "collage" in Kuenzli's definition and thus immediately recognize other possibilities. In fact, although the analysis of this classic collection was limited to movements within the experiments of the classical avant-garde, Kuenzli's description could extend to work that leads all the way up to the present, via Surrealism, to the work of Joseph Cornell, Maya Deren, Kenneth Anger, Jack Smith, Bruce Conner, and Jonas Mekas, infusing the West Coast New American Cinema, animating Warholian pop, inciting the Situationist International and the European Structuralists, and continuing to influence underground, queer, and performance and installation work. The fact that this description could extend to work in the present indicates not only that these works are centered on other aspects of the moving image than narration but also that they reveal certain general principles at work. A simple proposition that collage is defamiliarization is insufficient to apprehend the alternatives at work. This work points to a further structure of visual language.

Collage: Paratactic, Atactic, Heterotactic

But ultimately the discussion to this point has attended to a principle of collage that still organizes images sequentially, like montage. In film analytic discussions, collage has been used mostly as an alternate description for found footage films, like the work of Bruce Conner.[5] Collage in such descriptions addresses the reworking of film material, the cutting and splicing together of footage, and not any collage that might appear in the projection. Collage is thus treated as a form of visual parataxis, the sequencing/sequentialization of discrete visual units that nevertheless remain discreet. If the work of montage is to bring two images together into a cohering narrative producing structure, the segments of collage remain heterogeneous to each other; they form a radical alterity, a difference beyond immediate cognition.

The work of the historic avant-garde produced largely what we could describe as a paratactic collage.[6] Paratactic collage is a sequential collage, one image after the other, and the sequential/sequencing quality of film as film, a filmstrip, made this strategy the initial approach to filmic collage. But what about the classic collage as we know from the consideration of still images? We might describe this strategy as atactic or heterotactic collage: the collage of multiple images within a single frame in which no hierarchy of arrangement or multiple possible orderings arise out of the arrangement. Collage in this sense has the ability to offer a collision, colliding, contact and dispersion of image, symbol and information.

Stan Brakhage's *Mothlight* (1963) and *The Garden of Earthly Delights* (1981), in which he pasted material onto clear strips of film and ran them through an optical printer, take us a step further, from the sequential paratactic manipulation of footage to the formation of multilayered and multivalent atactic imagery. Both of these films are short films aiming to convey a visual experience while reflecting on indexicality and recognition. Perhaps most famously, both collage in this classic sense alongside montage play a central role to the project of Jean-Luc Godard's feature-length film *Le Gai Savoir* (1969). In that film, as part of the movement of 1968 and under the influence of the work of Dziga Vertov, Godard turned his attention to the language of film. As Eisenstein had once noted that it was impossible that the amazing artifice of parallel editing developed by the Americans should be used for nothing more than to depict another bank robbery, Godard sought to develop the language of cinema yet again in revolutionary ways. Discontent with the representational strategies of the New Wave, in *Le Gai Savoir* he undertook a grand project of rethinking cinema. In the film he depicted two figures, Patricia Lumumba and Emile Rousseau, and most discussions of the film focus on the dialogue between the two figures. In long sequences on a darkened stage with no prop but a plastic bubble umbrella, they discuss how to go about their project. They develop a three-year plan: year one to collect, year two to deconstruct, and year three to be reserved for the reconstruction of the language of cinema. However, before the end of the film, the project never arrives at year three. *Le Gai Savoir* goes beyond the dialogue sequences, actually undertaking this project as such. To this end, Godard included long sequences of images with collage elements. Photos, cartoons, advertising, in turn with text

102 · CHAPTER 6

written on them, other elements placed into them, including an advertisement for Ajax cleaning powder onto which is written "the kings of imperialism."

The primary form of collage is text on image, although there are some moments of image on image. All this work, as films ultimately consist of a strip of static images—one after the other, the images with their collage elements appear at a rapid rate making it difficult to read all the information. These sequences of collage require reading within the frame as well as the move of montage from frame to frame. As such, in the surplus of visual material, an ataxia, meaning a lack of ordering, or a heterotaxia, a multiplicity of possible orders, arises. And the viewer is incited to a freedom of reading/narrating practices. To be sure, this was not an absolute freedom. The first screening confronts the viewer with an unexpected excess of images from which the eye/mind can select primary semiotic units to construct meaning on its own. The viewer experiences the filtering and priming capacities of cognition being tossed off. It is as if lower-level consciousness tosses the film up to higher perception as a big question: We give up down here; what do you make of all this? It is a rather sublime experience in the Kantian/Schillerian sense; we experience in the moment of perception an act of consciousness wringing with the world that threatens to overwhelm it with too much input.

Of course, because *Le Gai Savoir* is a film and not a randomized database, the same viewer will see the same film each time, and the excess will slowly become patternized in the processes of individual cognition. Moreover, a viewer in control of the technology can stop the flow and engage stilled images. Ultimately an ordering establishes itself in which the initial freedom of the viewer gives way to a much more standard contemplation of artistic symbolism: Ajax the Greek mythological hero and the American scouring powder as a nexus of imperialism and advertising. Thus, although Godard deployed the strategy of collage here to dismantle the semiotic system of narrative montage, the project replaces it with a different system, one of non-narrative semiotics.

The deployment of collage as a means to open up a non-narrative returns in other work by Godard, perhaps most substantially his *Histoire(s) du Cinéma* (1998), a video project that returns to the collage of images to review the hi/ story of cinema. It is in some ways the accomplishment of year three of *Le Gai Savoir*, constructing a sort of poetics of cinematic language, connected to the voice of Godard, yet creating its own visual rhymes and alliterations. As with Godard's long relationship to cinema and the moving image, this exploration continues to highlight the potential of technology to open up new visual language. Likewise, Alexander Kluge has followed Godard and made collage a fundamental principle in his recent moving-image works, such as *Früchte des*

Vertrauens (Fruits of Trust) (2009), *Nachrichten aus der ideologischen Antike—Marx/ Eisenstein/Das Kapital* (*News from Ideological Antiquity—Marx/Eisenstein/Capital*) (2008), or *Mensch 2.0—Die Evolution in unserer Hand* (*Human 2.0—The Evolution in Our Hand*) (2011). Especially in *News from Ideological Antiquity*, Kluge relied on the full technological capabilities of DVD to bring together an almost ten-hour documentary, the episodes and themes of which connect through a principle of collage.

The beginning point of the documentary is Eisenstein's plans to make a film version of Marx's *Das Kapital* in the style of James Joyce's *Ulysses*. The capacity of the DVD allows Kluge to engage the project, reflect on its potential, and enact it in part, but it does so according to principles inspired by Eisenstein's montage theory as well as modernist collage.

Long sequences of photomontage and text collage run between interviews and performances that characterize Kluge's contemporary practice. The system of cinema is defamiliarized, fragmented. Narrative gives way to a form of fantasy that reopens the potentials of Eisenstein's project in the conditions of contemporary technology. In a key sequence, Tom Tykwer supplies a short film, *Der Mensch im Ding* (*The Person in the Thing*) (2008), for the project that used 360 recording potentials to explore Marx's discussion of commodity fetishism/Lukacs's extension of reification. The sequence begins with a pan down from the sky as Tykwer's voice-over locates the camera's image in space and time. It captures a woman walking down the street and then freezes the frame. From there the virtual camera spins and rotates around her on the street, reviewing her place in the material world she inhabits, from the clothing she wears to the manhole covers on the street where she walks. The voice-over provides a running commentary on the material origins, nature of production, and social significance of the objects. As such, it restores humanistic awareness, if not visual technical control, to the material world. The DVD project allows this sequence to be watched as part of a ten-hour sequential viewing—start the DVD and let it run. Or it can be called up and sequenced according to the spectators' interests and curiosities. The point of the project is not to create a sense of illusory completion and emotional wholeness through classical narrative, not to dynamize revolutionary consciousness in the spectator through the clashing conceptual montage of images, but to offer some insights about how to engage, via contemporary available technologies, with the fragmentation of that material world.

In a further technological advancement with impact on the ability of the moving image to appear in other than strictly sequential forms, Lev Manovich and Andreas Kratky sought to create a database film, the presentation of which each time would be a unique event. With their three short films—*Mission to*

104 · CHAPTER 6

Earth, Absences, and *Texas* (2005)—they created a new form of collage film in a tradition Manovich described as reaching back to Vertov via Peter Greenaway.[7] For the project they used a database of images and varying algorithms to generate randomly a film: "All the elements—including screen layout, the visuals and their combination, the music, the narrative, and the length—are subject to change every time the film is viewed."[8] For *Mission to Earth* the images used to tell the story are set in fields of rectangles and squares—that is, constructivist "elementary" shapes. The algorithm selects images based on a text read by a narrator who becomes the voice-over narrator of the film. A sentence like "She walked among strangers" may generate an image based on "she" or "walk" or "stranger." One run through the story, the image may be dominant in the upper left-hand corner, and in the next it may be minor in the lower right, while the rest of the frame is filled with fields of various size. The pastels of the fields are keyed to the tones of the image selected. Each viewing as unique is not simply unique because the images are drawn randomly from a database but precisely because they are set in a collage of corresponding colors and elementary shapes. The collage is neutral in meaning production per se but maximal in its randomizing of composition.

It might be the case that the images generated are random, so each viewing experience is unique; however, the text is not. Thus, as with Godard's project, there is a basic element of repetition. Whereas Godard sought to rupture narration with a symbolic semiosis, in Manovich and Kratky's project the images are selected and bound to a dominant text. Narrative dominates and each viewing experience will be of the same story with different images. Nevertheless, although bound to story, collage is again not a storytelling element here. It is a matter of ornamental stylistic arrangement.

Färblein (Colourette) (1991) was a project of two West German filmmakers, Rainer Bellenbaum and Bärbel Freund. They went to East Berlin from March to August of 1990, during the period of unification but also during the period of economic collapse of the East German systems of production. They recorded with a 16 mm camera on Kodak film the objects and places of quotidian existence in the German Democratic Republic (GDR). These images are dominated by a particular pastel color set that distinguished the GDR industrial design. The visual world of the GDR was separate from that of other countries in the Western and the Eastern blocs. The filmmakers then edited the images together into a collage of varying speeds. At times the shots are a bit longer; the camera lingers on a street crossing, an arrow on a road, or a simple board painted red, onto which tools, likewise painted red, are hung. Then the cuts come more quickly, images blur, become superimpositions, and follow a logic of series; for example,

Beautiful productive village, orange. *Färblein (Colourette)* (Freund and Bellenbaum 1991). Courtesy of Rainer Bellenbaum and Bärbel Freund

objects of the same yellow wheat color, all chairs, postboxes, reds and greens. Then the pace slows again, the camera seems to linger on a red sign reading *Leben* (life) in a field behind which a wheat-colored light rail train makes its way. The quickly paced sequences place the objects of interest generally in the mid-ground center, locking the eye into a tight focus on that spot of the frame. At times the objects or colors rhythmically move from the edge of the frame to the center, forcing the perceptive apparatus to search and grasp. The long sequences appear, then, as a bit of respite, returning some perceptive control to the eye. It is freed to look around the frame a bit and to catch a "cognitive breath."

Julien Patry, a young French digital artist, conducted a similar project for the now unified Berlin. *Berlin (Classified)* (2016) focuses on the colors and design of Berlin.[9] Indeed the repeated presence of the word "Berlin" in the frame underscores the specificity of the location. Where Bellenbaum and Freund produced a twenty-one-minute silent film, Patry's three-minute short digital project moves at a slicker pace set to an electronic mix that was popular in Berlin's club scene. The colors of Patry's project are more intense and in high definition. Yet the sequencing principles are similar. A series of orange garbage bins gives way to

Blue red shed. *Färblein (Colourette)* (Freund and Bellenbaum 1991). Courtesy of Rainer Bellenbaum and Bärbel Freund

a series of subway stops, to a series of crosswalk buttons, to purple objects via a purple minibus, to minibuses and then to campers and trailers, and then, via the VW logo on one minibus, onto a series of VW logos. Again, the eye seems locked in at times to the center of the frame, where the object of attention is located. One technique that Patry uses to give relief to the eye stands out as a digital editing technique advancing the collage of moving images. Patry periodically divides the frame into a four-by-four of smaller frames, each with an image; for instance, sixteen VW minivans in various colors. Each frame is itself a moving image. Action continues in each. And the project revels in this technique, using it to build to a form of crescendo. Doubling to eight by eight, then sixteen by sixteen, and then finally recalling all of the four-by-four screens into a meta-screen collage.

Unlike Godard's collage of "moving" still images in *Le Gai Savoir*, here the digitally edited collage is of truly moving images. It is a simple quadratic schema, not an elaborated form of juxtaposition and imposition into frames as one might know from Dada or Bauhaus collages. Again, here we experience a "lack" of storytelling. Bellenbaum and Freund described their project as an attempt to capture the evocative look, sound, and smells of the GDR. The fall of the Berlin

Wall in 1989 opened up a world, the quotidian reality of which had been separated and largely off limits to them for decades. And suddenly they could enter it. Their film is about entering into another space, an other space. Similar could be said for Patry. Although he shares a common post-Wall upbringing with the residents of Berlin, his film still relies on an appreciation of the unique qualities of a location. The Berlin press celebrated the film as a declaration of love by one of the city's new residents. For both films the strategy of collage rather than montage plays with space and time, offering a different sense of both. It is not one of narrative ideational unity but rather the aim to convey something of the totality of a place in its multifaceted and heterogeneous aspects.

Heterotactic Community Formation: YouTube Pooping

Collage of this strategy has gained a broad reach. It was already popular as remix and mashup strategies in music and easily flipped over into visual arts work. VCRs and tape-to-tape recording possibilities allowed for a new type of remixing of found footage already in the 1980s. Collage films in the classic sense, a paratactic series of found images, expanded rapidly as a practice. In 1992 the alternative group Was (Not Was) famously remixed George H. W. Bush's famous speech to produce the music video "Read My Lips" by A Thousand Points of Night. Found footage collage expanded especially when YouTube came online in 2005.[10] Offering a vehicle for moving-image work, the site rapidly became a platform of popular production that ranged from the banal pratfall and cat video to the experimental form. "Supercut" sequences, where similar actions (David Caruso taking off his sunglasses, various figures saying "nooooo," or lines from Bruno Ganz playing Hitler in *Downfall* [2004]) were edited together in quick succession, became a common practice in 2006. By 2011 mashup and remix YouTube channels began to emerge.

The development of new digital editing programs in established suites transformed what had once been an artisanal practice done on an optical printer. It became a ubiquitous digital technology. Free programs or tools bundled with hardware purchases made it possible in the new millennium easily to produce video in video, chroma key, and other creative projects. Often hailed as part of the democratization of the internet, what had been aspects of concentrated work turned into one of a range of effects deployed for popular practices.

Of particular interest for this discussion is how recycling images from videogames, especially games produced for the Phillips CD-I platform like *Hotel Mario*, became a new method of creating collage films. Certainly among "poopers" it is well known that with "I'd Say He's Hot On Our Tail" (2004, uploaded

108 · CHAPTER 6

2006) a gamer calling himself SuperYoshi inaugurated the strategy of YouTube Poop (YTP), reediting scenes from *Adventures of Super Mario Bros 3* (1990).[11] Fairly straightforward in its editing strategies, for "I'd Say" SuperYoshi relied on Windows Movie Maker; the project reedited the images to tell a different narrative with the simply drawn unsophisticated characters. The response to SuperYoshi was a quick formation of a subcultural genre emulating his project in which the full set of editing possibilities became deployed as they emerged. YTP at this point is an accretion of all audiovisual editing tech strategies.

The designation "poop" is suggested to have emerged out of the poor aesthetic quality of the work: another "shitty, crappy, poop" video. These projects thus align with the *détournement* practices of the Situationist International but also, later, punk and DIY Super 8 work from the 1970s, early music film clips, and eventually music videos. These projects as analog film projects depended on communities coming together in physical locations, cinemas, punk clubs, community centers, abandoned warehouses, and other venues. YouTube brought the phenomenon into cyberspace in new ways and allowed it to develop to new ends.

Irony, satire, puerile humor, chaotic anarchic pleasure (they are called poops and poopers for good reason) give energy to the community. Along with reediting, poops came quickly to deploy dubbing and voice to make sequences that had figures say or do something against character. In *jonathan swift returns from the dead to eat a cheese sandwich* (2010) madanonymous uses video in video (ViV) editing along with other forms of glitching and distortion.[12] The piece is often cited as a work that moved YTP toward artistry. ViV, lagging or stuttering images to get figures to say nonsense words ("SuS"), became popular.[13] Perhaps what was most important in the development of YTP was not any intention to artistry per se but how various YouTubers began to communicate via YTP uploads. By 2008 YTP "tennis" had emerged, in which the "players" make poop of each other's poop, until the videos become distorted sequences of chaos.[14] And by 2009 the practice of "collab" (collaboration) had emerged, in which various poopers joined together to produce one project that can last up to an hour. The former practice of tennis could draw in clicks and likes in the hundreds of thousands, but the latter practice of collab has had the potential to bring in millions of viewers; "Mickey Mouse's Clubhouse Catastrophe" (2017) has brought in close to four million hits.[15] The result has been multivalent collages. What appears as chaos, nonsense, or distortion to someone outside the subculture turns out to be a set of references added on as layers and layers of images. Using rapid forward reverse and word-splice editing to make someone else's project lag or getting a character to say "SuS" or "JoJ" becomes a form of legible code that has a multiplicity of possible orders. The insider viewer is incited to a freedom of reading/editing practices, expanding the heterotaxia of the poop. It is this form of visual communication, riffing on each other's work, that compels a turn to an ataxia (a lack of ordering) or a heterotaxia (a multiplicity of possible orders).

Indeed we can describe the YTP community as heterotactic in the rhetorical sense, where the architecture, grammar, and arrangement of topics opens asymmetrically through the reliance on others and differentiation. The YTP community develops not just through the making of collages (poops) but through the actions of processing and reprocessing poops in communication or direct collaborations with others. To be sure, tennis, collabs, and soccer have rules associated with them, but the moving-image projects became vectors for community development that can go in any direction. YTP draws together and renders apart participants (i.e., poopers) as they riff and remix (i.e., poop) popular culture, advertising, memes, music videos, and (most importantly) each other's work. The image itself is not the goal; rather, its pooping—that is, transformation, distortion, moshing, glitching, rendering, and other manipulation—is. The poop and its new iteration speak to the pooper as well as the pooped. Running gags are common across projects, "Easter eggs" and other visuals are inserted for the pleasure of the discerning viewer, and other devices are used that create connoisseurship. A text might appear completely uninteresting to the outsider viewer, but the visuals may reveal layers of reworking to the initiated pooper. The cyber community relies less on the mechanisms of traditional subculture formation and more on the production of image and (text) message, likes and clicks. The heterotaxia of its images creates the community in YTP.

Collage: Cognition and De/Fragmentation

Many of the projects just described retain a relationship to narration through voice-over narration or dubbing. Such a tying of the image to a narrator or directorial voice limits or counters the potential deformation of narrative made available by collage. We can consider such work as subordinating the potential of collage to the narrative principles of montage. If montage constructs a temporal-spatial unit and opens up emotional attachment and narrative engagement, then we can think of collage as deploying fragmentation. Thinking of this aesthetic specificity, Brian Henderson, one of the few film scholars to reflect on the actual distinction of montage and collage wrote: "[Collage] collects or sticks its fragments together in a way that does not entirely overcome their fragmentation. It seeks to recover its fragments *as fragments*. In regard to overall form, it seeks to bring out the internal relations of its pieces, whereas montage imposes a set of relations upon them and indeed collects or creates its pieces to fill out a pre-existent plan."[16] The reason much of the preceding work deployed collage was as a conscious strategy against narrative montage, hence the propensity to limit the potential of fragmentation as such. Yet, in making such an observation, a question arises as to whether there is any cognitive "reason" or "benefit" to fragmentation.

In cognitive and neuroscience, fragmentation is largely treated as a problem; cognitive processes "fragment" from sleep deprivation, Alzheimer's disease, or childhood sexual abuse.[17] "Dynamic core hypothesis" (DCH) and "information-integration theory" (IIT)—cognitive theories of consciousness that developed out of the work of Gerald Edelman, his colleague Giulio Tononi, and others—posit forms of complex cognitive integration in which neuron bundling pairs with external stimuli. In this activity "the brain can integrate the many different parts (modalities) of a scene to form a unitary view, which would be perceived as an integrated experience."[18] Developing these models, Fatemeh Bakouie and Shahriar Gharibzadeh have posited that schizophrenia and autism may actually result from a form of visual fragmentation. They have noted that dopamine in the brain is involved in dynamic core visuoperceptual tasks, which are difficult or impossible to accomplish for people diagnosed with schizophrenia or autism. Dopamine seems related to neuron bundling. This research is interesting, even groundbreaking, suggesting a possibility of integrated understanding of the relationship of systems of cognition all the way from the chemical to the objective. All of this research, however, positions fragmentation as negative and as antithetical to an ideal of continued integration.

Thus, in considering fragmentation in this research, one point that is not made or pursued is that fragmentation may have positive and constitutive capacities in cognition. Bundling, for instance, which seems to be an active creative process—that is, a process that requires some exertion of energy or incitement through forms of stimulation—is a transformation from one state to a different one. Bundling is the move from fragmentation to integration. This seems to suggest that fragmentation, beyond the negative dissociative states explored, may actually be the dominant mode of the brain. Fragmentation may not be a degeneration but a base state of the brain.

I am not in a position to pursue this point as a question of cognitive laboratory work; however, experience repeatedly has shown that the centers of concentration in discourses, the points of focus in systems of knowledge, tend to become blind to how their systems are constituted by their opposites. I state emphatically, then, that *there is no integration without fragmentation*, no IIT without fragmentation in some form, no dynamic core without. Something else, some other state, must precede integration. And, for that matter, in order to be truly plastic, the bundling process must also proceed through a process of "unbundling," or fragmentation. Even if neuronal bundles were permanent, the plasticity of the brain explored in DCH and IIT models suggests that such ordering must proceed through orders in which the bundled integration of the one order is a form of fragmentation in another. The neurons that bundle to learn language prove to be fragmented when a new language appears on the cognitive horizon. The dynamic core that integrates the complex information that allows us to walk is nevertheless in a condition of fragmentation vis-à-vis the order of movement we describe as dance.

Perhaps the state of fragmentation that exists in the cognitive system, that, by contrast, constitutes cognitive integration, has something to do with the fragmentation we find in collage. Perhaps, inasmuch as neuroscientists have posited that narrative cinema reflects cognitive processes, we can posit that collage cinema also corresponds to existing cognitive processes. If it could not, how could we perceive it? How could we enjoy the non-sensical provocations of Dada and the Fluxus movement? How could Surrealist work offer a profound disturbance? A sense of amazement must be able to arise from moving-image strategies other than the glorious narrative sweep and monstrational splendor of *Gone with the Wind* (Fleming 1939), mustn't it? Would not the world of marching silhouettes in William Kentridge's *More Sweetly Play the Dance* (2015), a forty-five-minute nine-screen projection of processing sequential itinerants, simply meet with confusion and misapprehension rather than contain the sublime appeal it seems to offer? Indeed, do not the reflections on the sublime offered by Kant and Friedrich Schiller, among others, already indicate the capacity of cognition to move from and back into fragmentation? And what about the work of installation? Is a project like Farocki's *Comparison through a Third* (discussed earlier) not a collage? It is not a narrative as such, even in its single-channel form. It does seem to rely precisely on the fragmentation of presentation through two channels in order to give the spectator a more engaged sense of the process of meaning construction. Is fragmentation here not constitutive of meaning as much as it is consciously deployed in the space of the installation?

Certainly we can identify one further form of "collage," or rather fragmentary film, in the work of the New American Cinema but also in the Structural/Materialist film of the Europeans. Bruce Conner, Stan Brakhage, Hollis Frampton, Michael Snow, Birgit and Wilhelm Hein, Jonas Mekas, Malcolm LeGrice, and others showed us that we can scratch the image, decompose it, and add and subtract forms of recognition by manipulating the material emulsion of film as such. In this way the moving image became open to collisions in the frame and

112 • CHAPTER 6

new forms of fragmentation in the frame itself. This work sought to provide a new experience of our visual intelligence. It may be possible to explore if this work corresponds to the kinds of dopamine levels in visual-perceptual tasks posited by Bakouie and Gharibzadeh. Such moving image work may actively explore some of the propositions of fragmentation and integration posited in IIT and DCH. It may give the viewer an experience of their own integration-fragmentation processes.

CHAPTER 7

Cine-Cognition: The *Kippbild*, Dis/Ambiguation

If collage and fragmentation has not been a focus on cognitive studies, the clearly related experience of ambiguous and multistable images has. Before the cognitive and neuroscientific turns took place, Gestalt psychology in particular attended to perception. Important in these studies was the function of the *Kippbild*, a German term designating those "images that suddenly switch."[1] *Kipp* means to tilt, lean, or switch, in the sense that a raucous sporting event can suddenly "kipp," turn into a riot. The term "kippbild" thus describes images that can kipp, switch, turn those multistable images and innumerable optical illusions that play on shifting cognitive recognition. We can think of, for example, the famous image of the old woman/young girl, or the simple black-white outline that represents either two faces or the outline of a vase. Here the kippbild can be understood in its broadest sense: as an image that switches back and forth, multistable, giving the viewer an experience of possibilities of recognition.

Multistable images have a long history. We can find these bi-stable or reversible figures, optical illusions of this form, in antiquity. They have been the subject of philosophical reflection but, more, they have captured popular imagination. They entertain because they play in part with a sense of the moving image—and they did so before the projected moving image took on its modern form. These moving images are part of a visual techne that preceded the era of cinema. The kippbild enjoyed such great popularity in the nineteenth century in the advent of cinema such that Joseph Jastrow, one of the founding figures

Kippbild "Cup or Faces Paradox." Bryan Derksen (https://commons.wikimedia.org/wiki/File:Cup_or_faces_paradox.svg)

of psychology in the United States, took note of their ubiquity and published studies of these optical illusions in the 1880s.[2] His discussion of, among others, the famous "rabbit or duck's head" image gained a great deal of notoriety and worked to popularize clinical psychology. The experience of multistable perception is not limited, however, to the perceptual apparatus of sight. Composers have developed techniques of play in harmonics, perfumers know that olfactory experiences can switch suddenly, just as cooks and sommeliers know that multistable taste experiences can bring pleasure but also disgust. The multistable haptic experience is a common goal of clothing designers.

Ludwig Wittgenstein in his late work "elevated" the kippbild from the play of popular culture to the heights of philosophical questioning. He explored the multistable image as a means to distinguish fundamentals of perception: "seeing" in its common form versus "seeing as." Reflecting on Jastrow's "rabbit or duck's head" image, Wittgenstein discounted the kippbild as having relevance to philosophical investigations of perception. We do not *see* the rabbit-duck-head image, we only *see* it *as* rabbit *or* duck head. We see only an aspect of it, and thus he discounts it given that perception can only be whole, a natural seeing of the entirety.

There are certainly other possibilities to approach kippbild philosophically. If the kippbild cannot be seen both at once, the viewer experiences the brain being

Cine-Cognition: The Kippbild, Dis/Ambiguation • 115

confused and searching. Precisely for Gestalt, the kippbild points to fundamental processes of perception, the activity of the mind in completing our world—hence an "error" in Wittgenstein's approach to perception. "The whole is greater than the sum of its parts" is a familiar principle of Gestalt; however, fundamental to Gestalt is actually the exploration of visual intelligence, the activity of the brain in structuring our perception of the world.[3] This experience recalls the Kantian sublime, in which "reason" wins out over confusion in the end.

Gestalt and cognitive psychology lead us to dismiss Wittgenstein's distinction, suggesting that there is no ability to perceive such a "whole" image; rather, the image contains two ambiguous contents that engage the actions of perception. We may not be able to see both the duck and the rabbit at the same time, and the Necker cube may project in or out at any given moment, but the viewing subject is aware of something else at work in perception. The viewing subject becomes aware that there is a larger apparatus at work in the perception of the world. Subsequent neuroscientific work shows how a recognition of the kippbild unsettles a certain naïve realism of the image. The kippbild reveals there is not an objective world that projects into a perceptive apparatus in renaissance geometry. Our eyes are not a camera obscura recording reality. If we attend well to the kippbild, it requires us to speak of a social *and* cognitive construction of reality.

Wittgenstein's presumption is that perception is stable, but as in the discussion of defragmentation in chapter 6, we could insist instead that the kippbild shows us that multistability is a constant to perception, or at least an ever present potential. Don Ihde famously set forward on a reworking of phenomenology—that is, Husserl's principle of "seeing phenomenologically" by focusing on multistability.[4] He was inspired to do so as a rejection of Wittgenstein's approach. This work led him to proclaim a post-phenomenology in which he collapsed Husserl's science and practical technology to develop "a pragmatically enriched phenomenology, a postphenomenology."[5]

Like the Necker cube, which projects outward but then from that given perspective switches and projects inward, the kippbild makes experiential aspects of our perceptive apparatus as it processes a three-dimensional world. In the still image, the kippbild does not vacillate; instead it shifts suddenly, suggesting something about perception as a search for stable recognition. We cannot see the cube extrude and intrude in our perception simultaneously. We can only see two faces or a vase; we can only recognize the old woman or the young girl. The image is perceived preferably in one way or the other, not both. Sometimes one of the variations proves more difficult to perceive, but once recognized, that perspective may also seem to expunge an ability to see the previous way: when

116 · CHAPTER 7

the hippo turns into a skull or when the stacked cubes switch from pointing downward to pointing upward. And with each kipp, each switch, we recognize something more at work in our acts of recognition.

The kippbild historically was a still image that moves in our perception. The form of drawn image that so fascinated popular culture in the nineteenth century is not a moving image in the cinematic sense. With the advent of cinema, however, everything changed. Since then the still image exists in a relationship to the moving. However, when the kippbild becomes a part of the moving image, something else comes into play. The moving image has the ability to play with the multistability of the image. The kipp effect can be prolonged. To the experience of recognition, an experience of nonrecognition or abstraction can be added. The possibility of multistability can be accentuated—in other words, recognition or meaning can be branched or networked in multiple directions, not only the bifurcation of the two, the either-or, of the still image. Thus the kippbild, as also a property of the moving image, has been deployed in various projects by moving-image artists. Like montage and collage the kippbild is a key component to the movement of image, yet also like collage it takes some effort to recognize it at work in the moving-image form. What happens to the kippbild when it itself begins to move in projection?

ABSOLUTE FILM (OCCLUSION EXPERIMENTS)

Hans Richter, Viking Eggeling, Walter Ruttmann, and Oskar Fischinger began their experiments with film in the 1920s. Richter, Eggeling, Ruttmann, and, tangentially, Fischinger comprised what is often called the Absolute Film movement. What truly unites this group of figures who, beyond Eggeling and Richter, only loosely associated with one another was that they approached the moving image through questions based not in cinema but in the fine arts. Richter, Eggeling, Ruttmann, and Fischinger came to the moving image as painters and not filmmakers. Thus, they were not concerned with the questions of narration, montage, and mis-en-scène that motivated their colleagues working in the world of narrative feature films. The history of this period is commonly dominated by discussions of German Expressionist film; however, these moving-image artists truly originated art film. Ruttmann explicitly described this work as "painting with the medium of time."[6]

This work was truly what we can call "experimental cinema." The much discussed and acclaimed German Expressionist film in this regard was the origins of art-house cinema. Expressionist film treated the questions of perception raised by Expressionism with little interest and instead drew from Expressionist painting, largely a form of depiction that represented a world out of

Cine-Cognition: The Kippbild, *Dis/Ambiguation* • 117

joint, a world in which the interior condition of nervous disruption and the exterior world of unsettled revolution and economic chaos of the postwar era aligned in filmic narratives: *Nerven (Nerves)* (Reinert 1919), *Das Cabinet des Dr. Caligari (The Cabinet of Dr. Caligari)* (Wiene 1920), *Von Morgens bis Mitternachts (From Morn to Midnight)* (Martin 1920), *Der müde Tod (Destiny)* (Lang 1921), and so on. By contrast, Absolute Film posed questions of perception and cognition, limits of representation, and possibilities of Gestalt recognition. Such questions were not interested in narration. Their work separated from the objective world into abstraction and in very precise ways sought to find the ur-forms of visual language a half century before cognitive scientists like David Hubel, Thorsten Wiesel, James Enns, Anne Treisman, Béla Julesz, and others explored the brain's mechanisms of edge recognition. Eggeling moved from scroll paintings of primary forms easily onto the film strip as medium via which he could make primary forms move in time. Eggeling was interested in forms that connected to music or displayed Kandinsky-like curves and flourishes, yet he wanted these movements to take place as music for the eye, not the ear. Eggeling cooperated with Richter on various visual experiments culminating in Eggeling's *Symphonie Diagonal (Diagonal Symphony)* (1924). For their part, Fischinger and Ruttmann were intensely interested in synesthesia, especially the relation between image, sound, and color. Fischinger explicitly sought a relationship between the moving image and sound, drawing on new sound recording possibilities. His light symphonies had broad influence from Disney's animation to expanded cinema and on to disco environments. These works eschewed narrative, and the artists in this moment concentrated on abstract nonobjective forms.

Although discussed in earlier chapters in conjunction with Dada film, Hans Richter's work in the Absolute Film movement is typically considered as undertaking groundbreaking work on abstract motion in time. His films *Rhythmus 21 (Rhythm 21)* (1921) and *Rhythmus 23 (Rhythm 23)* (1923) in particular are recognized as producing three-dimensional effects on the basis of occlusion.[7] These films put into motion the kinds of experiments that Constructivists and Suprematists were conducting with the still image. Movement, however, gave Richter the ability to experiment with stereoscopy.

Perhaps it is better stated in the inverse: Richter's experiments with the experience of stereoscopy allowed him to provide an illusion of movement. In the first film, Richter used black and white fields, simple geometric forms of squares and rectangles, to produce occlusion experiences for the spectator. Fields appearing to overlap, one square in the foreground and a rectangle in the background, provided a sense of movement as those rectangles and squares shifted in size. However, not unlike the work of Malevich, El Lissitzky, or Kandinsky, the

118 · CHAPTER 7

moving image here adds a dynamic to the experience. Through changes in size, shapes appear to move forward and backward, to create tunnels, and to overshadow each other repeatedly. The perception that they are moving within and across the screen derives from providing the eye with an outline that cuts into or is positioned against the outline of another field, techniques found repeatedly in the still-image abstract works of avant-garde colleagues. The second film brings in diagonal lines and parallelograms along with squares and rectangles. It moves into lines and shapes as well as animating techniques that are drawn from Richter's friend Viking Eggeling. In his 1923 film, however, Richter does not enter into this experiment with symbolic forms. He stays focused on the ur-forms, cognitive edge recognitions, and stereoscopy effects. Richter did not experiment with convergence of linear lines, foreshortening, or parallax as mechanisms of producing three-dimensionality. The effect thus accomplishes a play of depth—foreground, midground, and background—while at the same time remaining flat. The fields exist in occluded relations, which do not develop perspectival dimensionality neither of Renaissance nor of Cubist styles.

Unconsidered in these films is how we can also observe that the addition of movement puts into play an experience of the kippbild as well. Foregrounding and backgrounding, oppositions of white and black fields, these oppositions in the film not only provide a sense of movement; they also result in repeated sudden shifts in perspective. Indeed the film shows us that the sense of movement is interwoven with multistable perception, what Shai Azoulai explored as a kinetic depth effect.[8] His work focused on perceptions of rotation rather than the projection-introjection dynamic Richter accomplished. But in Azoulai's work we see how the sense of continuous movement through depth perception that Richter activated relies on a form of coherency in recognition. The shapes are perceived as objects in motion because the cognitive system is primed to expect change at certain points, precisely the kinetic depth effect. What was in the midground suddenly falls to the background; the opposition of squares and rectangles may project out and then in; the fields of black may form dominant images and then shift into a condition of background with the white fields constituting the foregrounded image—all because the perceptive apparatus is based on an expectation of motion in space. These mechanisms allow us to move about in space, but when we remain stable and we still see the "movement," it is because this cognitive expectation is still there.

None of this work is intended to narrate. If the collage strategy of Richter's Dada films aimed to provide a sense of fragmentation/integration, what was the aspiration? In his essay "Die schlecht trainierte Seele" ("The Badly Trained Soul") (1924), Richter discusses this work in terms that resemble aspects of

Cine-Cognition: The Kippbild, *Dis/Ambiguation* • 119

Eisenstein's theory of montage. Richter considers these images as having a direct impact on the mind. But here he is not interested in dialectics, revolution, or narration. He is certainly not working with images that involve the clash of images across cuts. His technique provides more a sense of flowing continuity rather than distinctive shots. The appeal to the "soul"—that is, unconscious cognitive processes—in his essay draws upon psychological considerations that go back to Georg Simmel's classic of urban sociology, "The Metropolis and Mental Life" (1903). Richter, following Simmel, notes that the modern urban experience has a deforming effect on the feelings of the modern subject. The modern subject is simply exposed to feeling without an awareness of the process. Conscious catharsis is no longer possible. The goal he pursues, then, in these films is recuperative to this modern experience. He seeks to provide awareness of the basic structures of movement and rhythm without those structures being tied to objective form. Richter eschewed the kitsch of preformed postcard images as having any recuperative value. By contrast, distance from the objective world and into a primary form could help the badly trained soul. He described a "vitality" available to the spectator in this viewing experience of abstract movement.[9] And he aimed through this experience of vitality to reveal the "inherent order" on which our feelings as a substratum generate our ideas as a superstructure.[10] The films educate the psyche, provide a "means of power to the soul," and provide "judgment and activity."[11] Having had such an experience in the contained environment of the cinema, the spectator can leave and reenter the rush of modernity better trained to contend with its inundation of form.

Richter's film as a project to train the soul is, as Michael Cowan and his colleagues have argued, an indication of Richter's participation in a high modernist project.[12] The suggestion corresponding to this description, however, is that this project is in some ways passé in our postmodern condition. We might have an interest in the historic connections, but such "entrainment" of the psyche posited by Richter has no contemporary currency. Entrainment, however, has become one of the dynamic aspects of cognitive and neuroscientific research. Bringing the natural waves of the mind into harmony with outside stimulation is being explored in conjunction with most cognitive systems from memory to recognition, as well as "disorders" from attention deficit disorder to schizophrenia.[13] Although typically entrainment takes place via binaural beats, the principle of using moving images to entrain the brain is neither far-fetched nor passé.

Richter's project does seem to correspond to contemporary edge recognition studies.[14] This direction of research has less interest currently—not because it is wrong but because the models that it was supposed to prove, models of two-system hierarchical brain functions, have been proven wrong. By contrast, considerations of occlusion and containment have likewise experienced a renaissance in cognitive studies. Shimon Ullman, in a work that transitioned out of the paradigm of passive vision, explored occlusion as a key challenge to recognition.[15] The ability to recognize objects in spite of occlusion pointed to more complex mechanisms of recognition than could be accounted for in the passive vision paradigm. The group around Rui Ni has studied occlusion and parallax as key to visual perception and judgment.[16] Working in a cognitive developmental paradigm, Olga Kochukhova and Gustaf Gredebäck recognized how in infants occlusion signals that the infant is participating in a "robust memory effect."[17] They described how moving-image occlusion in particular activates gaze tracking and relies on complex systems of extrapolation interacting with long-term memory. And while I am not suggesting it is a verification of Richter's precepts of urban overload, Brent Strickland and Brian Scholl used a display not unlike Richter's *Rhythm 21* to show that the kind of occlusion dynamic that transpires in the film is not simply a matter of childhood development. They identified that this form of recognition has long-lasting impact into adult judgment. Occlusion biases "do not merely get development off the ground but they also help structure adults' mature experience of the world."[18] Their research, however, appears unaware of its striking parallels with Richter's art film experiments.

To be clear, I am not interested in, nor capable of, verifying if such applications are indeed possible. I am not interested in arguing that Richter's films have a new import or increased weight because of clinical cognitive studies. I am interested in investigating other practices of cinema, critically unreflected potentials of the cinema that operate independently of montage. Thus we can offer here some form of initial résumé. If the use of collage was related to fragmentation/integration, we can initially posit that the use of the kippbild serves a different purpose, one related to recognition and memory. The fascination with or the sense of play derived from a multistable viewing experience, like that of other optical illusions, is that it presents an experience of the limitations of the perceptive apparatus. There may be reasons to ascribe to multistable images a therapeutic quality, as Richter did, because they do provide some meta-insight. Multistable images provide awareness to consciousness of its construction through unconscious systems.

Important to note about this awareness is its transience. If the multistable image or other forms of optical illusions reveal the unconscious construction of consciousness, it does not mean that this awareness undermines the ability of those systems to provide consciousness with a sense of seamless wholeness.

We may see how depth perception and edge recognition work, but that does not mean we cease to experience depth and edges.

The project of Absolute Film had a rather limited duration. By 1927 Richter had moved on to other modes—for example, Dada—and by the 1930s Ruttmann was cooperating with Leni Riefenstahl on *Triumph des Willens* (*Triumph of the Will*) (1935). Fischinger did continue on with his abstract film projects. With the ascent of sound film, he sought to provide a synesthetic experience through developing abstract moving sound images. Forced into exile by the persecution of the Nazi regime, Fischinger sought to collaborate with Walt Disney on a project that would become *Fantasia* (1940); however, Fischinger felt Disney's insistence on objective illustrations of music obliterated the significance of his abstract work, reducing it to animations for programmatic music. His later projects remained largely unrealized.

Artistic work with multistable images did continue. We can consider the visual dissections of space in Cubism making it a movement of multistable images at heart. Man Ray, Francis Picabia, and others deployed various techniques to fool the eye into seeing depth and movement. M. C. Escher and Salvador Dali in very different approaches drew on multistable images for their work in the '30s and '40s. In the postwar era, op art relied on optical illusions and multistable structures to produce countless works of painting, sculpture, and installation. For the moving image, projects like Paul Sharits's *T,O,U,C,H,I,N,G* (1968) relied on flicker techniques to provide optical illusions—in this case, of a glossectomy.

FISCHLI UND WEISS (SUPERIMPOSITION AND CHIMERA)

Peter Fischli and David Weiss—aka the Swiss performance, installation, and video artists Fischli and Weiss—reinvigorated the use of the kippbild as a central and multifaceted part of their artistic production. They engaged in a practice of superimposition of still images. Their slide show *Visible World/Sichtbare Welt* screened first in 1997 at *Documenta X* in Germany. It collected twenty-eight hundred of the still images they had been taking for decades in an eight-hour projection on three monitors. The images seem drawn from the repertoire of tourist and amateur photography, land and cityscapes, and are generally appealing, beautiful centrally framed and composed images. The one image fades in as the other image fades out; it lingers for a bit and then fades out as the next fades in. The images themselves are "pretty" in a way that critics have repeatedly found difficult to contend with in the artist duo's work. They are described as banal. Some critics have identified the images as kitsch, reproductions of tourist snapshots: the preformed image of what is beautiful that fits to the tourist eye on the proscribed search for nature or the monumental or the "special setting."

122 • CHAPTER 7

Some critics insisting on the work's value observed that the art lies in the ability of the artists to reproduce the position of the banal. They have a skill to take pictures that appear to be uncritical and without reflection from a position of critical reflection. Some critics have described the project and their work in general in terms of a postmodern citation, although some have pondered if "postmodern" is an accurate or useful descriptor. It is unclear to most critics if this is ironic or what is intentionally at play in the playfulness of the images. What happens when irony is ironic? Does it become serious? Some have simply noted that the very collection and presentation of twenty-eight hundred images is itself an art. Most critics have remained focused on the world that is being represented in *Visible World*. Few critics have gone beyond thinking about what is in the image and how the images are displayed. They may note the conditions of installation but then not ask further, What in this project of *Visible World* is being made visible? How does this project show us a world becoming visible?

I would emphasize, then, that the *how* of presentation is important here. The images are produced for us in a series, and one might first be inclined to consider this as a project of montage. However, the presentation seems to confound narration. It is not the story of a journey, although there are roads. The series does appear organized and ordered. The images seem connected, at times by one principle—the same location (all of Victoria Falls from different angles and at different times)—but then the principle seems to shift without warning, a series of images from similar locations (Kilimanjaro, Everest, Rainer, Hood, Fuji), and then again to all rain forest, all fields, all passages on highways. It is not a journey, or at least not only. As viewer, one senses that the series shifts as principles of organization come and go. And thus a sense of questioning repeatedly arises as the spectator wonders if the recognized organizational principle has come to an end or if perhaps the entire time the recognized pattern was not the pattern at all; perhaps a different principle was at play.

The spectator, in other words, comes to experience the "perceptual chunking" of learning and memory mechanisms. Fernand Gobet and his coauthors define perceptual chunking as an automatic and continuous cognitive process. We not only perceive the world of objects, but we also engage continually in the formation of "a collection of elements having strong associations with one another, but weak associations with elements within other chunks."[19] This capacity tends to take stimuli and group them "like letters into words":[20] these stimuli all belong to car ride, these all belong to nature images, these to fighting with lover on Sundays, and so on. In a more philosophical language, we might describe this as the process of bringing meaning into the randomness of the world. We actively "chunk" the world we perceive, and those chunks are stored

Cine-Cognition: The Kippbild, Dis/Ambiguation • 123

as such in memory. Recognition thus takes place by recall and comparison not to the mental outline of an object but to collections of stimuli we have already associated with one another.

Thus, with the project of *Visible World* the spectator has the ability to further experience how different cues can develop into chunks. The images also group according to color, distance, lighting key, place of horizon, time of day, weather conditions, cloud formations, time of year, populated/unpopulated, and so on. The banality of the preformed tourist image of the world confronts the reality of the preforming capacity of the brain. The critics who remark on how the images derive from the standardization of popular culture may need to consider that we produce our "culture" precisely in a process of standardization, of grouping, sorting, chunking.

Again, this is not a matter of montage of images. The principle of montage actually seems suspended or forestalled in this project. The critics' descriptions of the images as banal or pretty may better indicate that the emotional affective range is the same throughout. One image does not lead to the narration of emotion in the next. The spectator is not sutured into producing a story. Consider the fact of superimposition; especially important for the further work of Fischli and Weiss, this is not a side-by-side of images, one after the other, the typical process of a film. And it is also not the same as the practice of a slide show, especially not the multi-projection slide shows whose origins go all the way back to the nineteenth century. This practice reached its peak in the 1960s and '70s with slide shows using three to six projectors, frequently for educational purposes. The slides usually had soft edges, allowing for a projected still panorama that preceded the IMAX moving image. At times distinct edges set images against each other—rarely, however, in a superimposition. If they did, it was then typically in order to display the passing of time: a shot of an infant in a dress fading away as a slide of the adult FDR fades in would signal the maturation of the youth into the president/leader. These deployments of slides were generally for didactic purposes. If *Visible World* has a pedagogical intent, it is to offer an experience and not didactical information.

And it should be underscored that this ability we have to display to ourselves the working of our own consciousness is a fundamental response to biological determinism. In an apparatus that allows us to see the workings of the apparatus that encumbers our working, we come to supersede our own perception of ourselves and enter into a new apparatus. The process may not be liberation, it may not be progress, but it is transformation, if not revolution.

In this regard, especially remarkable is the process of fading in and fading out, which produces overlaps and superimpositions with often beautiful effects:

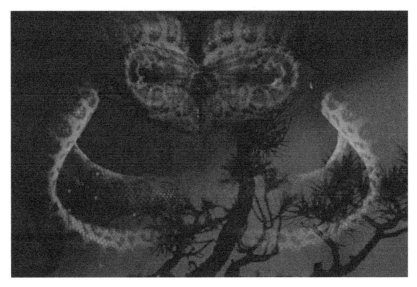

Eine unerledigte Arbeit (*An Unsettled Work*) (Fischli and Weiss 2000–2006). © Peter Fischli and David Weiss, Courtesy of Matthew Marks Gallery

Untitled (Fischli and Weiss 1997–1998) 1. © Peter Fischli and David Weiss, Courtesy of Matthew Marks Gallery

Cine-Cognition: The Kippbild, *Dis/Ambiguation* • 125

flowers in flowers. The superimpositions are also formed in the same chains; hence, flowers in flowers, flowers in sunsets, sunsets in sunsets, a sunset in high modernist architecture, architecture in a mountain, a mountain in the sea, a sea in an airport, and so on for eight hours.

There is something here we should note that defies the action of chunking. The superimposition is typically discussed only briefly and then often described bluntly as "mesmerizing," "kaleidoscopic," "transient," "changing," "time-based," "ephemeral," and "sublime." Analysis ends there—in part, perhaps, because these are moments of non-sense making. It is worth noting that although kaleidoscopy, spectralization, abstraction, cubification, and so on have been central points of exploration in the arts, neuroscientists have focused on the perception of the objective world and the process of sense making in perception. Neuroscientists have looked at fractals as a way of explaining the folds of the brain and not as a form of patterning that the brain seems to find pleasant.[21]

To pursue these considerations we can shift our attention to further work. In 1998 Fischli and Weiss began displaying selections of new work as superimpositions of still images, first as "Untitled (Flowers)" and "Untitled (Mushrooms)." These projects have a kippbild quality to them. The experience of depth perception is disturbed, leaving the viewer experiencing a multilayering. The experience of superimposition disrupts distinctions of fore, mid, and background. Shapes, textures, and colors interact in ways that lead into and out of abstraction. A sensation of dizzying unsettlement can set questioning or cognitive grappling into motion based on the images recognized out of the layers of the superimposition: Is it a frog or a strawberry toadstool? Is the bee on the mushroom or the grape? Is the flower in the cactus or is it in the stars?

Fischli and Weiss intensified this work with *Unsettled Work/Eine unerledigte Arbeit* (2000–2006). *Unsettled Work*, originally titled *Freakshow, Monsters,* relied on 162 slides recorded on a hard drive and played in a process of superimposition using two slide projectors. It followed on *Untitled (Flowers)* and *Untitled (Mushrooms)* (1998), an exhibit of still-image superimpositions of flower on flower or mushroom on mushroom. What is telling about these images is that these are not superimpositions in which the one image is a ghostly background to the other. They are two images of equal intensity, each on the cusp of perception. They are ultimately not just a superimposition but a kippbild, in which the act of perception switches between recognizing the predominance of the one and the other variously. *Unsettled Work* selected images from the body of work that went into *Visible World* but were considered too disrupting. In this project the process of transition, the process of fade in, linger, fade out, is timed equally so that each cycle of images is broken into equal quarters. There is a period

Untitled (Fischli and Weiss 1997–1998) 2. © Peter Fischli and David Weiss, Courtesy of Matthew Marks Gallery

in which the image is singular, a moment of equal imposition as it fades out and the other fades in, a singular moment of clarity, and then the beginnings of distortion as the process of fading takes place again. The moments of equal imposition are, interestingly, moments of abstraction in which the next image is not yet recognized, perceived but still on the horizon of recognition, while the fading image has moved out of clarity but is still recognized through an experience of recall. The memory of it retains it longer than the possibility of the eye to trace its contours.

The original title obviously alludes to chimera as creatures comprised of multiple species parts. Of course, the fascination with such creatures goes back to antiquity and still fascinates us in our myths and legends; the chimera has become a matter of intense debate in the biosciences, as genetic manipulation has famously allowed the splicing of fish and tomato and raised fears of the genetically modified chimera entering into our food supply unawares. However, the chimera as cognitive state, which Fischli and Weiss elicited in this project, has only very recently become a matter of investigation in computational neuroscience. Iryna Omelchenko and a team of researchers at the Technical University in Berlin have explored the chimera simply as a process of information processing in the structures of the nervous system.[22] They produce computational models but do not undertake application in actual psychological systems, physical cognition, or moving image projects.

Omelchenko and her colleagues describe "a dynamical bifurcation scenario for the coherence-incoherence transition which starts with the appearance of narrow layers of incoherence occupying eventually the whole space."[23] They coupled systems that were chaotic, periodic, and oscillating, and they revealed "that intermediate, partially coherent states represent characteristic spatiotemporal patterns at the transition from coherence to incoherence."[24] Jürgen Kornmeier and Michael Bach, at the University of Freiburg in Germany, undertook more applied research of the perceptive apparatus. Using electroencephalograms and fMRIs, they noted actual moments and times of such shifts from incoherence to coherence of ambiguous images.[25] A shift in perception takes two neural loops, 50 milliseconds: "Each reversal from one stable percept to another passes through a point of maximal instability when the perceptual state is on top of the barrier between the two related attractors."[26] What is perhaps most important in their research is that it discounts mono-directional approaches to perceptual reversals. It is neither a matter of bottom-up adaptation as a result of stimulus, nor is it a top-down matter of higher-level attention or fixation of perception. The brain seems primed to participate in ambiguity-disambiguation, to anticipate ambiguity and resolve it into coherence quickly. Surprisingly, Kornmeier and Bach discovered that "contrary to previous expectations, no circumscribed neural unit exists that decides about the perceptual outcome. Rather, perceptual reversals can be induced at different locations and levels of complexity along the processing of visual information."[27] Sensory and perceptual processing appear to take place throughout the cortex, without a specific site assigned. Kornmeier and Bach thus speculate that this experience of coherence-incoherence/ambiguity-disambiguation may be part of the overall insight process. The resolution of the multistable image into one form or the other may be a link to overall processes of insight and decision making.

What Omelchenko, Kornmeier, and others have charted Fischli and Weiss have realized. I am not trying to make the aesthetic experience provided by Fischli and Weiss into a scientific project per se. It is possible that Omelchenko or one of the other members of her team may have attended one of the many exhibitions of Fischli and Weiss's work in Berlin, at the major retrospectives in 2001 and 2004, or at the Sprüth Magers Gallery that represents them in Berlin and London. It is possible that Kornmeier and Bach were inspired in their research by the profound experience provided by *Unsettled Work* displayed at the Staatsgalerie in Stuttgart or at the numerous exhibitions in Basel. I do want to consider, however, that the image systems, which fade in and out, and the

128 • CHAPTER 7

experience they provide are well described by the coherence-incoherence calculations that Omelchenko and her colleagues have undertaken. Moreover, the observation that they make regarding characteristic neuron patterns suggests that Fischli/Weiss offered an aesthetic experience that activates that characteristic pattern. While the combinations of the 162 slides may be of an immense complexity of input for the human perceptive apparatus, the superimposition, the moment of the kippbild, that pattern of transition between coherence and incoherence, appears to be itself a mechanism of meaning making within the human cognitive system. The neuroscientists here create models that are strategically separate from the subjects' experience. Their knowledge of the experiment is limited lest that knowledge interfere with the results. Fischli and Weiss, by contrast, are oriented specifically to providing the spectator with an experience of their own perceptive apparatus.

The images of *Unsettled Work* are on the cusp between the moments of perception of this or that. They combine at the moment of incoherence, or what we may describe as abstraction—an ear and a mouth, frolicking pigs and octopus tentacles, a cat's face and a forest, a human shadow and a spiderweb of lights. These images, of course, then move into coherence, losing this monstrosity. Valentin Groebner's reflection on the work describes them as being in a tunnel rather than on a path of narration.[28] The objects glisten for him, but the moments of incoherence are of little interest to him. He experienced the projections as a quest of his mind to make coherent the incoherent. He does acknowledge a sense that his eyes are on a hunt of their own and that the stream of images is a stream of sense making in a repeated condition of non-sense:[29] "Everything is connected to everything else."[30] This final statement of his I would modify: *our minds have a capacity to link everything with everything else.*

Multistable Techne: The New "New Seeing"

Anyone who has used an analog terrestrial broadcast television knows that viewers have long been exposed to distortion and interference. Rolling bars, fog, clouds, and static could come and go depending on cloud cover or solar flares. Such experiences were typically understood as disturbances, although they could also be described as struggles for recognition. Households sat for hours in front of televisual images, looking past the distortion. The broadcast era in effect provided an image that often initiated in the perceptive capacity a search for recognition. Disambiguation became a conscious quotidian cognitive practice. Skype or Zoom on slow broadband offer contemporary experiences and make us aware of cognitive mechanisms of completing and filling in

Cine-Cognition: The Kippbild, Dis/Ambiguation • 129

to contend with distorted images and static in communication. The failure of recognition is not at the stall of an image or the moment of static but when the stall or static has duration that prevents a "chunk" of information from forming. And this experience has long been the subject of art intervention and reflection.

Although many viewers at home were frustrated in trying to watch the news or a favorite sitcom, Nam Jun Paik relied on such "distortion" to become central to his own television monitor and video projects. Playing with television perception, he inspired artists to play with recognition/nonrecognition experiences, making the recognizable into a barely legible image. In this environment, the deployment of multistable images intensified.

Famously, Paik, Warhol, Peter Campus, and Joan Jonas acquired the first generation of Sony's Portapak, the first portable video camera. Paik asserted that he bought the first one imported to the United States in 1965, but Wolf Vostell had already been exploring broadcast and video recording in the West German Broadcast (WDR) headquarters in Cologne in the late '50s.[31] Regardless who started, broadcast and video initiated an intense period of new visual technology and artistic experimentation in the 1970s. Video artists contended with a "messy" medium at the start. And they even garnered some disdain from filmmakers and art critics because of the "poor" quality of their images.[32] However, it became quickly clear that the video artists opened up once again a "New Seeing." And even as they initiated a new critical relation to sight and perception, the availability of cheaper video-recording devices also advanced new strategies of clinical psychological practice. (Subjects could be recorded in new ways.) Thus again we recognize in that historical moment of emergence that seeing is always a matter of techne, seeing through some technology, and that any new technology of sight transforms all manners of seeing as it calls forward new strategies of critical viewing. If the 1920s "New Seeing" project discussed in chapter 1 identified an effusion of experimental film and photographic strategies, we can consider the 1970s onward an era of a new "New Seeing."

To be sure, from the fuzziness and messiness of early video to the clarity of the digital image is a long way marked by rapidly expanding technology. And in these developments, we can actually chart a history of visual cultural transformations in which multistability becomes a dominant form of production. Multistability might seem counter to the popular image of technology as compelling precision and clarity, yet Peter Krapp described the move into the digital as a move of artists away from expectations of clean lines and clear interfaces.[33] Fuzziness and multistability only intensified with computing and networking. Rather than commitment to paradigms of information flow and disruption minimalization, the new data economy relied on lossy compression to limit hardware costs and investment in infrastructure. To immediately transport data across narrow bandwidth lines or onto limited capacity storage media, lossy compression led to reductions, loss of clarity, distortion, blockiness, and other problems. This period's artists were often concerned with activist jamming/hacktivism, but along with that work new artistry relied on distortion and non-communication. Pioneering digital artists, like video artists before, found a new form of creativity embracing "the mistake" of their technological media.

In tracing a history of video and digital moving-image art, practitioner of glitch art and theorist Michael Betancourt identified strategic video distortions in the 1970s of Paik and Jaime Faye Fenton as inspiration.[34] Betancourt noted also that all the early artists in the 1970s took inspiration from the Absolute Film movement and the works of Richter, Eggeling, and Fischinger in particular. Betancourt suggests it was the abstraction and repetition in the work that intrigued him. But as artists discovered new means in emergent technologies to produce fragmented and decomposed images, we can look back at the techniques like direct animation, photograms, double exposure, material distressing, and so on that Richter, Eggeling, Germaine Dulac, Fernand Leger, Man Ray, René Claire, and Jean Epstein developed. And we can find in that work lines of continuity.

It is important to underscore that in the history of experimental and avant-garde practice, technological innovation has had a fundamental impact on goals and possibilities. By comparison to artisanal handwork of a Richter and Eggeling, the new technologies allowed images to be produced rapidly and in volume. This dynamic increase in speed and output took on a greater significance as the technologies of production themselves become not only readily and cheaply available but also popularly accessible with standardized interfaces. If Fischinger could fight with Disney over the progressive revolutionary quality of his avant-garde strategies, the neo-avant-garde of the '50s and '60s witnessed a rapid dismantling of any sharp opposition between commercial and experimental interests. Technologically innovative work quickly became popularized. While first-generation video artists like Paik, Jonas, Campus, Warhol, and Bill Viola were still experimenting with color separation overlay, developing green screen and chroma key techniques, David Mallet and Nick Saxton were already taking on such new techniques to produce music videos for David Bowie, Michael Jackson, Peter Gabriel, and others. A direct connection between the high and popular began to compel work here, generating a venue like Andy Warhol's magazine, *Interview*. The revolution of music videos presented when MTV went live in 1981 was interwoven with the revolution in video arts presented in museum and gallery spaces. The rupturing of visual conventions to capture popular attention took place in galleries and on cable television, in media arts centers and Madison Avenue advertising offices. Teenagers in the US Southwest or the Scandinavian polar regions might not be able to make it to MoMA in New York or the Pompidou in Paris, but they could turn on the television and eventually dial into the World Wide Web. As such, the expectation to see differently and practices of critical perception became ubiquitous, anticipated, even expected. The 2003 introduction of commercially available high-definition video cameras ruptured the distinction between professional and amateur. The 2005 launch of YouTube became the global platform for amateur and professional digital images.

Nonlinear digital editing techniques, with their promises of ease and clarity, were particularly important in the move to multistability. In their infancy those technologies did prove a liberation from the expense of film material but also a relegation to a sort of glitch hell. An unintended consequence of the introduction of editing software like AVID Media Composer (1987) and Premiere (1991) was the possibility of key frame data loss or distortion, resulting in the image turning into random patterns. As with the television and video image before it, this type of image production was treated largely as degradation and hardware failure. However, a practice developed of combing "distortions" as holding new potential for artful image production. Such practice directly influenced then emergent digital artists like Pipilotti Rist, Bjørn Melhus, and Kirsten Winter, who began working with video in the 1980s.

It is easy to recognize that in this era of digital images, this era of installation work—at a moment when chroma key techniques have become easy and ubiquitous, allowing compositing of multiple layers of images—in this moment our moving images have changed. The dynamic of montage comes to increasingly share a role in the presentation of the moving image alongside collage and multistable imaging. A long way from the Jastrow duck or rabbit's head, the kippbild play of non/recognition and fragmentation/integration dynamics became a central aspect of contemporary digital moving arts. Indeed in experimental and popular work we could announce that the era of the multistable moving image had arrived.

Kirsten Winter: In/Coherence

Consider Kirsten Winter's digitally edited film *Just in Time* (1999). It appeared at a transition moment, the end of the high era of the MTV music video. Winter describes this film as a reflection on a traumatic accident, a car crash. Even though she had been living for sixteen years with the physical impact, while traveling by train across the US she suddenly had to confront the emotional impact of that experience.

132 • CHAPTER 7

For the project she worked closely with composer Simon Stockhausen, whose score interacts with the images, and together they give the film, which constantly vacillates between the recognizable and the abstract, a structure. It is one reminiscent of a pop tune, with lyrics and refrain.

The film reflects the travel on a train in its soundtrack and its images. We hear a characteristic clacking of wheels and see tracks at times. However, the film is not a narrative as much as a visual presentation of a memory effect. Winter overlays images through chroma key. Nothing remains stable; the piece continually turns to a superimposition of images. Images morph in medial form; moving images and oil paintings intermingle. Photoshopping turns the recorded moving image into partial drawings. The effect is such that multiple layers of images, not just one or two, rest on top of each other. Perspective constantly shifts as a result of this layering. When a new image appears in the background, midground becomes foreground only then in turn to separate from the photographic image.

The speed of images is variable. At first like a slow train, we can recognize countryside images, clouds, a bridge to nowhere. But then at 3:46 in the film, nature suddenly gives way to heavily processed and rapid strobing, flickering images. The strobe creates a kippbild experience, a moving forward or backward that can alternate rapidly. The soundtrack accelerates the sense of a speed of images picking up its own tempo. And in this speeded sequence, urban images predominate but at a speed so rapid that it is impossible to absorb the information.

The urban environment is marked too by a collage of text, which remains on the edge of recognition. Suddenly the speed gives way to a singular image, like a quartz rock, yet processed in such a way that it has multiple layers outlined like a Cezanne still life. Within the outlines of shape, the color glows iridescent in faceted surfaces. And then, as if traveling into a tunnel, marked again by the sampled sound of a train, the film seems to move back out into nature. We are back to lyric, or is it refrain? The nature we are given to see, however, is a nature more akin to Rorschach silhouettes than to any scene from nature photography. The film provides no narrative, only experience, and that, like a traumatic memory, is always only ever on the verge of recognition.

Pipilotti Rist: Dis/Ambiguation

Deploying similar strategies Pipilotti Rist developed into one of the best-known Swiss artists on the international art scene—along with Fischli and Weiss. Highly productive, certainly Rist ranks as one of the most celebrated of contemporary video and installation artists. She is sometimes compared to Nam Jun Paik in terms of creativity and innovation in these areas. In part because Rist grew up in a small village in Switzerland, her introduction to the contemporary art scene came via its points of intersection with popular culture. On her early influences, Rist cites precisely John Lennon and Yoko Ono, as pop art and pop music icons, or the emergence of MTV as vectors by which she entered into art production. Rist's cultural production thus does not bear a particular antipathy to the art market, nor does it struggle against popular forms. Her work does not derive from a notion of artistic genius and radical individualism but from the artist as *technician remaking the world*.[35] The outsider status is not celebrated as a radical alternative to the existing social order; instead, the status of the outsider allows the artist to discover radical alternatives within the existing social order. The artistic reimagining of quotidian space is interconnected with the imagining of the impossible perspective or the ridiculously impracticable space. They are utopias that rupture the everyday with an awareness of other possibilities. But what form does this work take?

Flowers in vase kipp between fore and background. *I Want to See How You See or a portrait of Cornelia Providoli*, 2003, video by Pipilotti Rist (video still). © Pipilotti Rist Courtesy of the artist, Hauser & Wirth and Luhring Augustine

134 · CHAPTER 7

Rist's work is visually pretty, lush, and lascivious, often relying on intensification of color, tone, and hue. It is formally playful. From her days in Basel, Rist has experimented with new technologies in video, projection units, and even motion-detection sensors, to create installations that are fun events, humorous experiences. The breakthrough video, *I Want To See How You See* (2003), begins with the title text appearing first as the words "I want," and then in a following shot "To See How You See."[36] The video bears as an alternate title "a portrait of Cornelia Providoli." Providoli is a curator and director of Zürich's prestigious art house Hauser and Wirth, which represents Rist, yet the video certainly does not contain a traditional portrait. It is a music video that begins with a canted frame traveling shot on a terrace, with a figure in the background, Providoli, but, typical of a Rist video, the colors are intensified. The video then moves to an interior space, and the images of the hotel are edited with two layers of signal overlapping. Relying on chroma key, certain colors of the interior space are processed out, made transparent, so that the two signals are composited; in effect, the background image bleeds through into the foreground. The effect is not a double exposure nor a dissolve but a simultaneity of images. The second signal comes from nature scenes. All the while, set to electronic music, Rist sings, "I see, you see, I see you, you see, me seeing, I want to see how you see." The use of pronoun shifters, both to address the spectator and spectating, adds another layer to the images, drawing the video into a postmodern exploration of multistable image and subjectivity. A shift takes place as the video, maintaining the same overlaying effect, focuses on a body part: toes. The soundtrack shifts in quality, as if it were a phone call or voice message, adding multistability into the audio component. And ideationally the voice announces that "the toes are Africa." The breast will be identified with Europe, and then the teeth with Asia. The video, in a further move that is characteristic of Rist's work overall, inspects the female body: doing so in close-up—naked, distanced, extreme close-ups disembodying the subject as a breakup into body parts. All of this becomes increasingly abstracted as the layers expand to four, and the colors intensify until finally, as if oversaturated, the colors become floating bubbles with the video ending in a black screen. The project exemplifies all aspects of multistability dis/ambiguation, non/recognition, in/conherence.

One capacity of multistability in these projects that should be underscored is that in the speed of images, the layered density, the shifting between figurative and abstract, the multistability of imaging results in a condition in which each screening of Rist's and Winter's films are a unique screening for the spectator. The same visuals cannot be seen twice in this level of ambiguation.

Cine-Cognition: The Kippbild, Dis/Ambiguation • 135

Providoli kipps between fore and background. *I Want to See How You See or a portrait of Cornelia Providoli*, 2003, video by Pipilotti Rist (video still). © Pipilotti Rist Courtesy of the artist, Hauser & Wirth and Luhring Augustine

Technology Popularization Dependency Cycles: Distortion and Reappropriation

Moving-image artists like Cory Arcangel frequently rely on the experience of recognition/nonrecognition. Much of this work deploys digital editing to play in the realm of popular form, calling up recognition through the reference to common popular cultural experiences or places. *Urbandale* (2001) was a rendering into ASCII/ANSI code of filmed images of food prep in an upstate New York strip mall.[37] The repetitive activity of line cooking becomes recognizable through the reduction to outlines of repetitive code text based on spectator familiarity with the ubiquity of the form. Dis/Ambiguation is key to the viewing experience. In the new millennium, Arcangel began remixing Nintendo or Mario games before YouTube remixing, supercuts, and YTP expanded the practice. In his work *Clouds* (2002) Arcangel removed the characters from a Super Mario Brothers video game, leaving behind only the sky with its iconic clouds jerkily scrolling for five minutes.[38] Bereft of interaction, the project reduces the spectator experience to the experience of recognition. Although the work relies on the principles in effect in the kippbild, it would be hard to describe Arcangel's work as such. However, I want to underscore this commonality of the popular image in such work. In the discussion of remixing projects and YouTube Poop (chapter 6), we saw how the popular form functions in these circuits of production. They certainly represent transformations in cine-cognition, in which an underlying history of moving-image culture is part of the project itself.

In that discussion I mentioned in passing glitches and glitch art. I want to focus on this form of representation as a key to the contemporary deployment of multistable moving imagery. Glitch art as a phenomenon has many forms—from Paik's distortion of a television image using a magnet to the active disruption of CD playback. Betancourt cites *Digital TV Dinner* (Fenton, Zaritsky, and Ainsworth 1979) as a primary project of emergent glitch art.[39] Fenton disrupted the playback of the Bally video game console, which resulted in the television screen filling with patterns that had nothing to do with the original intent for the hardware. Various strategies emerged to ambiguate recognizable images into defamiliarized patterns, with hints that pointed to the source code as in the persistence of the words "select game" in the *Digital TV Dinner* still.

Digital TV Dinner (Fenton, Zaritsky, Ainsworth 1979). Courtesy of Jaime Fenton, Raul Zaritsky, and Dick Ainsworth

In the new millennium, filtering, rendering, deformation, and ambiguation all became strategies and effects layering on possibilities of multistability in moving-image projects. Datamoshing, a particular form of glitch art, exemplifies the emergence of multistable techniques. As a form it took off in the second half of the first decade. In an event often cited as the first moment in which the failure turned into a new representational form, Owi Mahn and Laura Baginski began playing with "corrupted" images they had shot on digital video, turning a common problem with the software of the period into a new opportunity for representation. Their project *Pastell Kompressor* (2003) transformed footage of Southern France, the countryside, clouds drifting on the horizon into a de/recomposition experience.[40] Relying on Sörenson 3, a compression codec that competed with early releases of QuickTime, they forced a datamosh in an organized fashion. The video they produced retains indexical reference to Mahn and the setting, but they give way to abstraction, melting distorting, and then suddenly reemerging into a moment of recognition. It recalls the projects of Winter and Rist, but as the colors kaleidoscope, they do so not as chroma key overlay but as patterns that are more globular and effervescent.

Betancourt noted that in the work of datamoshing, the move from recognition to abstraction plays a central role: "A recognizable image is repeatedly transformed by a glitch process called 'datamoshing' that renders its initially familiar forms as progressively more unstable and abstract graphics."[41] For Betancourt, in the move from video or digital "clarity" and indexicality to an abstract unrecognizable abstraction, the viewer perceives the artifice of the image; its coding/decoding key is revealed as constitutive. Betancourt, ascribing to a Frankfurt School aesthetic focuses on this revelation as key to the import of glitch art. Not once does the word "pleasure" appear in the study; "viewer" and "spectator" appear only marginally. Betancourt focuses largely on the education

Pastell Kompressor (Mahn and Baginski 2003). Courtesy of Owi Mahn and Laura Baginski

138 · CHAPTER 7

of the audience to a critique of materiality that inheres in the morphing of the work as such.

In the contemporary moment, however, Betancourt's Adornian position seems out of place, anachronistic. Adorno's considerations of abstraction were focused on painting and poetry and based on a Hegelian/Marxian notion of art history. Adorno described a moment in which the medium, the materiality of representation as such, and not the representation of reality, the act of depiction, had become central to art practice. In the visual-technological innovations unleashed in the '60s and '70s, the manipulation of the technology becomes increasingly central. Showing images to be manipulated by technology is of little interest, but showing your technological skills as you manipulate images (and sound) is core to contemporary audiovisual artistry.

Rosa Menkman, like Betancourt a practitioner and critical theorist, has been at the heart of organizing glitch artists. She takes the understanding of the potential of glitch or datamoshing into new directions. The glitch is always present in the new technology. It is not a revelation of the artifice but a part of it as such. Standardized commercial hardware always opens up other deployments. Menkman's advocacy for PAL (phase alternating line, a method of video recording) recalls the punk reappropriation of obsolete Super 8 technology for new purposes. As amateur video cameras became more readily available, punk artists recovered Super 8 cameras from secondhand stores and even dumpsters. They deployed the cameras against their original intent. Devices sold to make home movies of birthdays and graduations became technologies of unintelligibility and ludic illogicality. In the ongoing never-ending progressions of visual technologies, Menkman looks back on an ever growing mound of visual technological detritus to advocate for its reappropriation. Further, Menkman takes up a notion of randomness inherited from John Cage and the neo-avant-garde. Menkman writes actively about the refusal to "let the syntaxes of (a) history direct our futures."[42] Glitching disrupts code and works against intent. The unintended effect opens up new syntax as well as new horizons of expression.

Menkman's hopefulness is infectious, but the production of nonstandard work is always only a creative liberation within the given. The work she describes is always developed out of technologies that are already fulfilling intended purposes, typically surveillance and war. And the productions of glitch artists have typically relied on the popular cultural image, the Nintendo game, the music video. The interaction between representational experimentation and the popular, between technological artistry and technological change, seems

Cine-Cognition: The Kippbild, *Dis/Ambiguation* • 139

Compression Study #1 (Untitled data mashup) (Davis 2007). Courtesy of Paul B. Davis

a constant—and that is suggestive here. Critical artists like Menkman and Betancourt may be the source of the problem they identify.

Datamoshing artwork went seamlessly from the gallery presentation "Intentional Computing" (2007) of Paul Davis, artist and theorist, to Kanye West's "Welcome to Heartbreak" (2009) music video.[43] It is reported that West got the idea for his video from a visit to the show, although by that time datamoshing was a highly active form even in YTP. Nevertheless, in work like *Compression Study #1 (Untitled data mashup)* (2007), Davis had developed his own codec to mosh images from Rhianna's music videos.[44] West used the same strategies to mosh his own image. In effect, West took back to mainstream the form that Davis had developed to critique the mainstream flood of images. Davis found this an appropriation of his work and a form of pilfering that pointed out the inherent weakness of moshing and mixing's critique.[45] It resulted in his setting out in new directions. In the end it is unthinkable that this glitch strategy of Betancourt, Menkman, Davis, and others can find any way out of this cycle of dependency on popular culture and new technological innovation. They produce in a closed universe, and it would be as if we found out that Neo had always been the programmer of the matrix. However, the work is beautiful. And people seem to find great pleasure in looking.

140 · CHAPTER 7

Multistable Community: Gaming, VR, and Augmented Reality

Don Ihde explored cyberspace as a multistable environment.[46] His discussion, however, is less about perception as such and transformations in behaviors, because the cyberspace environment is multistable, both real and virtual. This "here and there" of cyberspace, he argues, impacts ways of knowing and behavior, evidencing itself in, for instance, attention; Ihde suggests it becomes limited, although we could consider how multitasking sets up conditions for inattentional blindness. In the YTP phenomenon discussed in chapter 6, we noted how the YTP community develops not just through the making of images (poops) but through the processing and reprocessing of poops in YTP tennis; the moving-image projects became vectors for community development. Similar can be said about other forms of cyber networks, especially the gaming community. Multiplayer gamers, inherently socially interactive even if through avatar, also form community through methods that are distinct from the traditional subcultural tactics. Switching between concentrated play and multitasking, talking with other players or about the play while playing, moving between views—all seem to suggest that multistability plays a part in community formation.

It should not surprise us that video games, both in multiplayer networked and the single-player forms, rely on multistability in image and interaction. The design of video games is dependent on rendering and design that goes back to the Renaissance debates of *prospettiva naturalis* and *prospettiva artificiale*. The Necker cube illusion, with its rapid switch between projecting out and in, inspired a great deal of design work. Video game designers learned to deploy multistable images along with other optical illusions to induce perceptive dissonance. Standard games like *Mario*, *Legends of Zelda*, and others often ruptured the flatness of their 2D worlds by including optical illusions and multistable play. Arcade games like *Ms. PAC-MAN* appeared in 3D version, which often involved occlusion experiences. Games like *Hocus*, *Perfect Angle*, *Endochrome*, *Anamorphosis*, and *Portal* incorporate explicit optical illusions and various forms of play with perspective. *Portal* (Valve Corporation 2007) relied on a principle of shifting planes and portals, requiring the players to think through vectors. *Fez* (Polytron 2012) established a multiplayer game based on an ability to move between and across 2D and 3D universes. The 3D game world is played in one of four 2D views.

While movement in these games is complex, many games seek specifically to break apart Euclidean space, taking inspiration from M. C. Escher drawings. Are the stairs leading up or down? Does the pyramid point out or in? Such

Cine-Cognition: The Kippbild, Dis/Ambiguation • 141

insecurities in recognition compound the play in the games. *Monument Valley* (Ustwo 2014) was an indie game first released for the iPhone in which the player guides a figure (the Princess Ida) through tunnels and across bridges that move across Escher-style space distortions. Almost the inverse, *The Witness* (Thekla 2016) relies on a multi-perspectival universe to solve it. Moving about and advancing in levels allows players to gain different perspectives and see new aspects of the game's map; those new angles require the players to reanalyze what they thought they had seen and hold the key to advancing through the puzzles at the heart of the gameplay.

Recognizing that forced perspective can actually create multistable experiences, Pillow Castle Games' *Museum of Simulation Technology* set forward a project to create a surreal first-person puzzler using play with forced perspective.[47] It was celebrated from 2013 to 2015 with various awards and finally went live in late 2019. By contrast, *Antichamber* (Demruth 2013) came out on the market accomplishing some of what Pillow Castle Games had announced for their project. It is a first-person single-player game with a traditional maze concept. The game's designer, Alexander "Demruth" Bruce, relied on Escher to build his images but also to create the core of the play itself. Reviewer and gamer Jeff Marchiafava describes the experience:

> Like Portal, Antichamber's puzzles exist in an environment where the laws of nature don't apply, allowing players to think in ways that reality doesn't require. Whereas Portal "only" bent the rules of space, Antichamber throws everything you know out the window, stripping you of your preconceptions before building you back up with a new set of skills and rules to play by.[48]

The rapid expansion of the play with perspective has continued on. But to be clear, it is not just a play with perspective; these games have the goal of playing with the experience of recognition itself.

Likewise, virtual reality (VR) loves multistable optical illusions. Light propagation, shading, optical distortion, foreshortening, hazing and resolution, and other techniques are all elaborate questions seeking resolution in VR. The artificial immersive environment and the 360-degree recording could both be described as optical illusion on a grand scale. In their playback they offer a creation of a perceptually immersed environment. VR viewers report a variety of experiences in playing the game, including the experience of entering into altered states and identities.[49] At the same time, VR has the ability to evoke a form of nausea resulting from the sense of immersion in an environment that is in conflict with the preconscious experience of the body's position in the real world. Vection, the dissonance between a virtually moving body and a real stable

142 • CHAPTER 7

body, can induce a specific form of motion sickness. Multistable imagery can intensify these mismatches and increase visually induced motion sickness. At the same time, because VR is still developing transition strategies that are distinctive from the cinematic cut, multistable experience is a place of exploration, providing the viewer with a sense of transport.[50] The experience that can create mismatch dissociation and nausea in one instance can be deployed creatively in another setting. Ultimately, multistability is distinctive from montage's ability to drive narrative and collage's ability to de/fragment. We can anticipate that multistability as a principle of image experience will increase in VR projects.

*   *   *

As with all genealogies—I could draw lines differently, more or less complexly, but clearly from the Absolute Film occlusion experiments to the present—a great deal of the pleasure of these projects derives from the visuals they produced. The deployment of datamoshing is in line with the long history of image production/deformation, a line that includes kaleidoscopy, fractalization, spectralization, abstraction, cubification, split screen, infrared, and so on. Datamoshing exists in a complex connection to hypnogogic pop, glo-fi, new rave, shoegaze, and other aspects of neo-psychedelia in the first half of the twenty-first century. At this point there are datamoshing video compressors that create the effect by taking out the keyframe, and where the technique was once proprietary and artisanal, a short decade later it became easily manipulatable and generally available.

Datamoshing is now only one of a host of visual effect filters and renderings available on social media apps and directly in the processing capacities of smartphone cameras. Not just in museums, or galleries, on television, or streamed images, we can actually move about in a world that we can record and render on the spot and immediately see differently. Augmented reality does not do justice to describe the rapid expansion of the new New Seeing. With the popularization of visual technology, we do not need to wait for the artist to render a world for us; we can turn our lenses on our own environments.

CHAPTER 8

The Apparatus of Difference

Xenophobia/philia

Knowing the Other Next Door

How do we know the Other? If truly and fully alterior, the Other is unknowable, beyond cognition, outside experience, outside communication, at the boundaries of self and society. Thus, if an answer to this question exists, we must distinguish an unknowable Other from the others that we can know. This other proves to be closer, part of our limits, tangential, divergent, but also convergent, touching. The Other, in Hegel's vision of the development of *Geist*, allows spirit to know itself precisely because it is contact with others. Absolute spirit diverges, leaving behind its absolute state, so that precisely in an other it can experience its self. For the sake of this knowing, it gives up its absoluteness and becomes limited, but it also becomes social. The Hegelian narrative of Geist begins in a rarified binary state of idealist reflection, but it describes the very real material process of *sociation* and helps us recognize that the basis of social organization is differentiation. The process of sociation opposes the self not with an Other but places the self in a field of *others*. Like the narrative of Geist, the very real material narratives of self-knowing are social narratives of convergence and divergence, contiguity and tangentiality. How do we know these others? We know them because they are part of our cognition, our experience, our communication, part of our selves.

A complete answer to the question "How do we know the Other" must make distinctions not simply about the other but about knowing as well.

144 • CHAPTER 8

Knowing—that is, knowledge of—does not necessarily mean understanding. We can live with or next door to a person whose behavior we know but do not understand. We must be aware of them, as other, but we do not need to understand them. We can even have more knowledge than simple awareness without necessarily understanding. We might know, for instance, that a certain behavior will provoke the other in our house without actually understanding why. Such awareness might lead us to remove ourselves from contact so that we can continue those activities that provoke and our living conditions remain tolerable, or such awareness could lead us to modify our behavior vis-à-vis others because contact with them is more important than insisting on a particular behavior. With very simple knowledge, we can tolerate the other right next door without requiring understanding or accommodation. The amount of knowledge we have does not derive from the distance or proximity of the other. To be sure, the proximate and convergent proves easier to know, to tolerate, even to trust and integrate, but it does not follow that the distant and divergent is therefore de facto its opposite; it is not necessarily intolerable, to be distrusted nor taken as unreliable. Can we overcome distrust and rely on the divergent? The answer must be: we do not yet know. Only if we know others better can we really answer the question of trust.

Since we can know our others more or less, we should be able to distinguish others. We might want to make a distinction between the others we know more or less and those we do not yet know because they are strange, foreign, *xeno*. Again, however, such strangeness does not derive directly from distance or proximity. That which lives next door can be more foreign than that which lives on the other side of the planet. Strangeness derives from the lack of knowledge, a lack that can take many forms: geographic, historical, culinary, physical, ideological.

The techne of knowing is social. To maintain itself every social organization must reproduce itself materially, from which it follows that the process of differentiation is not solely or even primarily an ideational process. Thus our knowledge of the other is embedded in the material forms and institutions of our society. However, no reproduction is exact, and thus in its material reproduction every social organization is constantly exposed to transformation. The material practices change, institutions change, the forms of communication change, the borders change, new forms of experience arise, new methods of cognition occur, the relation between self and other changes.

The problem of knowing the others becomes all the more urgent within the process of globalization and transnationalism, migration and displacement, global dislocation. We exist in a world with new possibilities for material and ideational reproduction because it is a world in which changes in borders, communication, intercourse, and exchange have accelerated. We experience the more rapid transformations of social reproduction more acutely. We feel how the material weft of affective relations that constitutes our knowing of the world constantly rends. We seek to repair it and to experience the new knots we weave as positive opportunities, not constant damage to the social fabric. Yet, honestly we cannot help but feel a sense of bewilderment. That divergence that was once distant is now proximate, without, it would seem, having lost any of its divergence, and we are suspicious. That which once touched is now distant and leaves behind an ache of incompletion. Globalization opens up new material connections while at the same time foreclosing others. Transnationalism redefines our borders and leaves our selves in new fields of association where we are newly attracted and repulsed, where we are newly philic and phobic, where we find our selves wanted and unwanted.

Neither xenophobia nor xenophilia are attributes of our relation to the other; rather, they derive from the discourses that determine social dynamics of proximity and distance, knowing and unknowing.

The Stream of Refugees

As I write this, a global pandemic has hit, making the questions of location, shelter, and movement all the more urgent. Shelter-in-place and lockdown measures have trapped people in inhumane conditions in camps. Global economic shutdown has also forced millions of people to take to the road to get "home." In this year records for displaced persons have repeatedly been broken. The United States has shifted from being a country of refuge to become a gated community. This year asylum seekers from all over Latin America's troubled regions were turned away from the southern border of the United States. Haitians, Puerto Ricans, and Bahamians all experienced forms of diaspora because of natural disaster and climate change devastation. The Rohingya, still facing ethnic cleansing in Myanmar, are confronting attacks in Bangladesh. And Turkey invaded Syria to start a conflagration in Kurdish regions with the goal of displacing and replacing populations and then went on to military interventions in Libya. These people, displaced from their homes and places of livelihood, add to the more than 70 million people currently displaced. This number is the highest ever recorded by the UN High Commission on Refugees. The majority of those on the move are refugees within their home countries. Turkey is the largest refugee country in the world, with 3.7 million combined refugees, mainly Syrians, and displaced persons, mainly Kurds from the eastern

146 · CHAPTER 8

regions of Turkey. The current conflagration has stated as its goal a return of those people to Syrian territory in a safety zone. Other countries especially have taken in great numbers; following Turkey we can count, in order, Jordan, Lebanon, Pakistan, Uganda, Germany, Iran, and Ethiopia. If we consider per capita, however, then Jordan, a relatively tiny country with scarce natural resources and water of its own, has accepted refugees in numbers equivalent to 25 percent of its own population.

Yet when I attend to the news, the discussion of a refugee crisis or a migration threat is a discussion posed in the US and by populist politicians in Europe. The threat to these displaced people is not what US politicians are considering. The threat that drives them into rapid forced migration is overshadowed by the fact that they are seeking safety and shelter, looking for hospitality, simple respite. Thus, the discussion of refugee crisis in the US contrasts with the statistics of peoples granted asylum in the US; it is significant that over the last forty years the US, the world's most prosperous country, has admitted about 3 million refugees, less than 1 percent of its current population. And plans by the current government have restricted the number of admissions for 2020 to ten thousand people. In the current refugee crisis, Germany, with the strongest economy and the most prosperous country in Europe, has taken in roughly one million refugees, just more than 1 percent of its population. Yet Germany is in the top five weapons-exporting countries, earning more than $1.25 billion per year. (The US is the top weapons exporter.) The connection between profits made and the instability that the weapons cause is seldom discussed, and even then not as a question of responsibility: missiles don't kill people, people kill people.

So when we speak of a refugee crisis, do we focus on the displaced persons and the regions from which they are fleeing? Do we mean the state of crisis that is causing people to flee social and political instability, flee for fear of their lives and livelihoods—refugees fleeing a state of crisis? Do we mean the conditions of trauma and grief that these people on the move bring with them—refugees in crisis? Or do we mean the refugee crisis is a crisis for the United States or Europe? Is the crisis the drain on resources to the US, one of the largest economies in the world, or the EU, one of the richest regions in the world—refugees as causing a crisis? Is the crisis a condition of alarm resulting from an influx of people amounting to less than 1 percent of their respective populations— refugees as themselves a threatening crisis? Our answers to these questions depend on the critical assessments of the world and our local communities that we make as individuals. But our answers also depend as much on the way that the media frame the question posed to us.

Borders as Abjecting Apparatus: The US and EU

I have discussed extensively the border as abjecting apparatus. Borders are always permeable. Attempts to close or control them require significant investments of energy. The border makes that which is proximate appear distant. It constructs a community on one side by abjecting bodies onto its other side. It establishes barriers to entry for certain bodies. It defines its interior through the expulsion of bodies from a defined region. Although the discourse around borders seeks to suggest that there is a clarity of belonging, two sides, this is not the case. The act of border abjection constitutes an us and them, defines a communal self and other.

There is no doubt that currently the southern border of the United States is an abjecting apparatus. It is a place of massive resource investment, humiliation, criminalization, and degradation. But these activities of the border extend throughout the territory of the US, policing and terrorizing populations with and without papers, employees and employers, elderly and adolescent, criminalizing regardless of behaviors. And it moves out globally into airports and embassies and other points of contact between some one created thereby as belonging and an other. The southern border is not a barrier, although there are natural obstacles—deserts, rivers, gorges, and other obstructive land features. Historically it was an interzone, a space of dynamic interaction and complex connectivity, multilingual, multistable. The creation of the southern border wall is part of a long trajectory to rupture this interzone that plays a more important role in constructing a nationalist polity for populist purposes than it does for economic or criminological rationales.

By contrast, the EU is known as a region dedicated to lifting borders and developing complex connectivity. The EU in many ways aspires to expand the interzone as counter to national sovereignty. The year 1992 set off the lifting of borders and the formation of the Schengen area as a space of semi-sovereignty. And in the 1990s, the EU famously began projects to expand that zone. Best known is the eastern expansion that incorporated the former Warsaw Pact countries. But at the same time as those countries were being prepped for ascension, the Euro-Mediterranean Partnership program, or EUROMED, emerged. This program derived from a recognition that the Northern and Southern Mediterranean had historically constituted a region of interaction and trade, fostered by ease of transportation over the sea and a history of grand empires that lined the shores, uniting rather than dividing them. This state of commonality was understood as a kind of basic normalcy and that the division between united Europe in the north and the various regions to the south and east were not

148 · CHAPTER 8

natural. The distance between the Mediterranean north and south is in spots quite close: a distance of 70 kilometers separates Tunisia from Italy, the Straits of Gibraltar separate Morocco from Spain by 14 kilometers, the Greek island of Kos is 4 kilometers (2.5 miles) from the Turkish mainland. Discussions began in 2003 to build a Chunnel-style tunnel across the Straits of Gibraltar in order to intensify communication of the region.

The EUROMED project led to a liberalization of the economies in North Africa. But the outcome of the trade liberalization was an asymmetry that created an imbalance to the benefit of the EU.[1] This condition in turn led to massive unemployment and a stream of labor migrants looking to get to Europe. Well before the global refugee crisis of 2015, Italy especially was receiving waves of refugees crossing the Mediterranean without papers, without official state permission. Where once the aspiration had been to restore a vibrant coherency to a divided region, a shift began. The Mediterranean is truly a difficult barrier, and where once an open orientation existed, now massive energy had to be invested in separating distinct sides. Although just like North and South America, the Northern and Southern Mediterranean regions are connected complexly within a political and economic apparatus, recognition of this complex connectivity had to be ruptured. The 70 kilometers separating Tunisia from Sicily had to become a passage between different worlds. The abjecting apparatus had to be put in place.

In 2005 the EU established Frontex. Also known as the European Border and Coast Guard Agency, this agency, whose primary task is to police the EU's southern coast, has its headquarters in Warsaw. Poland, a country distant from that territory, was made into the headquarters of policing that border. The abjecting apparatus has no need to know its other.

The Medial Barrier of Images

How is it that our media can make the refugee crisis or the caravans to the Rio Grande a proximate experience, raising with alarm a sentiment that "they are coming"? And how is it that at the same time the brutal slaughter of populations actually proximate to us and the devastation of climate catastrophes of peoples with whom we have complex connections barely receive notice in the media? How are they made proximate in one setting and kept distant from our living rooms, soliciting little compassion on the screens of our social media?

How was it that caravans constructed to protect people from danger and profiteering as they traversed difficult terrain and exploitative conditions were constituted as threats to the US, conveying the idea that these people were criminals who were endangering US citizens? What massive devotion of resources

The Apparatus of Difference · 149

had to be deployed not to build a wall on the US-Mexican border but in the heads of people who would otherwise never come into contact with asylum seekers from the south?

There is a direct ferry connecting the Greek island of Kos to the Turkish mainland, one of the main crossing points in 2015 into the EU. The distance the ferry travels is 4 kilometers (if it were a land journey, five thousand steps, a forty-minute moderate walk). The service, relatively empty and inexpensive, regularly traverses this stretch. Yet why is it that refugees are required to cross via makeshift means? Is it only political logic that requires the abjecting apparatus to be in place?

Why are reporters traveling with caravans and not showing the conditions from which the people are fleeing? How does that position the spectators watching their screens, waiting for the refugees to arrive? What are the media and the political logics that require humans to place themselves in a precarious condition and risk their lives when available transport and secure means of conveyance are available instead? Was it a need for a story, images to toss into the flood in order to feed a twenty-four-hour news cycle? Was it a need to fulfill a political logic that requires refugees to be a threatening mass? Or a political logic that wanted to keep displaced persons in a state of illegality, deny them orderly refugee status, criminalize them in order to claim a right of control over a sea of humanity literally rising out of the waters of the Aegean Sea and the sands of the Chihuahuan Desert? How is our compassion framed and directed in a medial environment, even encouraging us into a spectatorial passivity, so that we remain glued to our screens rather than become active in our world?

The European Media Apparatus and/as Political Apparatus

In the classic period of apparatus theory, the questions that were posed focused critically on the depiction of reality. Now, however, we may agree that this current period of fake news and alternative fact debates calls us to focus on the reality of depiction. It is a worn observation that our media technologies have taken on new forms of surveillance and control, but they have also unleashed new forms of expression and creativity. How does a modern media apparatus act as technology of the other?

On September 8, 2015, Petra László, a camerawoman working for N1TV was filmed by Stephan Richter, a German reporter working for the TV channel RTL Germany. They were at the Serbian-Hungarian border where at that moment a group of refugees was rushing the border patrol, trying to get across into Hungary. Although the internal EU border had been opened at certain points to an orderly crossing, here the Hungarians were trying to keep further refugees from

150 · CHAPTER 8

entering, and they had been deploying brutal methods. Richter caught László kicking children and tripping a father holding his child. Richter posted the footage to social media, where it went viral. László was eventually fired from her job and brought up on charges of breaching the peace. She received a sentence of three years' probation. Let us consider for a bit the European media apparatus behind these images.

Television without Frontiers (TVWF)—this title is the designation for the EU directive No. 89/552/EEC from 1989. The expressed goals of the directive include "establishing an even closer union among the peoples of Europe, fostering closer relations between the States belonging to the Community, ensuring the economic and social progress of its countries by common action to eliminate the barriers which divide Europe, encouraging the constant improvement of the living conditions of its peoples as well as ensuring the preservation and strengthening of peace and liberty."[2] Beyond those lofty goals, the directive concretely opened up broadcast transmission across borders and frontiers; in doing so, the directive directly resulted in the end of any public monopoly of radio and television throughout Europe. By pushing for a common European program of production and distribution, the directive broke the state control over media, a control based on the presumption that the media are there to educate the citizens and inform the electorate. The directive also broke national markets open to outside and private media groups, promoting free market competition in the broadcast media and accelerating the expansion of popular cultural entertainment on television and radio.

The opening up of new markets fundamentally transformed European broadcasters, most notably in Luxembourg, where Compagnie Luxembourgeoise de Télédiffusion (CLT) had long broadcast beyond Luxembourg's territory. CLT became a pan-European media giant. Fueled by private advertising revenue and a series of mergers, CLT began broadcasting as Radio Television Luxembourg (RTL) and reached into national markets throughout Europe. Not unlike the appearance of FOX TV in the US in the 1980s, RTL offered least-common-denominator popular entertainment shows of a sort once eschewed by pedagogically oriented European public media.

Clearly some benefit must have offset the loss of state control politicians from across the spectrum agreed to with the TVWF directive. We can find this benefit in the expansion of the private economic stakes in the audiovisual free market. By 1997 CLT combined with Hamburg-based UFA Film und Fernseh GmbH, and then in 2000 CLT-UFA combined further with German Bertelsmann, Belgian GBL/Electrafina, and British Pearson in order to form RTL Group. This move transformed what had once been a regional station broadcasting in the Luxembourgeoise dialect into a media conglomerate spanning nine countries.

I have discussed the broader impact of these transformations elsewhere.[3] Here I want to underscore that the dynamic transformations to the European media apparatus have had little to do with the lofty goals put forth in the TVWF directive. But it did result in a new form of media conglomerate. By the end of the 1990s, RTL expanded ever further, especially eastward to RTL Croatia and RTL Klub in Hungary, and then further beyond the borders of Europe. Currently RTL Group is a global leader across content and digital broadcast with interests in sixty-six television channels and thirty radio stations. It is "a global business for content production and distribution, and rapidly growing digital video businesses."[4] RTL's Fremantle division supplies 12,700 hours of TV programming broadcast each year and distributes more than 20,000 hours of content in over two hundred territories. RTL's success as a media apparatus is based on a dynamic of simultaneous globalization and localization. This takes place through a strategy of format that came to the fore in the 1990s. Formats are structural programming platforms that can be tailored to appeal to local tastes and genre patterns. The best-known examples are the formats developed by the Dutch company Endemol. Endemol developed the *Big Brother* series, which grew to have local productions in more than seventy countries. Endemol is not a broadcaster; rather, it sells its formats to broadcasters. And to be clear, it did not succeed by trying to sell episodes from the container in Holland; it was the series format itself that went into syndication. *Big Brother* appeared on RTL affiliates from Belgium to Hungary. Importantly, such formats allow for a flexibility to appeal to local interests and cultural specificities. RTL expanded its holdings to include its own content provider, Fremantle, which has gone on to develop formats like *x's Got Talent* or *The X Factor*. These formats appear on RTL holdings or are sold to local broadcasters from the US to India and Australia.

Formats such as "I'm a Celebrity . . . Get Me Out of Here!," "Hell's Kitchen," "Bachelor," and "Bachelorette," which were developed first for British audiences, resulted in spin-offs: "Americanized," "Germanized," or "Frenchified" formats such as "I'm a Celebrity. . . . Get Me Outta Here!," "Hilfe ich bin ein Star-Hol mich hier raus!," "Je suis une célébrité . . . sortez-moi de là!," and so on. The B-level stars in these productions are from local popular film and television. The exploits to which they are subjected are tailored to local sensibilities. Nudity or vulgarity is trimmed or expanded, and other community-based changes are made. The basic reproducibility and localizability of the formats leads to a transnational structural uniformity. Not everyone watches the same *Bachelor* or *RuPaul Drag Race*, but through formatting, all viewers across regions watch similar shows. Facebook pages, Twitter feeds, and Instagram accounts allow fans in each country or region to not only discuss their show but also compare the show across formats.

152 · CHAPTER 8

In this media apparatus, refugees were not stories of individuals as such; they are potential content to be entered into formats. The kicking and tripping Petra László was employed by the online-only station N1TV (nemzeti1tv), which was founded in 2011. The station is closely aligned with the extreme right Hungarian populist party, Jobbik. It is financed by the Balanced Media Foundation (Kiegyensulyozott Mediaert Alapitvany), which is in turn funded by the Growing Hungary Foundation (Gyarapodo Magyarorszagert Alapitvany), a foundation of the Jobbik party. This broadcaster is an outstanding example of the localization of news. The station couches its political alignment in a hip style that is set to appeal to local youth. It includes popular segments with former party leader Gábor Vona going undercover in the popular *Undercover Boss* format. For these segments he disguised himself as a vegetable seller at a market or a kindergarten teacher, testing the sentiment of the Hungarian people. The *Two Knights* show enjoyed popularity, a format where two men dressed as medieval knights go to Budapest's party district and interview Hungarian youth on topics such as ISIS threats and foreign migrants invading Hungary. MediaPower-Monitor.com reported in 2015, "The channel has over 16,000 subscribers and its videos almost 12 million views."[5]

N1TV signals an important development in the ability of Jobbik to create a populist appeal. Jobbik was founded as a far-right party in 2003 and remained largely on the fringes of Hungarian politics, capturing only 2 percent of the vote until 2009. That was the first year it was elected to the European Parliament. Jobbik reached out to the British Nationalist Party and with it formed the Alliance of European National Movements, which also included Marine Le Pen's National Front. In 2010 in national elections the party won 16 percent of the vote. N1TV was founded in 2011 as part of Jobbik's broader media strategy and an attempt to compete with the far-right Echo TV, a television station that aligns itself with the ruling Fidesz party of Viktor Orbán. Where Echo TV uses television broadcast, N1TV relies on YouTube and formats designed specifically to appeal to a younger voter: slick, hip, ironic. In the 2014 elections, Jobbik rode the growing populist momentum and rose to the status of third party. It set its sights on overtaking the ruling Fidesz party. In 2018, when it could not achieve those goals, Vona stepped down and the party has struggled with its course. Thus in 2015, as refugees began crossing the Serbian border into Hungary, they arrived in a country whose ruling political class could treat them as pawns in yet another power struggle.

At this point it is worth considering that the emergence of such an antidemocratic, authoritarian media entity is directly an outgrowth of the TVWF directive's liberalization of the media market. But it also parallels the development of other organizations such as Breitbart or One America News in the

USA. The expansion of multiplatform broadcasting and formatting of content has moved as a strategy for reality and popular television programming over into the news: infotainment and "newsy" formats. In effect, these stations are following on a very minor scale the format of RT (formerly Russia Today) or other propaganda wings of parties and authoritarian states. Even though she was fired by N1TV, László was not kicking refugees on the Hungarian border because the actions went against the station's editorial policies; rather, it was because it went against their slick, hip, ironic format.

News is typically highly localized, and even global news is trimmed to the interests of the local. Weather is very site specific, and sports is typically a vehicle for local patriotism and even overt nationalism. Consider, then, what the dynamic between the local and the global means. A transnational conglomerate specializing in crossing borders, RTL functions very differently than N1TV, for which Petra László worked. RTL does not pursue overarching explicit editorializing, although I would suggest that it does support a liberal approach in its affiliates. For instance, RTL Klub, the Hungarian RTL station, regularly reports critically on government policies vis-à-vis refugees and is anti-Jobbik in its approach.

Stephan Richter, the person who filmed Petra in the kicking incident, was actually a reporter for an RTL affiliate. But ultimately, in a sign of further shifts in the media apparatus, Richter's recording of Petra did not get incorporated initially into a news story about refugees. Instead he posted the images online to Twitter, where it went viral. As a result, it only then became a story in the mainstream media. And then the story was not about refugees; it was a story about the media and media ethics. The refugee crisis became a crisis for a European reporter. László was fired; however, she became a hero of the European far right, and N1TV skyrocketed in number of daily views for a month.

*　*　*

The perceiving and organizing of difference as fundamental to perception must occur in an interaction of perceiver and perceived positioned somewhere and somehow in a relation. This positioning in a relation we can call a regime, the mechanisms of positioning we can call an apparatus. Chains of signification, codes of representation, the images of us and them are formed in apparatuses. Consciousness—the brain, the mind, the visual intelligence that allows for recognition, and so on—exists not in and of itself but arises along with the object of perception in dynamic chains of signification within an elaborate apparatus of perception. Our technologies (of seeing) are as much a part of that apparatus as are our eyes, ears, sense organs, objects and hallucinations, light sources, and so on. Seeing is dynamic. Visual alterity is a dynamic—but what kind?

CHAPTER 9

The Cinematic Face

Interior Recognition, Gay Surface, Queer Multistability

> The discovery of printing has gradually rendered the human face illegible. People have been able to glean so much from reading that they could afford to neglect other forms of communication. In this way, the visual spirit was transformed into a legible spirit, and a visual culture was changed into a conceptual one.
>
> . . .
>
> Now another device is at work, giving culture a new turn towards the visual and the human being a new face. It is the cinematograph, a technology for the multiplication and dissemination of the products of the human mind, just like the printing press, and its impact on human culture will not be less momentous.
>
> —Béla Balázs, *Béla Balázs*

The Techne of Recognizing the Face of the Other: Cognitive Psychology's Evolution

Faces: to see faces is to perceive at once difference and a connection. In visual alterity the face plays a particular role. The face of the other is the emotional mirror but also the limit to the self. The face of the other is proximity to the other: to perceive the face of the other means one is close enough to read the emotions signaled by the typically forty-three muscles that make the face plastic. Showing emotions entails incredible muscular and motor coordination. The face without the movement of those muscles is a mask. Facial paralysis forecloses the easy conveying of emotions. Yet the perception of the face and the movement of the muscles is also an experience of distance from the person. To see the faces is also to read the face. We experience our foreclosure from being "in"

The Cinematic Face • 155

the consciousness of the other, from the conscious being of an other. Recognition as a face turns into recognition of the face, the other becomes an other in a cognitive process. To see the face of the other and to recognize it as neighbor, as friend, as family, as threat is to enter into society, to place self and other in a relationship, in an ethical relationship. To see the face of the other and to recognize it is to negotiate our responsibilities to the other.

We know that the face has a particular role in human cognitive development. Complex cognitive processes are involved, and special areas of research emerged early on for both cognitive and neuroscientists. For example, as cognitive psychology emerged in the 1960s, it emerged along with new cybernetic modeling, and we can recognize a connection in the direction between the advancement of cognitive theories and computers. Cognitive psychology, which was understood as an antidote to behaviorism, sought to attend to the brain's cognitive mechanisms rather than treat mental processes as unobservable responses to exterior stimuli. Cognitive psychology sought to establish models focused on the detection of perception, attention, memory, and emotions. It was not the input so much as the mechanisms of processing, storing, and recalling that input. Both the cybernetic model of the time and cognitive psychology treated the brain's memory functions as a kind of archive, a library, a set of files in folders. Memory could call up what was stored there. And in this way research on facial recognition developed. The same model was applied to cognition as it was to cybernetic research on facial recognition technology.

The problem for cognitive psychologists, however, is that as this project developed good algorithms for use by the FBI and Homeland Security, it did not provide an accurate model for the understanding of cognitive processes of facial recognition. By 2005 neuroscientists Andrew Calder and Andrew Young published critiques of the prevailing cognitive model.[1] Since then new models have developed to account for the fact that the brain does not perform facial recognition like a simple recall mechanism in an archive. It is too fast and specialized for that. Neuroscience has likewise helped us understand that facial recognition differs from object recognition in the brain architecture, with its own fusiform face area (FFA).

The rupture with the cybernetic model of facial recognition that is so useful in contemporary surveillance technology is not the only paradigm shift in cognitive theory's approach to the face. Although a great deal of cognitive work on facial recognition arose in a paradigm of evolutionary psychobiological essentialism, I already discussed how this approach has been contested and even overthrown within the community of researchers. Indeed a number of cognitive and neuroscientists have been impressively active in considering context

156 · CHAPTER 9

dependency in facial-emotional recognition. Their work makes clear that there is not a simple hardwired strategy as has been developed in cybernetic facial recognition technology. Rather, context dependency has led some researchers to identify the processes of facial-emotional recognition as a link between the psychical and social.[2]

The understanding of facial recognition as a link between the psychical and the social, however, requires a careful consideration of cultural expectations and social categorization. In chapter 2 I also discussed at length how cognitive research in general needs to attend much more carefully to the constructedness of race and gender. In studies devoted to gender and racial recognition, blackness and whiteness and male and female are taken as givens and not understood as social categorizations constructed within long histories of power. *The Handbook of Categorization in Cognitive Science*, focused on a US study, simply notes, "Racial categorization is a ubiquitous phenomenon in our judgments and perceptions of ourselves and others."[3] And I already noted that the terms "white," "black," and "Asian" are treated as if they are globally consistent racial categories and not describing very different social constructions. I have undertaken a survey of the literature on this point beyond the work noted in the handbook and have found the state of research to be consistent, even in articles where the discussion turns to paradigms of multiculturalism and migration or where researchers themselves might have experienced differing constructions of social categorization.[4]

Facial recognition begins at very early ages, with the advent of visual processing. It is a matter of complex feedback loops and top-down/bottom-up processes. Consider that the face of the other has a particular ability to draw out an emotional empathic response. Facial recognition begins in the first month after birth, and recognition of facial emotions follows quickly. It begins with the mimicking of facial emotions, and by four to eight months recognition sets in as the infant starts to categorize various emotions they read off the face.[5] These feedback loops develop out of complex social and cultural contexts. The process continues well into adolescence and entails regions of the brain that are specialized for this purpose. The feedback loops drive specialization of familiar facial patterns.

Facial recognition thus entails multiple functions, including emotion reading, and it shows plasticity evidenced by recognition of various culturally specific forms of emotional expression. There are not racial or gendered faces that do or do not show something to someone; there are gendered, raced, classed, aged, and other faces that have developed cognitive capacities in their determination. That these capacities and patterns of facial legibility develop at the earliest ages is clear but to what extent over a lifetime patterns can be retrained is not. Further, the capacity can be impaired by various illnesses or conditions, many of which are on the autism spectrum.[6] When and how emotions register on the face is in part determined by cultural feedback in cognitive development. But the faces of some individuals display emotions differently than the surrounding cultural codes; some people laugh when others would commonly cry, or cry when others show no emotion, and still others show no emotion when the crowd is roaring. Further, cognitive differences in the areas of facial recognition can lead to various behaviors that set the individual at odds with their society.[7] A failure to recognize normative gender types in faces can result in ostracism. A propensity to misrecognize fear or desire can result in misaligned approaches to the other.

And what happens when the forty-three muscles of the face confront conditions in which they should and must remain still? What happens when the face is explored by an anti-Semite for particular qualities? What happens when the face is exposed to the color-discrimination paper bag test? Do the muscles move when the fag basher raises a fist? Seeing difference and the paradigms of differentiation are related but separate. We may not determine the circumstances in which we come to recognize difference, but we have the ability to change the way we differentiate. That these patterns of differentiation develop at the earliest ages is clear, but we must learn over our lifetimes to break with the given patterns. We must learn how to see difference differently.

The Face and Film: *Photogenie* and the Birth of the Cinematic

Cinema, the modern technology of differentiation, from the start showed us the different and exotic. The *actualités* were a staple of the Lumières offerings from 1895 to 1908. Already in 1893 Thomas Edison's Kinetoscope had offered individuals quick peeps of the other. Whether a simple display of the coworker at the factory, Herald Square in New York, Czar Nicholas arriving in Paris, a Kazimierz Prószyński view of Warsaw, or the Sioux Ghost Dance, cinema made the image spectacular. Whether proximate and quotidian or distant and exceptional, cinema set the image up to be viewed as fascinating, other. That film already developed preferences for subjects like men boxing and women doing serpentine dances reminds us that these images emerged in codes of representation that were already in place. Gendered, raced, colonial codes placed limits on not what could be shot but what was presented.

However, we could say that film became cinematic as it learned to show the face, as it learned to present the face as a key to an emotional response. It

158 · CHAPTER 9

took a bit before cinema became a key feedback mechanism in our cognitive development. This function that made cinema cinematic had to be learned. It was not part of cinema's early history. Faces took a while to appear in cinema. For almost the first two decades of the cinema, the camera stood at a theatrical distance. It was not until 1911 that the moving image began to incorporate what was common in the language of the still image. Tom Gunning has detailed how especially with the work of D. W. Griffith the camera moved to a proximity in which one could read emotions off the face.[8] A new ensemble of visual language developed that was focused on the face, like the iris as a technique for introducing a character, inserted like a playbill, or for emphasizing an emotional state.

Béla Balázs based much of his early film theory on how the cinema had rediscovered the face, the physiognomy. His work detailed how the language of early film quickly discovered the power of the close-up in creating the appeal of silent screen divas such as Asta Nielsen, Lillian Gish, Pola Negri, Greta Garbo, and Louise Brooks. Balázs observed that silent pictures did not need dialogue; they had faces. The face became the passionate face. And cinema rapidly gained a new interiority; it was a short decade from the introduction of the close-up to Lupu Pick's *Scherben* (*Shattered*) (1921) or F. W. Murnau's *Der Letzte Mann* (*The Last Laugh*) (1924), in which the expressive face and the envisioning of interior subjective processes became central to cinema. The cinema and the close-up created a new language of expression. Eisenstein and Vertov would develop their theories of montage based on this insight.

In his work Balázs understood the cinematograph as providing a visual language that set civilization on a new path that had been dominated by the culture of the book. Cinema's faces created a culture of the face. Balázs, along with Germaine Dulac, and Jean Epstein propagated the theories of the visual idea or of *photogénie*, placing the face, the close-up, the interiority of the subject, as a key to the language of cinema. Dulac and Epstein were active behind the camera and were themselves cinematographs. They explored cinema's ability to represent emotional and intersubjective recognition in avant-garde classics like *La Coquille et le Clergyman* (*The Seashell and the Clergyman*) (1928) or *La glace à trois faces* (*The Three-Sided Mirror*) (1927).

The Face as Interior: Dreyer

Faces in film came to reveal an interiority. In the same way that cinema learned to show the face, we learned to read off of and into the cinematic face the motivations and emotions of the character. The display of the face remains one of the important aspects of visual language, but it is not the only potential of the

The Cinematic Face • 159

cinema. Faces like those of Griffith, Murnau, and the photogénie movement were recorded as the image to portray the interior state of mind of the other. They sought to overcome in visual language our foreclosure from knowing what is in the minds of others. They preceded Theory of Mind (ToM) research by a half century. It was not until the 1970s that psychologists began to catch up to filmmakers and film theory by exploring the mechanisms whereby humans develop the potential to recognize thinking in other humans.[9] Long after the century of cinema was under way, psychological and social neuroscientific research recognized that starting at age three humans develop an understanding of another person as having an interiority, other beliefs—that is, a mind of their own. Subsequent research has shown that this ability to mentalize or "mind read"—in other words, project an interiority onto other subjects—arises as a result of being able to explicitly represent the other's belief in relation to one's own knowledge.[10] What cognitive psychologists began to explore through neuroimaging at the start of the new millennium, filmmakers had been exploring in cinematic images since the first half of the last.[11]

Other neuroscientists consider the face central to the sparking of the mirror neurons. The mirror neurons give a viewer a sense of doing what they are seeing. When I see a smiling face, I sense myself to be smiling. When I see a desperate face, I am filled with anxiety. And much cognitive film theory had been based on the idea that the viewing of the face in films connects with a deep biological system that is central to the prompting of empathy.[12]

Torben Grodal has considered the face extensively from a particular cognitive standpoint in film studies. His work underscores a central importance of the face. He writes:

> The centres for the regulation of facial expressions are placed with other evolutionarily late features in the anterior part of the cortex, and it is generally believed that facial expressions for basic emotions such as happiness, sadness, anger, surprise, fear, and disgust are innate and therefore transcultural (see Ekman and Friesen 1975). The facial expressions of fear, sadness, joy, or other emotions often directly evoke the displayed emotions in the beholder. In visual narration, close-ups of persons that either indicate their emotions or their perceptions (and thus the possible emotional impact of the objects of their perceptions) play a very prominent role (see Carroll 1993).[13]

But this assessment is wrong. It sees the face in the moving image as activating a cognitively hardwired transcultural human emotional response and is out of step with approaches to cognitive plasticity. This approach ignores the long history of the face emerging in cinema. It sets up the dynamic as transhistorical.

160 · CHAPTER 9

And it ignores the mechanisms of difference-to-be-seen in the technology of cinema. Quite the opposite is the case.

Carl Theodor Dreyer's great silent film experiment of 1928, *La Passion de Jeanne d'Arc* (*The Passion of Joan of Arc*), relied largely on faces, especially that of lead Renée Falconetti. Famously, Dreyer recreated a medieval town at great expense, but at the first screening of the film his producers were alarmed when the set did not even appear. Dreyer created it for the actors to experience a certain realism, but the authenticity he was exploring was to be found on their faces. Central to the film was the authenticity of passion. From cognitive theory, one might expect that the experience of the film would be to suffer along with Joan, to feel her fear and sadness, to be tortured as she is tortured. This expectation would certainly be in line with a bias in cognitive film theory for analyses of classical Hollywood narrative cinema. Sometimes the orientation toward classic Hollywood is explicit, as in the work of Peter Wyeth.[14] But in other work, like that of Grodal, the bias for popular narrative fiction goes largely unreflected, as when he observes the following:

> Central to the film experience—one that expands language-based storytelling with its added audiovisual dimensions—is the portrayal of the lives of other human beings in such a fashion that viewers are invited to share their cognition, emotions, goals, situations, and social environments. . . . Because films are produced to capture and sustain viewers' attention, they magnify all kinds of possible human behavior, virtues as well as vices.[15]

The Passion of Joan of Arc is certainly a narrative; however, I would dispute that its goal is to portray Joan's life so that we can share her emotions or goals. This film hardly belongs to the traditions of popular fiction films that Grodal privileges. Indeed the suffering in the film eschews precisely the melodramatic narration of films on which he prefers to focus—for example, *Sophie's Choice* (Pakula 1982), *Stepmom* (Columbus 1998), or *Titanic* (Cameron 1997). What happens to cognitive approaches if we take up a film like Dreyer's, in which he sought a different goal than to share a melodramatic moment? What happens if the quality aimed at by the film we analyze was, as in *The Passion*, to accomplish a moving image of passion in the traditional religious sense? What if Dreyer purposely eschewed the instilling of an emotional mirror response because to do so would have been to make banal the suffering of the saint? In order to carry its religious meaning, Joan's exquisite martyrdom has to remain outside our quotidian experience. Dreyer in effect creates moving images that function less like bourgeois emotive portraiture and more like Orthodox religious icons, less attempts to elicit empathic response and more an attempt to represent the transcendent or an aesthetic sublime.[16] And this point is important: if we want to reflect on the full possibilities of the face as moving image, we cannot neglect attending to the aesthetics of the film, which is to say the great apparatus of film should not be limited to a machine for the production of banal forms of empathy.

The Homosexual Face to Be Seen: Magnus Hirschfeld

There is nothing inherent on the face that marks passion or desire. The desiring face must be shown and the particularity of the desire must be revealed. A face, a bowl of soup, Kuleshov showed us that cinema has a technology to reveal desires that are unstated, interior. It gives us a technology to read passions off the face. Cinema allows us to see otherness. However, the face *as* other and the face *of* the other are two different matters. Consider the face of sexuality, the sexualized face. "Gaydar" as a popular term aside, you cannot see "the gay." You cannot see same-sex desire in a face. Same-sex desire, gayness, homosexuality has to be made visible. Queerness is a strategy that can be seen only in or against a code of images. Film has been deployed to establish that code, to show us the face of the homosexual, to reveal its passions, to open its interiority, to build sympathy for its desires or condemn its very existence. There is no homosexual other; the homosexual other must be produced, seen, recognized. The face of the homosexual must be envisioned. Difference to be seen requires a technology to produce it.

The 1919 film *Anders als die Andern* (*Different from the Others*) (Oswald) is the first homosexual emancipation film in the world. This film, censored and for a long time unseen, nevertheless sought to give a new sexual scientific face to the homosexual. In effect this film sought to produce a modern vision of the homosexual. There were other films that presented homosexuals. This film, however, participated in and worked against various traditions of differentiation, seeking to produce something new. Richard Dyer has so eloquently written about these long histories of differentiation in film and photography—I could never do better.[17] Not the least of these traditions is that of the "sad homosexual," typically a tragic character whose primary option in society is to commit suicide, or maybe to survive in a state of artistic sublimation in order to become a productive member of society. *Different from the Others* reveals features of the sad homosexual. It relies on iris shots. Its main character does commit suicide. It shows us, however, a new face—the face of the sexual scientist (Magnus Hirschfeld), who enlightens his audiences with information and truth and reconfigures the other images of the homosexual out of sadness and into. . . . If we had the complete version, we may be able to say into emancipation.

162 · CHAPTER 9

Hirschfeld—Jewish, homosexual, socialist, and preeminent sexual scientist—was behind the film. It was to provide a counter to dominant images of the period. The censors of the Weimar Republic prevented its broad distribution, limiting it to medical scientific audiences. Finally the Third Reich intervened, for whom Hirschfeld represented all that was antithetical to the National Socialist vision of society. The National Socialists promoted a very different vision of homosexuals, one that dominated the perception for decades, that persists and, in many places, even dominates to this day.

I point to this film to note precisely how film, how the technology of cinema, has a potential and how Hirschfeld sought to deploy that potential to revise dominant social categories. Through the technological capacity of cinema, *Different from the Others* was to change the differentiations that were dominant in society. This film, along with others, seeks to show the face of the homosexual. It does not seek to show homosexual acts as such; rather, it seeks to show the condition of the homosexual, the interiority behind the face. Once called into existence, once entered into our ways of seeing, our capacities for recognition, the face of difference does not go away. Once we have learned to recognize otherness in this way or that, we cannot easily unlearn that recognition. How, I want to ask, is it possible to see the face of the homosexual differently?

The Face as Surface: Andy Warhol

In 1999 the Wadsworth Atheneum Museum of Art explored the function of portraiture and the face of Warhol in its exhibition *About Face: Andy Warhol Portraits.*[18] There are few artists who are as well known for their images of faces as Andy Warhol. Rembrandt and the entire tradition of bourgeois portraiture in the Low Countries did not produce as many faces as the one artist did in his serialized formats: endless Jackie Os, Elvises, Marilyns, Debbie Harrys, Deans, and other popular cultural icons. Nicholas Baume argues that Warhol directly countered this tradition of painting the Burghers of the Netherlands; his seriality revealed the artificial aspects of public identity.[19] Warhol recognized the transformation of portraiture for the middle-class elites to popularized superstardom for all in modern mass society's creative industries. And long before the modern YouTube influencer, Warhol attended not just to the still image of prints and paintings but also to the face in the moving image. There is something uncanny about Warhol's faces, though. They seem the opposite of Dreyer's Joan. The stylization of Warhol's work seems to eschew, even foreclose, the emotive response anticipated in cognitive theory. They remain surface to any attempts

The Cinematic Face · 163

at identification. And yet they do attract our attention, fascinate, even in their artifice, like an icon.

In about two years starting in 1964, Warhol produced 472 three-minute films, "Screen Tests," of 189 people, mostly in black-and-white, some in color.[20] If you walked into the Factory, you sat for a shoot. Three minutes, one reel of film, the Screen Tests largely focused on the face. Silent, they sometimes show conversations, responses to voices off frame, but largely they focus on the face. This project was deeply embedded in both technologies of visualization and traditions of representation. Callie Angell noted that Warhol drew inspiration from photo-booth photos. This technology had been around since the nineteenth century but was set up in its modern form in the 1920s on Broadway. Warhol had used the photo booth to do a fashion shoot for *Harper's Bazaar* and had become enamored with it and with the behaviors, popularized in the contemporary as selfie mugging, it captured.[21] Angell also noted as influence the mugshots Warhol developed for his 1964 World's Fair project, *13 Most Wanted Men*. The Screen Tests were a mixture of culture industry stardom and surveillance technologies. In addition to the Screen Tests, there are also a number of longer films that likewise focus on the face, most famously *Sleep* (1963) and *Blow Job* (1964). These multiple-reel films followed a similar principle: the film reel ran through an entire exposure without a cut, fading in and out to white at the start and end of each reel. The longer films (for instance, *Sleep* was 311 minutes) were constructed as a series of the entirety of the film reels being edited together. They thus have a rhythm to them as the fades to white mark a standard of time from reel to reel.

Sarah Boxer describes the Screen Tests as "3 minute eternities."[22] And for anyone who has enjoyed the automated digital screen test at Pittsburgh's Andy Warhol Museum, this seems an apt description and explains why the contemporary selfie is so brief. To be in front of the camera for longer than a snapshot threatens to empty out subjectivity. David James describes the films as a demand to self-construction in which the sitter's awareness of the camera becomes an awareness of the self as image.[23] James describes this condition as calling out a fantastic self-projection. Out of the painful loneliness and anxiety one experiences with the three-minute-long take, it makes sense when Reva Wolf sets the project not in relation to an ego-centered individualism but into a communal undertaking: the project of Warhol's Factory.[24]

Richard Dyer explored the project under the term "gay." Careful to consider this project as part of the larger development of underground cinema, Dyer notes that these strategies of filmmaking were not unique to a gay underground, "but it is no accident that gays were so central to the development and definition of the tradition as a whole. Underground cinema provided a space and an opportunity for gay men and . . . lesbians to represent themselves in films in a way that mainstream film-making . . . did not."[25] Dyer continues on to assess the general dynamic of identity construction in the underground in its connections to the emergent gay identity of the time:

> The concerns of the underground—with personal identity, with self disclosure, with gender roles, with subversiveness—have a particular urgency in a lesbian and gay context, and even more so in the context of the development of newly assertive gay identities in the period. What makes underground cinema even more fascinating, however, is the way it also seems to problematise those identities.[26]

And he characterizes the emergence of this form as a key to the attempt to deploy the cinema in a construction and dissolution of new (gay) identities.

Douglas Crimp likewise considered the project as a gay project, asking extensively to what ends Warhol recorded these faces. In the faces he also finds something more than a Warholian superstar precursor to contemporary celebrity culture. These films are not all superficial and plastic as often approached. Concentrating especially on the face in *Blow Job*, Crimp considers an ethics of representation, a quality based in a "face not *for us*."[27] Crimp develops this analysis to counter the typical analysis of Warhol as voyeuristic and his actors as exhibitionists, all of them as narcissists, and so on. Of course the charm of the film *Blow Job* is that we never see the titular act, thus we are left to read the act off the action of the face. And the face we are given to read is lit by one lightbulb that poses challenges to the film's spectators. It is not a film of easy facial recognition or emotive mirroring.

Crimp insists that this strategy of lighting points to an explicit intention on the part of Warhol to turn the face into a mask, just as Jonathan Flatley argued that the still portraits are all stylized to appear as "fictive."[28] We might pick up on his use of the term "mask" here as suggestive. Crimp sees this strategy as putting forward an "ethics of antivoyeuristic looking."[29] He seems inclined to find in Warhol the antidote to the "to-be-looked-atedness" of women in Laura Mulvey's exploration of visual pleasure. We are refused any direct (pornographic) view of the blow job and the pleasure it brings. There is no interiority per se; we are given just the face. The face in Warhol's work, Crimp argues, draws us toward it and beyond. He cites Emmanuel Levinas on the face's propensity to draw us to think about the You, the other of the face. For Crimp, Warhol represented a paradigm shift in representation, a non-evaluative interest in everyone and everything they did. Warhol was not interested in the fellatio but in the young man as such, his face, what his face was expressing.

Andy Warhol, *Blow Job*, 1964. 16 mm film, black and white, silent, 41 minutes at 16 frames per second. © 2020 The Andy Warhol Museum, Pittsburgh, PA, a museum of Carnegie Institute. All rights reserved. Film still courtesy Andy Warhol Museum

I am not convinced by the quest for an ethical Warhol, nor am I impressed by the elevation of Warhol's famous "superficiality" to a position of more than just tolerance. Certainly important is the refusal of interiority. Dyer described this as a discarding of notions of authentic self that dominated more earnest gay political filmmaking.[30] I am very sympathetic to my former colleague and friend's attempt to find a queerness before gay, to recall a heterogeneity of possibilities before Stonewall produced a homonormative identity. Crimp wants Warhol's presentation of difference to be that, a provocation, because it makes difference visible.[31] But there is nothing inherently positive in showing difference. Warhol's seriality, his Marilyn or Elvis prints, repeated the same image over and over and showed us that no image was the same in its repetition. Serializing difference is not an ethical gesture; it is a fact of perception. Ethics here is a question not of seeing difference but of how our seeing differentiates.

Importantly, in other projects Warhol also reflected directly on the perception of difference, or rather he allowed the artifice of the audiovisual project to create its own commentary. Warhol shows how seeing works as a project of social categorization in films like *Harlot* (1964), *Eating Too Fast* (1966), and *My*

166 · CHAPTER 9

Hustler (1967). These films were sound projects and contain for almost their full duration a running commentary, typically by three voices from off frame, while the camera focuses on an image. In *My Hustler* the voices discuss the hustler Paul America sunbathing on the Fire Island beach or primping in the close quarters of a bathroom, and their dialogue forms an audio commentary on the visuals, sonically enfolding it. In this particular film, the bitchy campiness of the voices portrays a sociability based in negative affect: vicious, cruel, camp, arch, mean, and competitive. It is a world that invites either laughter or repulsion. Four years later, Rosa von Praunheim would use this strategy to film the classic of gay liberation cinema, *Nicht der Homosexuelle ist pervers sondern die Situation in der er lebt* (*It Is Not the Homosexual Who Is Perverse but the Society in Which He Lives*) (1971). The backlash against that film's negative portrayal of homosexuals actually led to the formation of openly gay groups making demands for liberation. The backlash against *My Hustler* led to its being censored and confiscated by the police.

To be sure, Warhol was fascinated with faces himself. How does Warhol ask us to see the face? Jonathan Flatley observed about the Screen Tests that "in the way that they encourage sustained, close gazing at another's face, the Screen Tests recall an infant's mode of looking."[32] Rhyming with contemporary cognitive theory, he calls it "interocular gazing" and "obligatory attention." Such gazing is important for the child, but what does it bring the adult? In this gazing, affect is lost. The Screen Tests do not ask us to identify with the people seen. They recorded basically everyone who came in, and it was a slice of New York City that showed up at the Factory—from socialite to homeless, artist to academic to banker. Warhol's films present to us various ways in which film technology constructs other beings. But what they seem to eschew is the being of the other.

Difference is visible, seeing is differentiation as such, the other is seen, and in our focus on perceiving otherness, the same is glossed over in inattentional blindness. It is not a question of *if* we see difference but of how our differentiations arise in the apparatus of seeing. The Warhol Screen Tests in their seriality show different differences. The art of Warhol is there in that moment when we see sameness differently.

The P/operatic Intensity and the Multistable Face: Werner Schroeter

As Warhol marked a reconfiguration of the face and our relationship to the perception of difference, across the Atlantic Werner Schroeter was undertaking similar explorations. Schroeter, a generation younger than Warhol, was nevertheless part of the complexly connected underground scene. The 104-minute

Two faces in proximity. *Der Tod der Maria Malibran* (*The Death of Maria Malibran*) (Schroeter 1971). Screen captures

film *Der Tod der Maria Malibran* (*The Death of Maria Malibran*) (1971) begins with sequences of faces, typically two faces. These are static moving images often set against a black backdrop in relatively long takes. The camera is frequently in a medium shot at a slight low angle looking up at the two faces in high-contrast lighting. But the camera may also be in a close-up at eye level. The faces are of a pair of people pressed together in proximity. They appear as couples because of their physical proximity. One of the two often turns toward the other; one of the two often tries to kiss the other. The face being kissed typically remains just out of reach. The face being kissed may respond to the attempt with an operatic facial gesture, as if setting into an aria, as if to signal an ecstatic state. Yet one of the two often cries, one of the two seems to suffer, one of the two seems to pull away. These shots repeat, for 7 minutes right at the start of the 104 minutes of *The Death of Maria Malibran* and then again and again throughout the film.

The film defies easy description. The title is based on the legendary nineteenth-century opera diva who literally sang herself to death on stage at age twenty-eight. The film presents this story as a part of its many episodes; however, more than the story, the film thematizes the representation of all-consuming passion and art. *Malibran* thematizes the cinematic representation of passionate desire. It confronts us with the question of seeing from its very first

Desiring bodies in contact. *Der Tod der Maria Malibran* (*The Death of Maria Malibran*) (Schroeter 1971). Screen captures

image. Taking up the legend of Malibran, it shows her as the face of a woman with blood streaming out of her eyes. At the end of the film we return to this image with her collapse on the stage. But the image gives way to the faces, dyads, triads, single close-ups of faces. And it also inspires other moments in the film—for instance, a nightmarish fairy tale of the traveling apprentice who gives up one of his eyes to the evil Hugo in return for food. Blinded, the boy (played by one of the women cast members) finds redemption at the foot of a cross in a cemetery, where he overhears crows who reveal that if a blind person washes their eyes with the morning dew, their sight will be restored. His piety rewards him with a new romantic vision.

Schroeter appeared on the scene at a time when Brechtian language dominated theater and film production and analysis. Hence his early work is often discussed in conjunction with alienation techniques and Brechtian *Geste*. Likewise, early on in his career Schroeter's work is often described in connection to the opera and operatic, a distilling out the operatic effect.[33] *Gestus* and opera remain the dominant mode of discussing Schroeter.[34] Certainly there are reasons to discuss his work in conjunction with these terms, but their predominance in the critical literature should be understood as deriving more from a perspective that dominated the analytic schools of the period, not explicitly from Schroeter's own approach. The concentration on Brecht masks his fascination with Warhol. His passion for opera masks Schroeter's equal fascination with popular music. Before he admired Maria Callas, Schroeter was a fan of the 1950s pop chanteuse Caterina Valente. The soundtracks to Schroeter's films, right up to his last, combined precisely and explicitly the high and the mass, elite and popular culture equally. To single out Brechtian alienation is to ignore Warholian seriality. To single out the operatic is to ignore how Schroeter recognized in both opera and pop a tendency to escalation and intensification of emotional states, and it is this quality of his films that interests me here. They span an arch back to Dreyer's *Joan of Arc*.

Thus, while the contemporary culture industry may keep the popular and the operatic performance typically separate, we can observe that Schroeter understood that long before there was pop music, there was "op" music. The propensity to engage in emotional intensification, to activate emotional states, is a matter of operatic *and* pop performance. Reveling in this quality, Schroeter, especially in his early films, set about to distill such highlights, creating films that show one moment of intensity after the other.

These couples, these faces—what do they want? As with Warhol's project, the film relies on surface, not interiority. Although the shots rely on the language

Lighting for desire. *Der Tod der Maria Malibran* (*The Death of Maria Malibran*) (Schroeter 1971). Screen captures

of cinema, they do not make clear what is desired, what is thought. These faces, in close-ups, in dyads, triads, monads—what do they want of us the spectator? What do they want us to know? They certainly give us ample ability to consider the experience of visual alterity. Yet to be clear, these are not images of an Other, a single other, or a class of otherness by which I constitute my subjectivity. The images are not woman to my man, heterosexual to my homo, black to my white. The tableaus of faces and figures that constitute the film give us something else to recognize.

What do we see, how do we recognize, how do we apperceive, how do we apprehend? Like Schroeter's other work from the period, *Malibran* actively relies on the familiar and iconic. Its characters, the faces of the others, are primarily posed in stances that make up the repertoire of nineteenth- and twentieth-century opera and melodrama: crouching, observed from high angles, point and backlighting to highlight features, surrounded by lush interiors and curtains, arms outstretched, encaged, wailing sorrowfully at the bottom of a stairs, singing out one's love pain, *Liebeskummer*, through the blues. Such images have a clarity within a narrative context. We need only think of when Billy Wilder's Norma Desmond descends the stairs for her close-up, or Douglas Sirk's Astrée Sternhjelm walks out in her costume to sing "La Habanera," "better than any

The passion of Ingrid Caven. *Der Tod der Maria Malibran* (*The Death of Maria Malibran*) (Schroeter 1971). Screen captures

native"; these are filmic moments that draw out our emotions and render the image a point of desire and projection. Thinking back to Balázs, these are moments in which the characters' interior lives are made most filmically explicit for the spectator. We know what she is going through; we know how much she suffers by the hand gesture, by the smile, by the glance upward to someplace off and outside the frame.

Schroeter decontextualizes these images. He removes the narrative around the icon and offers instead the stance, the mise-en-scène, the framing. He strips narrative of its action, leaving behind only alterity and the point of projection and desire. To these images he adds a grand soundtrack that moves between the most elite and the most popular of music—for instance, motifs from Bizet's *Carmen* find their counterpart in country singer Marty Robbins's "Tonight, Carmen." At times the music loops and repeats, and at times it cuts out entirely into silence. In those moments the spectator is reminded of how the music has served as film score, briefly offering context and familiarity. We know the gesture is romantic because Brahms accompanies it. And when the Brahms cuts away, or when "Tonight, Carmen" plays again for the third time, we lose our reveries and confront how much the act of viewing is not simply about an act of Kuleshov narration but of subjective investment, emotional commitment, and engagement with the images, identification and feeling. While narrative might contextualize, the icon draws us out to a place where we feel. The face of the other does offer us a potential to recognize, feel, emote, cathect, cathart. It does not function here, however, as Grodal or Theory of Mind cognitive scholars have largely postulated.

In Schroeter's film the play of gender and sexuality takes off in a different direction from Warhol's presentation of difference. The film plays not only with the artifice of operatic and popular culture; it also plays with the performance of gender in culture. It makes differentiation difficult. The faces belong to all genders. The first couple in the opening sequence is a female couple presented in a frame that could be described as drawn from fashion photography. The women barely move, as if it were a still image. The two women are played by Schroeter's longtime diva Magdalene Montezuma, diminutive alongside the larger Manuela Riva, a Munich drag queen superstar. The couples who follow include various divas with high drama baggage: Christine Kaufmann, back from her decade in Hollywood and recently divorced from Tony Curtis; Ingrid Caven, married at the time to Rainer Werner Fassbinder; and Candy Darling, fresh from her work with Warhol. Sometimes distinctly masculine faces appear, but gendered and sexual appearances are fluid. On occasion there are three figures, two women and a shirtless youth. There is also one face, tear-streamed and awash in gold.

If Warhol was breaking with the paradigms of the 1940s and '50s and projecting forward a popularized superstardom, in its turn Schroeter's work points to a queerness, a fluidity of gender and sexuality, its performance in ways that have come to dominate the contemporary moment. Important for this study, these faces create a gender kippbild; they underscore a multistability in gender and sexuality. The spectator can experience a struggle to locate, determine, normativize the faces and assign them to their proper genders. Or it can indeed experience the vacillations of the image. Long before Judith Butler was highlighting gender as performance, a year before Esther Newton wrote her foundational essay "Mother Camp," Schroeter was displaying a long history of visual representation and aesthetic genre tropes that stretched from the ephebe androgyne of antiquity to the renaissance theatrical cross-dressing and Romantic performances of gender up to indiscriminate modern pop sexuality.

Like the images of Warhol's Screen Tests, the faces in *Malibran* do not require spectator identifications. The spectator is not required to do anything. If they want us to know anything or identify with anyone, it is to identify with instability and an unease of identity. In a contemporary moment when cis/trans identity is a central part of sexual liberation efforts, where queer identification "as" and allied identification "with" is key to a sense of political progress, Schroeter's work is not easily available to this direction. The multistability of the images

Desiring others and gender fluidity. *Der Tod der Maria Malibran* (*The Death of Maria Malibran*) (Schroeter 1971). Screen captures

The Cinematic Face • 173

dislodges not only binary but also third gender, third sex models of describing gender and sexuality.[35] Stability and instability play in the image as much as they play with our perception. They make us feel an uncertainty vis-à-vis socially trained gender-normative perception.

At a moment when we have been trained to recognize historical and local specificity of gender and sexual expression, the visual language of *Malibran* provides an experience of flux within a long historical-cultural-civilizational trajectory that seems to suggest gender and sexual instability as a constant of cultural production and by no means an aberration. This is as much a matter of the staging, mis-en-scène, where the figures appear in setting and costumes from a range of human history. It is also in the sound of the film. The sequences are accompanied at the start by Maria Callas signing a rhapsody by Brahms with arias from Puccini and Rossini, eventually giving way to pop songs by Marty Robbins and Julie Rogers, blues songs, tangos, ballads, and back to opera. The audio and the visual push the instability. The single faces sometimes lip-sync and we grasp at an experience of playback. But then the sound moves from the lips. The sound moves from diegetic to extra-diegetic. Sound is ever at best only loosely synced to the image. There are texts that speak of ecstatic desire, loss, longing, passions. However, more common than direct synchronization, the faces mouth words that do not relate to the sound. Sound bridges across disparate shots and gives way at times to silence, repeatedly underscoring that the sound is not bound to the image. The disjoining of the sound and image repeatedly disrupts the *melos*-drama, the song drama of the melodramatic. Whatever differences you expect, *Malibran* disrupts. Regardless of how you are used to differentiating, *Malibran* offers new possibilities of perception.

Film-Philosophy Foucault: Queer Opacity

At the release of *The Death of Maria Malibran*, Michel Foucault first took note of the work of Werner Schroeter. In 1981 Gérard Courant, under the auspices of the Goethe Institute in Paris, arranged a conversation between Foucault and Schroeter.[36] In the discussion Foucault noted in the filmmaker's *Malibran* and *Willow Springs* (1973) a tendency that could describe all of Schroeter's subsequent films. Ostensibly they appear to be about love, but in reality they are about passion, where passion contains that double sense of desire and suffering. Foucault described passion as something into which one falls, that takes hold, and does not pause and seems to have no origins. Passion is always a mobile state but one that does not move in any given direction. Passion is a moment of varying intensity. Foucault describes passion as in effect a state of radical alterity: "in

174 · CHAPTER 9

the moments of passion one is not oneself. There is no sense of being one's self. One sees things entirely differently (*tout autrement*)."[37]

Foucault describes in passion a "suffering-pleasure" that he distinguishes from desire or from the experiences of sadomasochism. In passion there is no explicit causal relation in which one desires to cause the other to experience pain. Foucault notes how in Schroeter's films, the dyads or triads of suffering-pleasure experience it all simultaneously, equally. In effect, where love can take place one-sidedly and narcissistically, without the response of the beloved, passion requires a partner. Love is egocentric while passion is a form of intense mutual communication.

In a highly personal moment of reflection on his own life, Foucault suggested that while he could not say if two men experienced passion differently or more intensely than a man and a woman, homosexuals are frequently in a state of opaque communication (*communication sans transparence*).[38] This obscure communication is the basis of passion, when one does not know the pleasures of the other or what motivates the other. This type of opacity and obscurity as an aspect of homosexual experience could be understood as an experience that extends beyond simple male-male desire and forms the foundation of queer experience.

Foucault points to a queer visual language that is distinct from what Balázs ascribed as key to cinema. Balázs was enamored of cinema's ability to convey knowledge about the figure, to convey Theory of Mind. The image has personality that we know and read; we read the mind of the image. Queer visual language would suggest that the image has no mind; it is image. The emotions of love it conveys are image and no guarantor of behavior. The emotion of repulsion it represents does not mark clearly a pattern of desire. Where Balázs underscores clarity, Foucault and Schroeter and Warhol point to opacity.

QUEER OPACITY

The Screen Tests and *Malibran* represent desire as something hermetic. It is opaque because we do not enter into a Theory of Mind. The figures on the screen do not draw the viewer in, even when their gaze directly addresses the camera—or more so when their gaze is directed elsewhere. We often confront the faces we see in decontextualized spaces, against a neutral backdrop. In the Screen Tests the faces perform self. In *Malibran* it is a Romantic desire presented in these sequences in the sense that the faces represent longing, torment, or unrequited passion to us iconographically; however, we only read the sign of such desire off the face. The film does not provide entrée into an interiority. No voice-over describes to us the feelings. No actions other than a turn of the head

The Cinematic Face • 175

appear to indicate direction or movement to some culmination or resolution. No contextualizing narrative appears to provide depth to these *tableaus vivant*. We see what we see, we look upon what we see, without the usual filmic apparatus that supports our ability to "desire with" or "desire as."

This opaque communication results from a social organization dominated by a hetero-coital imperative in which all other pleasures are subjected to censorship, silencing, screening, and concealment. Foucault is alluding to a condition in which it is not just the possible pleasures of contact between men but the fundamental communication with another person toward a pleasure that cannot be expressed—to paraphrase, "passion arises out of the pleasure that cannot be immediately named." This opaque communication can be taken as a fundamental principle of Schroeter's or Warhol's films. In Schroeter's work we find such communication establishing a queer aesthetic not just in the representations of the films, figures who move and turn, wordlessly expressing unfulfilled longings, but also in the condition established vis-à-vis the spectator. The viewer of a Schroeter film enters into a state of opaque communication. In all of his films there are various forms of dependencies that are already in place at the opening, without there being any clear exposition of the backstory.[39] The spectator enters into the diegetic world as if entering into an unconscious configuration. The outcomes of actions on the screen are clear, but the motives that initiate and drive them are at best opaque. If the Kuleshov effect describes a fundamental aspect of cinema, whereby the mind has a tendency to narrativize two images that follow each other (a woman's face, a bowl of soup = she wants to eat the soup), then Schroeter's technique creates a constant provocation to the expository desire of the conscious mind. Where typically the language of film follows tacit conventions and commonplace understandings (a car, a child on the road, a car, a close-up of the child = an accident), Schroeter's work eschews the customary. The images that sequentially progress continually elude the spectator's narrative potential, and yet it is clear that in the structure of the film and the actions of the figures there is a logic of narrative at work.

In this regard Foucault distinguished the work of Bergman, who, like Schroeter, he saw as equally "obsessed" with women and the love between women. In Bergman's work there is a lack of a queer aesthetic precisely because, as Foucault assesses, Bergman believes that he knows and can portray the states of pleasure, desire, and consciousness of a woman, and hence his films offer "evidence" of psychological states.[40] By comparison, Schroeter's films leave behind such psychologism and instantiate a psychological state in the act of spectating. The states represented elude names and categorization. Foucault described it as a process of creating something that cannot be

176 · CHAPTER 9

named but at each moment is given a different coloration, a form, an intensity that never has to confess what it is (*ce qu'elle est*).[41] Foucault, suspicious of his contemporary gay liberation movement's demand for coming out, a form of gay confession, a quest to produce an authentic self, finds in Schroeter's work what we can describe as a queer production of self without confession.

The Instability of the Image, the Complexity of the Self

Warhol's and Schroeter's faces present a possibility of an alterity that unleashes the potential of desire. It is not an eros of essential otherness. *Blow Job* is not pornographic, requesting me to desire the image. It is an image that performs pleasure that is not mine. In *Malibran* the first shot of Montezuma and Riva sets up a performance of gender. *Both* women are in gendered drag. They are costumed in high fashion, wearing overdone makeup. Both women perform femininity that is seldom seen outside of certain *en vogue* social events. They perform a desire for each other that has nothing to do with physical configuration. The surface of the image suggests a lesbian couple. Whether the spectator recognizes Riva as a drag queen or does not, the image that presents Riva as an actress alongside Montezuma leads to an overdetermining of the signifiers of gender and an "underdetermination" of the essence of sex. In the repetition of the self and stammering of passion, an "essence" of the body fades away behind an actuality of the image. These images swat away any sense that social codes are ordered according to a primary sex-gender differentiation. They undermine the presumptions of what I have elsewhere called the "linguistics of heterosexuality" and the possibilities that arise when the essentialist figuration is ruptured into a myriad of queer possibilities (see charts 1 and 2[42]).

Signifier		Masculinity		Femininity	Gender
───────	= Sign	───────	= $\male \leftrightarrow \female$ =	───────	
Signified		Male		Female	Sex
		Sexual Desire			
Gender: masculinity/femininity					
Sex: male/female					
Sexual desire: a "natural" force of attraction between these two gender/sex morphemes					

Chart 1. The Linguistics of Heterosexuality

1. $\dfrac{\text{Masculinity}}{\text{Female}}$ ↔ $\dfrac{\text{Femininity}}{\text{Female}}$	2. $\dfrac{\text{Masculinity}}{\text{Male}}$ ↔ $\dfrac{\text{Femininity}}{\text{Male}}$
3. $\dfrac{\text{Femininity}}{\text{Male}}$ ↔ $\dfrac{\text{Masculinity}}{\text{Female}}$	4. $\dfrac{\text{Femininity}}{\text{Male}}$ ↔ $\dfrac{\text{Femininity}}{\text{Female}}$
5. Male ↔ Masculinity	6. Female ↔ Masculinity
7. Female	8. Male 9. Masculine

Chart 2. Elaborated Semiotics for Dimorphic Configurations of *Sexual Desire*

In chart 1 we have represented an essentialist approach to sexuality that presumes a natural attraction between masculine male bodies and feminine female bodies. These films, however, undo sexual and gendered dimorphism. They open up possibilities of desire that do not align gender and sexuality, that do not even require another body for the expression of desire. The films discussed here point to and envision a lively *combinatoire* of possibilities (chart 2).

I may write about alterity generally, and we may consider alterity universally, but the work of Warhol and Schroeter here reminds us that each instantiation of self is unique. There is no absolute alterior experienced as such in a feminine essence. "The subject" never experiences alterity as such, but it does experience alterities in themselves. Alterity is always a unique opposition, and in each self/other opposition a new aspect of self arises into being. The self would be stable only insofar far as the other would be stable, never changing, the same, intractable. We can develop this insight even further to recognize that the experience of each new other, of each new moment of an other results in a complexity—that is, a making more complex—of the self. Each other brings with it a unique perspective of the self. That complexity of the self is unknowable, inexperienceable, without the unique perspective of the other. To close oneself off into a-stability must be based on a foreclosure of the experience of the other. The complexity of the self is a property of the perspective available to it only in the gaze of the other. It is not just that the gaze of the other sees me; it is that the other is always positioned uniquely occupying a gaze that no other can occupy. The other multiplies, augments, compounds, extends, and intensifies the self: the other complexifies the self.

CHAPTER 10

The Ethics of Visual Alterity
The Face of the Other, the Faceless Other

Recognizing the Other: Surveilling the Face

In 1886 Arthur Conan Doyle popularized modern criminal science with his character Sherlock Holmes appearing serialized in print. In 1888 Alphonse Breillart took the first mugshots and brought visual technology into the standard practice of criminologists. Facial databases became a staple of modern criminology. The deployment of this type of apparatus is displayed to great effect for the first time in Fritz Lang's classic, *M* (1931). In 1963, sponsored by the CIA, researchers Woody Bledsoe, Helen Chan Wolff, and Charles Bisson began work on facial recognition technology (FRT).[1] In 1967 Ulric Neisser published *Cognitive Psychology*, bringing together various influences like Noam Chomsky's critique of behaviorism and the rise of cybernetics and investigations of artificial intelligence (AI). While the project of FRT relied on an archive of mugshots to mine for biometric data, it also relied on cybernetic models of cognition being developed. A strange combination of archaic physiognomy and modern artificial intelligence developed to measure the distance between points located on the mouth, eyebrows, hairline, eyes, chin, and so on. By the 1990s breakthroughs in computing allowed the biometric data that had been relied on to expand to roughly one hundred points, along with color and thickness.

FRT marked its entry into the new millennium with a first major deployment at the Thirty-Fifth Super Bowl, on January 28, 2001—more than seven months before the September 11th attacks.[2] This deployment was secret. The next year, however, under the promise of protection from terrorism, the deployment was public and it proved a general failure; with the detection of a number of "deadbeat dads" being the catch, presumably the predominantly male audience felt themselves, not the terrorist other, to be the object of unnecessary surveillance. Nevertheless, for the developers of the systems, that year was a great leap forward because post-9/11 law enforcement opened its databases. This move provided an archive that could assist the project of facial recognition. In 2020 FRT was ubiquitous in the mass protests in the US in the cell phone and camera technologies of protesters and police.

I noted in chapter 9 that by 2005 neuroscientists Andrew Calder and Andrew Young published critiques of the prevailing cognitive model of FRT.[3] FRT in its cybernetic applications and FRT cognitive and neuroscientific research separated. That does not mean they have stayed separate. But looking away from the cognitive theory, we can see that FRT is now pervasive; cameras surveil public spaces across the globe, and our own private technologies are increasingly relying on FRT for security, even more so than passwords and fingerprints. In March 2017 US president Donald Trump issued an executive order requiring all international passengers to have their identity verified by biometric identification by 2021, including US citizens. That same year Indian prime minister Narendra Modi fostered the Digi Yatra scheme aiming to require biometric-based digital processing of passengers at all airports in India. In 2019 facial recognition kiosks began to appear to facilitate check-in at the Beijing and Chengdu Shuangliu international airports. By various accounts, these kiosks already have the ability to recognize the faces of international travelers. This capacity to register people even before they input information suggests a leap in technology and an unpublicized amalgamation of various databases. It is unclear if the facial information comes from international law enforcement agencies or (also) from public social media such as Facebook, WeChat, Weibo, and Instagram. Have Apple and Android allowed the fingerprints and face prints of our smartphones and other personal devices to be included?

On March 3, 1991, George Holliday used his home camera out his window to shoot a video of five Los Angeles Police Department officers beating Rodney King. In 2000 Samsung introduced its first camera phone, and in 2005 YouTube went live; by 2010 camera phones were being used to upload scenes of rebellion and conflict in revolutionary movements across the Arab world and beyond. In 2013 the hashtag BlackLivesMatter appeared on Twitter and took off in 2014 when the recordings of deaths of Eric Garner, Tamir Rice, and others at the hands of the police spread rapidly through social media venues. In 2020 Derek

180 · CHAPTER 10

Chauvin was recorded kneeling for eight minutes on the neck of George Floyd, which caused Floyd's death. The video went viral and unleashed protests across the US and throughout the world. Recording the violence of the state has become a tool to oppose that violence, mobilizing hundreds, thousands, and millions of protesters at various times.

In 1992 IBM introduced a quaintly clunky first-generation smartphone, and in 2007 Apple introduced the iPhone. The prominence of screens in everyday life took off. In 1999 the first broadcast of *Big Brother* took place. This first reality television production took as its name a reference to George Orwell's classic *1984*. It quickly spread, expanding to fifty-four franchises present on every continent. In 2016 the former star of a reality TV show was elected to the presidency of the United States. In 2002 the *Oxford English Dictionary* noted the first documented use of the word "selfie" and in 2005 the first documented use of "sexting." With Facebook, Instagram, and YouTube influencers, the rapid inversion of reality TV to televised reality was taking place.

In contemporary times the societies of control have become societies of alterity, determining our community through a responsibility to the face of the other.[4] To be sure, state facial recognition technology confronts the use of visual technology to give a face to state violence. Yet the actions of resistance arise in an imbalance of control over visual technologies. China's social media firewall and the ability of countries like Egypt and Turkey to shut down entirely and consistently censor social media points to precarity for those who want to dismantle the house of state authority with its own tools. The cell phone camera may stream scenes of police brutality, but the state apparatus can also identify protesters from the same phones. The very techne of facial recognition celebrated in the selfie flips quickly into the negative of anxiety-driven racial profiling. The never-ending war on terror, the battle against global forced migration—these frame the face as a threat, and our social responsibility is differentiated by the faces of our friends and our foes: like our people and dislike their enemies, swipe left for us and right for them, *gens envers et contre tous*. We bear responsibility only to the other we recognize and not to all the others we might perceive.

Breaking away from cybernetic models of AI and FRT, cognitive psychology was freed from the model of surveillance and obtained a renewed freedom to explore the face of the other with new potential but also new responsibilities. Nevertheless, the potential for cognitive and neuroscientific research to be deployed in the service of the state to offer new models of surveillance and control is realistic. The state has the ability to drive research with funding if not direct coercion. It is a caution for us to be wary. We must not allow our models of the brain to determine how we use the critical capacities of our minds. It is an opportunity for us to consider how we recognize the other and how we might do so in a more responsible way. Such is the topic of this chapter.

Film-Philosophy Emmanuel Levinas: The Face of the Other and Ethics

Alterity, the other, the face of the other, the face and the other—there is no other philosopher who has attended so specifically and fully to the term "alterity" than Emmanuel Levinas. From his death in 1995 and into the new millennium, we have witnessed a surge in the engagement with Levinas's philosophy on the other. Peter Atterton and Matthew Calarco note that in 2006, on the centenary of his birth, thirty-two international conferences in thirteen countries on five continents took place. They note that Levinas's ethics of the face have "served as inspiration for religious leaders, writers, dissidents, statesmen and artists the world over."[5] Indeed, as Simon Critchley noted, it was Levinas as humanist and ethicist that kept him in obscurity for the first part of his career and then won him great notoriety in the second. The end of the revolutionary aspirations of 1968 and the new social movements, and ultimately the end of the Cold War, opened up a space for ethics, once rejected as bourgeois and voluntaristic. By contrast, in 2006 the globalized world seemed in need of a new ethical ordering, for which Levinas seemed well suited.

One of these conferences was "Levinas and Cinema," which took place at the Institute of Germanic and Romance Studies in London in May 2006 and was collected as a special issue of *Film-Philosophy*. Sarah Cooper organized the conference to bring Levinas's work to bear on the questions of cinema, in part because his work challenged "questions of vision and the phenomenological world of appearance" but also because it never directly spoke about cinema and because it tended "towards the anti-ocular and revealing an iconoclastic approach to images."[6]

The majority of those papers delivered considered Levinas's ethics and the matters of cinema. They sought to apply Levinas to cinema, reading various films for the ethical questions they raised in the light of Levinas's philosophy. The project of thinking film and philosophy, film as philosophy was subordinated to applying philosophy to film. Here by contrast in this study the goal is indeed one of film philosophy and sets out to ask the question of visual alterity: How does the face of the other appear?

182 · CHAPTER 10

THE ETHICAL OTHER/THE ETHICS OF THE OTHER

My own thinking about visual alterity has of necessity been incited by Emmanuel Levinas, especially his critique of Hegelian alterity. For Levinas, knowledge, which rises out of reflection, begins with the sight of the face of the other. Alterity is this moment of recognition, of seeing the other. Alterity is visual, is in visibility. I become aware of my self in the face of the other. The being of a being may be for it-self, but self-conscious being is being for the other. Where Hegel developed the phenomenology of this consciousness, however, Levinas developed an ethics. Knowledge, then, which arises out of reflection through the other, should take up responsibility for the other; however, we know that does not (always) take place. It is likely that the response to the other, which makes us aware of the self, can lead to the opposite of responsibility: abjection, violence, murder.

Certainly Warhol's and Schroeter's films discussed in chapter 9 seem to represent the extremes of such propensities vis-à-vis the face of the other: love/ abjection, passion/destruction, artistic creation/death. Schroeter's traveling apprentice episode seems to be drawn directly from Levinas's considerations of the sojourner. Thinking of the precarious condition of someone on a journey, displaced, considering especially the condition of the Jews in fascist occupied Europe, Levinas observes that "a responsibility for my neighbor, for the other man, for the stranger *or* sojourner" does not arise from being itself; "nothing in the rigorously ontological order binds me—nothing in the order of the thing, of the something, of number or causality."[7] Not bound ontologically, *I* must want or will or fear or desire or commit or accept a responsibility to the other. Why take up a responsibility to the other? Why not kill him? Why offer protection? Why care? Why would the subject "want" to take up a responsibility to or for the other?

In the Face of the Senseless Death of the Other: Rabih Mroué

Although Levinas may not have devoted much attention to cinema, in "Signification and Sense" (1964) he turned to the eye and embodied vision. Perception is not just the eye and not just the senses. However, vision is a specific and primary form of perception. Vision, furthermore, is embodied from a position. Vision is not from the eye or from any eye but an eye. And Levinas understood vision actively. Vision is not a passive reception of the spectacle of the world. The bearers of vision are not spectators, as was modeled in classic apparatus theory: "The Spectator is the actor."[8] Subjects are actors, and vision orders the

The Ethics of Visual Alterity · 183

world in which they act. Levinas's active perception overcomes a problem posed by notions of unidirectional cognition; prior thought does not guide expression outward. The subject expresses in the world: "We are not subjects of the world and part of the world from two different points of view; in expression we are at the same time subject and part."[9] Thought, perception, expression—these are not prior or outside but part of the world. Signification is the totality of being.

Levinas repeatedly invokes the face of the other, this specific moment of vision and perception. He invokes "the face of the Other" as *the* ethical relation. In the face of the other, face-to-face with others, the *I* "loses its sovereign coincidence with self."[10] The other is a particular form of engagement, enactment, or expression. He repeatedly couples the subject to the other through desire for the other and notes that we desire the other because the other is a bounty of resources. *I* experiences those resources in relation to the other. *I* is more because of the others. And because all the others are unique individual resources, each other offers *I* an epiphany. The diversity of others makes being "scintillate" with "inexhaustible wealth."[11]

Rabih Mroué's *The Pixelated Revolution* (2012) challenges this proposition. The project appeared at Documenta 13 as a performance lecture and installation the centerpiece of which was an eighty-three-second YouTube video titled by Mroué "Double Shooting." The title refers to the fact that the man doing the recording—that is, the shooting—was recording the shooter in the moment where he himself is about to be shot, not by a video camera but by a gun. This confrontation with the murderous other was recorded with almost alarming frequency as the nonviolent protests that overthrew the government in Tunisia and Egypt spread further and met with increasing state repressive force. Exposed to murderous violence, the protests in Libya and Syria flipped into armed struggle as the "sides" received weapons from outside sources. The conflict escalated as the combatants turned into proxies for competing geopolitical struggles between the US/EU, Russia, Iran, Al Qaeda, and eventually ISIS.

Those protests and the battles were recorded and uploaded to YouTube as streaming videos intended as documents of resistance and rebellion. What started as a form of encouragement to others to join the uprisings against corrupt dictatorial systems quickly turned into testimonies of the violent oppression that those systems undertook on their populace. And in turn the videos themselves became evidence of violence that spread on all sides. YouTube, the internet, and the nightly news were flooded with moving-image documentation of carnage and destruction. The faces of various actors and the faces of repeated deaths streamed on the web. A figure runs away from a tank attack or assault weapons fire, only to fall as a result of shrapnel or a bullet. The cell phone lands

184 · CHAPTER 10

on the ground and remains still. A friend, family member, or comrade finds the cell phone and then, to honor the dead person, uploads the moving images.

Mroué's installation contained a wall with seven blown-up pixelated images of murderers caught in the moment before they shot the holders of the camera phones. This is a face-to-face event in which ethics are gone, the responsibility to the other does not exist, and, by contrast, the drive to annihilate is the quest of an all-consuming I. The act of shooting, the video itself, was replicated in seven flipbooks in which the spectator is returned to the early days of the moving image, the pre-cinematic era. They linked, however, to the YouTube video, drawing a long arch to the present expanded cinema era. The toy that once fit in the pocket connects to the recording device that again fits in the pocket, the mobility of the flipbook images now alluding directly to the cyber ubiquity of YouTube. On a further wall an eighty-three-second YouTube video plays of a man being shot, in the act of falling. The man, holding his cell phone recording potentially his own killer, being himself now recorded by the other, falls to the ground. He then leaps back up as the video rewinds in a loop, back and forth, up and down. The first time Georges Méliès deployed this strategy, it was comedy; here it is beyond tragedy, beyond horror. This installation is a confrontation with a condition of representation, indexicality, visual technology, real lives, and bodies that keep piling up. It overwhelms understanding and reason.

The *I* here. Is it the eye of the recording subject about to be killed, robbed of existence?

Mroué inserts himself in this condition. It is he who takes up a responsibility to the other. He explains this project arising as a result of citizens becoming the only journalists available.[12] The state apparatus prevents fact-based reporting, replacing it with positive propaganda. Foreign journalists are controlled or not in the region. And locals with the tools of social media and low-grade technology move in. What they report, what they show, however, is indeed confusing. In the absence of "official" reporters, Mroué saw it as his duty, as the duty of the artist, to take up the condition of the other, to speak about, to re-present the conditions. He does so with a certain resigned futility: "Revolution cannot be done with images," he observes.[13] If in the past it was possible to take the radio or television station to control the message of the state, now the condition of the internet is too diffuse. It creates a different condition, a flood of images, a sea of faces.

In this vein, Katarzyna Ruchel-Stockmans focuses her analysis of Mroué's work on the recording subject and sets their videos in the contemporary condition of a medial production of self and not news reporting:

One of the most significant results of this new situation is the way image production steers the comportment of people involved in the events. Ordinary participants become actors performing certain roles, while the events themselves are being seen as cinematic. This increased theatricality of mass protests can thus be seen as an instance of blurring the lines between video and photography on the one hand and performance, theatre and cinema on the other.[14]

Ruchel-Stockmans ignores that there is another component to the project. There is another *I* at play in these films and the project. It is the *I* of the killer. The wall of the installation is covered with the seven images of the killers and gives the entire installation its name. The flipbooks show them in action. Hegelian alterity described a struggle of consciousness with an other, feeling this consciousness to be robbing the self of its universality, its egotistical sense of being all and everything. In confrontation with the other, it realizes its limits, experiences its self, and becomes suddenly not everything but just some one. The combatants, struggling at this point in Syria against the repressive state apparatus, confronted an other with this all-consuming claim. The troops, the thugs, the agents of the state allowed for no other. Their claim to a universality was based on wiping their other out of existence.

Mroué's project as a response to this flood of images is indeed tenuous. It is perhaps in the confrontation with this *I*, the violent *I*, that the ethical response of Mroué is strongest.

THE FLOOD OF IMAGES AND THE FACELESS OTHER: BIRGIT HEIN

At first glance Birgit Hein's *Abstrakter Film* (*Abstract Film*) (2013) is the radical opposite to Mroué's project and to Levinas's philosophy. The face does not appear. It is an abstract film. Like *The Pixelated Revolution*, it is based on cell phone recordings from the Arab Spring uprisings but draws on the images of both Libya and Syria. Having been uploaded by a friend, the world is able to repeatedly see people in the act of recording their own deaths, unaware that they are about to be overcome by the violence they are filming. If they filmed as a last gesture against the violence that was about to overwhelm them, then, sadly, their documentation on the web, the spectacle that they provided, the fascination that they met, rather than lead to a subsiding of violence, a return to an "ethical" relation, seems to have only contributed to the violence. The two sides, state versus protesters, collapsed into factionalism and sectarianism. Hein, born in the last years of World War II, a child of war, was fascinated, even overwhelmed, by this flood of images of war and sat obsessively viewing the loss of life, feeling helpless.

Hein noticed in these films that a great portion of the image was "abstract." The cell phone cameras were not able to contend with the speed of movement. In the hand, the cell phone cameras were an extension of the body, an embodied camera. In the movement of the hand, the cell phone cameras repeat the motions of the embodied eye. They move to pursue; they converge on or diverge from objects and people. What is missing is the vestibulo-ocular movements that stabilize the eyes relative to the external world. While vision is constantly compensating for head movements, here the camera is in no position to compensate for hand and arm movements. Frequently the hand raises the cell phone to observe in place of the eye; frequently the cell phone swings in the rhythm of the arm as the holder runs away from danger. During these moments of rapid movement, the images pixilate into abstraction. They act as the saccadic eye movement, the rapid eye movements that abruptly change the point of focus. It is a *ballistic movement*: the flailing hand holding the cell phone. During that moment there is no actual visual recognition.

The cell phone images do not have the brain to mask the saccades, so the abstract moments are replaced in the activity of perception by some form of cognitive continuity. Thus for long periods the cell phone videos are screens of unrecognizable color. Hein noted these as accomplishing the abstraction that was the aspiration of much of the structural film movement, the movement that was denounced by the political activist movements of the '60s as apolitical, lacking in realism, lacking in message. *Abstrakter Film* excerpts the abstract moments of numerous videos and strings them together into an eight-minute and thirty-second collage of image and sound. Where the structural films were frequently silent, Hein retained the soundtracks here. The opening, a silent fade in from white with the title of the film, breaks away quickly to a cacophony. Screaming, gunshots, yelling in Arabic, and breathing overlay a screen of reds, blues, colors that belong to the hands and faces and colors that belong to the street and hiding places, strobing light. It is not until the second clip that the camera comes to a momentary stillness as the bearer of the cell phone is shot, collapses, recording the ground, a last kick of his leg. The eyes of the viewer have little opportunity for respite. The shots continue.

The abstraction is part of the recording. The excerption, however, does not extract the images from reality. The soundtrack makes it clear that these are shots of life and death. Hein's excerptions, however, refuse to take sides. The uploaded images themselves frequently lacked clarification or were presented as scenes of martyrdom, political pathos serving to make sense of the images, to give meaning to the death of the comrade. These images were also frequently drawn into the twenty-four-hour news cycle to display carnage and loss of human life to viewers in distant locations. They were deployed in the flood of news items to raise a sense of pity or alarm or fear. They bolstered a sense that "they are always fighting over there" or "we need to do something to stop them." They were often incorporated into arguments about intervention, pro or con.

The Ethics of Visual Alterity · 187

Hein's excerption resists this sense making while at the same time offering abstract images that have a more profound connection to the reality of life and death. A focus on the pixelated image moves us into the fog of war, not to make sense of war but to display its cognitive senselessness. The moment of the real experience captured in pulsating lights conflicts with the rationales that placed bodies in harm's way, that exposed individuals to conditions that would lead to their deaths, countless times—literally so many uncounted times.

Levinas emphasized that the face of the other is not the same as the physical face, an important distinction we want to consider. The relationship to the other does not derive from a mundane relation to the physiognomy. Likewise, Hein's film suggests that the relation to the other need not rely on the face. The condition of a body in flight, itself facing death, confronts us with basic liminal human experiences. We sense emotions, but we are not given the opportunity to have sympathy, to empathize. Levinas suggested that the face of the other is the key to the ethical relationship between humans. The lack of faces in Hein's abstract film suggests that the lack of face, the facelessness of others, is itself a call to ethics. In the middle of the desensitizing stream of images, the abstract sequences open up a new possibility of reflecting on ethics. The conditions of violence do not foreclose ethics, but they do make it clear that the possibility of ethical behavior is constituted by more than a voluntarism deriving from the face-to-face relationship to the other.

The Limits of Levinasian Ethics: The Radically Alterior

EROS AND ENSLAVEMENT

Setting Mroué's and Hein's moving-image projects as philosophical retorts to Levinas makes clear that this chapter is not based on an easy appreciation of Levinas's ethical alterity. It is not an exegesis of Levinas. Visual alterity does not align easily with ethical alterity; indeed visual alterity—the process of differing and differentiating—while part of the human gaze is also part of the human power to persecute, harass, afflict, repress, coerce, extort, torment, torture, or abuse. It is also thus part of the human power to do the opposite: to free, welcome, support, aid, assist, encourage, comfort, cheer, grant, or delight. But is Levinas the right place to consider an ethics of alterity? Certainly an uncritical application of Levinasian ethics would be ill placed. Unfortunately, Simon Critchley, one of the foremost scholars of Levinas, notes that in the explosion of interest in Levinas, "much of the work on Levinas tends to confine itself to exegesis, commentary, comparison with other thinkers, and, at worst, homage."[15] Critchley admonishes us to be critical, and indeed I take up Levinas here based on a radical skepticism toward the ethical turn, which his work represents and effects.

188 · CHAPTER 10

Levinas rejected the intersubjective quasi-utilitarian relationship that Hegel considered in his discussion of lord and bondsman and instead sought to reconceptualize alterity as a form of humanistic mystery. He took up a proposition that being-for-the-other is better than being-for-itself. The relation to the other, the difference of the other, establishes a relationship, which Levinas suggests can be considered as voluptuous, as a promise of fullness, as "eros."[16]

Right from the start I will say that while the problem of enslavement is a significant insight, it is (1) based on a reading that does not go beyond the few pages of the lord and bondsman passage. (2) Its arrival at a proposition of eros as distinct from Hegel does not contend with Hegel's turn to bourgeois marriage as the reconciliation of the unhappy consciousness.[17] (3) It replaces a material determining system—for example, the economic conditions of lordship and bondage—with an ethics of humanistic *mystery*: "The relationship with the other is a relationship with a mystery."[18] (4) This ethics appears as voluntaristic: thou shalt but likely you won't. Nevertheless, with eros Levinas seeks a rationale that can function equivalent to Hegel's proposition of self-preservation (one preserves the other in order to have an awareness of self). Eros, however, is a failed basis for alterity. I am thrown into a world in which I am other to countless other selves and I am not attracted to all others. My relationship to all others is not dominated by the term "eros," but in their multiplicity they generate an equivalent multiplicity of desires and repulsions, needs and disdains, reliances and indifferences. (5) And as much as Levinas speaks of the relationship to the other, the individuals' experiences of alterity are based not on a relationship to the other but to some other. We exist in the world surrounded not by the other abstracted but with others in conditions that we have not freely chosen. (6) Finally, Levinas's answer to his critique of Hegel itself arrives at a condition of enslavement. An approach that reduces the complexity of the relationships of the individual to all others, an approach that considers a singular relationship of an *I* to the other, in turn risks itself "enslaving" all the others. In spite of all our legal histories, our catalogs of manners, our archives of human interactions, each relationship of self and other is a specific relationship. Each relationship of alterity exists within a here and now. There is never an interaction with the other from which we can abstract a universal ethics; that universal ethics demands of all others that they behave as the same. I begin my approach to Levinas's ethics of alterity with a deep critical skepticism.

ANDROCENTRISM

I am not alone. While celebrated by many, Levinas has also been the object of very thorough criticisms. The philosopher of the ethics of the other proves to deploy essentializing sex-gender paradigms. In *Totality and Infinity* the feminine

The Ethics of Visual Alterity • 189

other appears as foundation to heterosexist essentialism. The relationship of eros is not one of desire to the other as such; it is the "essential" desire of "the man" to "the woman." In *Totality and Infinity* the feminine is described variously with all the same worn paradigms of essentialism the Greeks wove, the Enlightenment and the Romantics stitched up, and Freud mended. She is virginal, an enigma, an animal, indecent and wanton, an equivocator, and loved by a male.[19] While many have treated these passages as marginal and insubstantial, numerous feminist critics have taken exception, putting them into the center of Levinas's project.[20]

Critchley identifies this as the problem of androcentrism in Levinas.[21] And Luce Irigaray in particular has engaged in extensive critiques of Levinas's engendering alterity. In her essay "What Other Are We Talking About?" she challenges the presumptions of universalism that Levinas asserts. She considers gender difference and Levinas's treatment/degradation of femininity as a pre-ethical difference. In doing so, she seeks to show how his discussion of the other and the self are by no means universal but rather instilled with a monologic that assimilates the others of the world. Ultimately, she charges, Levinas's ethics subsumes the difference of other cultures through integration into a single subject, representing a norm. Irigaray counters understanding alterity as a fundamental and incommensurate difference. She critiques Levinas *and* Hegel for positing alterity as the essence of the other, an alienation from the subject/me, observing how this approach necessarily encloses the other in a space defined by me. The other as "not I" entraps the other in my egocentrism. The feminine other is bound to a masculine me. Irigaray's critique suggests that it is insufficient to expand the Levinasian subject/other relationship to "include" women. Her critique of Hegel's and Levinas's notion of freedom of the other reveals it not to be freedom as such but freedom in assimilation to unity, the extension to the other of a freedom in the irreducibility to my world—accepting the freedom of the other as freedom not to be in my world. The other is other and therefore *not* reducible to an ethical relationship.

EUROCENTRISM

Other scholars have noted how in different passages Levinas has proven quite prepared to advocate for a Eurocentric world order. He repeated in his interviews an observation on Europe using similar phrasing in each. Perhaps most illustrative of the position was this: "I always say—but under my breath—that the Bible and the Greeks present the only serious issues in human life: everything else is dancing. . . . There is no racism intended."[22] Numerous critics have approached this statement as likewise opening up a point of fundamental critique.

190 · CHAPTER 10

The offhand gesture of "there is no racism intended" is recognized as precisely the indication of a fundamental and unreflected racism in his work.[23] It rings in the sentence like the telling phrase "some of my best friends are. . . ." If there was no racism intended, why is there a need to say it? Robert Eaglestone sees "these spoken comments [as] clearly dismiss[ing] all culture outside the European-ized Hellenism/Hebraism axis."[24] He identifies the statement as embedded in colonial racist analytic paradigms. Yet he goes on in his analysis to find a form of usefulness that redeems Levinas. He reads Levinas "in spite of." Certainly, when one inhabits a racist, heterosexist, Eurocentric world, this practice of reading "in spite of" is common, even an uncomfortable necessity. We cannot think radically outside the world we inhabit. Our thought must pass through a terrain of lega-cies and accretions to arrive at new shores. Yet Fred Moten, who understands the invocation of dance to be in line with Hegel's dismissal of Africa as a continent without history or culture, counters precisely with the potential of dance. Moten, a scholar of performance and himself a poet, contends about Levinas's dismissal of the rest as dance that this statement not only stands in for a dismissal of an entire continent but also as a failure to recognize dance as offering a profundity of ways to experience/overcome alterity. The inter- and intra-subjective potentials of dance themselves offer a radical alternative to the foundations of Levinas's ethics of othering. And indeed this is the key point: Levinas's ethics of the other is itself an ethics of othering, othering under the term "ethics."

Perhaps most profound in Levinas's ethics was his willingness to set a limit to the infinite responsibility of the face-to-face. While he could write in 1984 of a "responsibility for others (that) therefore comes to be for man the mean-ing of his own self-identity," two years earlier he had made it clear that this was not a universal responsibility for all men and women toward all people.[25] On September 28, 1982, Levinas participated in a public debate with Alain Finkielkraut lead by Shlomo Malka, broadcast on French radio. The conversa-tion was one among leading French Jewish humanist intellectuals who were themselves central figures in the ethical turn in philosophy. The debate was in response to the Israel Defence Forces (IDF) allowing Lebanese Phalangists to enter into the Palestinian refugee camps of Sabra and Shatila. Justifying the presence of the IDF as a protective force in the Lebanese Civil War, Ariel Sha-ron, the leader of the IDF, allowed the massacre to take place over two days, during which anywhere between four hundred and thirty-six hundred people were killed by the Phalangist militias. An international outcry arose. Sharon would be tried in Israel and removed from his post, convicted by Israeli courts as a war criminal. Shortly after this event, Malka drew Levinas and Finkielkraut together for the interview.

The Ethics of Visual Alterity · 191

Asked by Malka to address Israel's responsibility in the massacre, Finkielkraut saw it as his responsibility to address the war crime, not in order to condemn the project of Israel but in order to improve the promise of the real existing state. Like Hannah Arendt and many other Jewish intellectuals, Finkielkraut viewed Israel as a universalizing project of modern statehood. Levinas, by contrast, turned to notions of closed groups, kin, family, and people out of his commitment to a majority Jewish state and an understanding of the Zionist project to protect the Jewish people. Taking up his long-standing theme of the neighbor, Levinas suggested "my people and my kin are still my neighbors."[26] Such propositions surprised many who were engaged with what was understood to be the universalism of his ethical thought. The following exchange took place between Malka and Levinas:

> S. M.: Emmanuel Levinas, you are the philosopher of the "other." Isn't history, isn't politics the very site of the encounter with the "other," and for the Israeli, isn't the "other" above all the Palestinian?
>
> E. L.: My definition of the other is completely different. The other is the neighbor, who is not necessarily kin, but who can be. And in that sense, if you're for the other, you're for the neighbor. But if your neighbor attacks another neighbor or treats him unjustly, what can you do? Then alterity takes on another character; in alterity we can find an enemy, or at least then we are faced with the problem of knowing who is right and who is wrong, who is just and who is unjust. There are people who are wrong.[27]

Let us be clear in this exchange: Malka has posed a question that presents two peoples in a relationship of alterity—the Palestinian as other to the Israeli. Levinas's response is to use the word *gens*, people generally, humans, and not *peuple*, a people as a genus of humanity—for example, the Jewish people. This gesture seems to refuse Malka's essentializing; nevertheless, Levinas poses this question of a neighbor attacking a neighbor in response to being asked about Sabra and Shatila. And with that he inverts the condition of who was attacked, who was massacred.

"There are people [gens] who are wrong [tort]." What does it mean to identify the people of the refugee camps of Sabra and Shatila as "wrong"? As juridically wrong? What does it mean to discount their claims to justice, in effect to resist the inquiry that the state of Israel would eventually conduct, and to discount those people who were massacred, reducing them to an essentialist state, a status of *being* wrong? Are they wrong because of their *being* Palestinian? What does this say about Levinasian ethics? His ability to discount people as such requires a radical critique of Levinas's project.

192 · CHAPTER 10

RADICALIZING ETHICS VERSUS RADICAL ALTERITY

Judith Butler unleashed a sizable debate when in a critique of Levinas she turned to this discussion specifically.[28] She observes a distinction in Levinas's work between the people of the face-to-face relationship and what she then describes as the faceless. The term "faceless," which seems attributed to Levinas, likely resulted from a bad reading, a misremembering of the quote, at the least poor editing in the choice of punctuation. Her critics took this point up frequently and vehemently, using it to dismiss her entire argument without having to engage it. The reason Butler made the distinction between the face and the faceless is that it allows her to separate out a "good" Levinas, concerned with the face as key to the ethical relationship to the other, and a "bad" Levinas, for whom politics, the negotiations of ethics in the real world, was a problem. Butler's critique of Levinas follows an analysis: if the face is key to the ethical imperative "thou shalt not kill," then the enemy one can kill must have no face. Pointing to how Levinas identified the Palestinians as enemy, she contends that they are faceless, a further category she inserts into Levinas's work, a gesture toward the project of radicalizing Levinas. Butler contra Levinas thus seeks to return their face to the Palestinians with a goal of preserving Levinas's ethics, bringing them into politics in a move that Levinas himself eschewed. As discussed above, the physiognomy of the other is not the same as the other's face, but the recognition of the other as human, evoking our ethical-political engagement—what does that require of the face?

I am actually concerned with the project of radicalizing Levinas. It aims to preserve his philosophy into a different practice, fundamentally an act of Hegelian *Aufhebung*, with its double meaning of preservation and abolition. Why do we need to preserve Levinas's ethics? What, in the face of these "problems," necessitates us to pick and choose among his good passages, excluding those we do not like? The interview should give us cause to reflect thoroughly on the project, on the proposition of ethics as such. Some have suggested that this is a minor statement in a minor interview and should not be used to judge his entire oeuvre. However, Levinas's is not a statement at the beginning of his career but at the end, and it certainly allows us to trace a line of thought, a trajectory in his thinking. On a basic level we can ask, What does it mean that a Holocaust survivor and a philosopher of the profundity of human responsibility in the aftermath of the Shoah, an ethicist of the self and other, should deploy simplistic distinctions of right and wrong? What does it mean that he does so in order to justify a massacre?

Remember that the reason the discussion took place was the massacre of Sabra and Shatila and not a general discussion of the confrontation between

Israel and the Palestine Liberation Organization (PLO). The other is distinguished into others who are neighbors and enemies, who are right and wrong. This observation is not made about the members of armed forces, about people in the PLO's Fatah. Hamas and Hezbollah did not yet exist, so he could not have been talking about people in belligerent groups. Rather, it was made in confrontation with the bodies of hundreds if not thousands of refugees, humanity's most vulnerable. The people in the camps of Sabra and Shatila were not people attacking but fleeing, displaced from Palestine and then displaced again in the Lebanese Civil War. These were precisely the individuals who should call out the most profound of ethical commitments, if there are such things. And instead, the massacred are discussed with a blanket term, "enemy," and described as wrong. Levinas observes the possibility of identifying an entire people, gens, as enemy. The philosopher of the Holocaust should have known that such gestures have a history, a long history that goes back through the Holocaust, colonialism, into the wars of classical antiquity. The advocate of Hellenism/Hebraism/Europeanism should know the long history of words like "barbarism" and "annihilation."

Butler's response? To think about "the face of the enemy," to return the face to the Palestinians seems to follow this error. Butler slips into her own effacement of the Palestinian. The Palestinians as enemy, as people who have been living for more than half a century under a condition of enmity, Butler's own designation risks effacing the complexity of the conditions in which people live in Israel/Palestine. It risks making the refugees in Sabra and Shatila stand in for all Palestinians. As much as Levinas should stand in for all Israelis, the residents of Sabra and Shatila should not be the face of a Palestinian gens. It risks a simple inversion of Levinas's own ethics, turning Palestinians into the Palestinian: survivor, refugee, victim of war, occupation, apartheid, innocent, *right*. The solution Butler seeks to the conflict is certainly not to be found in *radical alterity*.

"Then alterity takes on another character." How are we to understand this statement? It seems to point to two aspects or two kinds of alterity. How are we to understand the other possible character of alterity? Is there the other and the "really" other, the alterior and the "very, very" alterior? In Levinas's statement and in Butler's response a radical alterity appears. There is the alterity of the other neighbor who is right and just, who behaves as potential kin. And then there is a radically alterior other, who is wrong, unjust. The paradigm of radical alterity that we find in Levinas and that adheres to Butler's argument risks a radical othering, the radical alterior: *an other who is not object to my subject but is abject to my being*. What makes this distinction? Is it in the *being* of the

194 · CHAPTER 10

Palestinian refugee? If they are not located in the actual ways that people are treated, where are the ethical criteria that define just and unjust? In the case of Sabra and Shatila, what are those criteria that place the massacred into the condition of wrong? Does a distinction here of right and wrong serve to justify the massacre? And does it accomplish anything to radicalize Levinas by an inversion that constructs Israel and Israelis as the radical alterior?

IDENTITY POLITICS VERSUS ALTERITY POLITICS

I am not interested in the project of radicalizing Levinas. I am interested in the project of radicalizing alterity. I agree with Diane Perpich that there is much to be gained in a move from identity politics to alterity politics.[29] There is no need to retain a debt to Levinas or any other philosopher as such; rather, the point of critique is to overcome the limitations of human thought. I am living in a moment when the question of refugees is more pressing than at any other time in recorded human history. More people are fleeing war and destruction than at any other time. In Europe one speaks of the "refugee crisis" and means with that phrase the crisis wrought upon Europe by the influx of so many desperate people seeking refuge. The crisis is not in the places of origin, the war, bloodshed, impoverishment, and material and climatic devastation that sets them out on dangerous roads where they may as well meet their death. In the phrase "refugee crisis" these people do not arrive as enrichments, possibilities, humans filled with resources and individual potentials. They arrive marked as the crisis themselves. And in Germany, where I sit at the moment, weapons exports are at an all-time high. The media reports constantly on politicians and citizens who wonder about how to end the "crisis," and I have yet to see a debate in which a discussion of war profiteering as a benefit to the German export-based economy comes up. Rather the current discussion focuses on the position of NATO in the region and impact on the German armaments industry—a very lucrative responsibility. Those who are here are innocents. Those who come are in crisis. In alterity perhaps we are indeed faced with the question of who is just and who is unjust. Perhaps when we confront the Nazi, the slaveholder, the racist, the anti-Semite, the point of alterity is that it calls us out to consider justice and injustice, an ethics of response. Perhaps alterity requires us to face ourselves. Indeed, the image in the mirror is alterior. But is not the goal of the recognition of the face in the mirror somehow an attempt to reconcile with the other? Is not the goal of the ethics of alterity an overcoming of the irreconcilable differences? Is not a truly radical response to the diversity of us versus them, the overcoming of the difference, finding the root of humanity that unites in difference. I am not suggesting that *tout comprendre c'est tout pardoner*. Rather, I am suggesting that our ethics moves to a higher order when we overcome an unjust diremption, when we overcome racism, anti-Semitism, slavery, misogyny, exploitation, coercion, extortion, torture, murder, war. The other is a call to be just in our human relations. To insist on othering and refuse a responsibility to reconcile difference is a refusal to seek universal justice. What might it mean to suggest that in alterity I is unjust?

Facing Effacement

What happens when the other is actually faceless? I ask this question pointedly of Levinas and of Butler. Again, the face is not the same as the physical visage. What does it mean when the visage is absent? Do we have a better ethical world because we can see the face of the other suffering twenty-four hours a day on CNN, N-TV, or Fox? What does it do for ethics when cognitively abstract images provide a more direct compelling relation to the human tragedies that challenge our thinking of our "proper" role in the world? What does it mean when we confront images of the other that seem to show behaviors that elude our own ethical order: thou shalt not kill, thou shalt give shelter to the homeless and comfort those in distress?

Horizon across mid-screen. *Havarie* (Scheffner 2016). Courtesy of Philip Scheffner, Pong Film GmbH

What happens when the other does not behave as expected, arrives at our doorstep legally wrong? What happens when the others are faceless because we refuse to recognize their arrival as belonging to our system of justice?

Philip Scheffner's *Havarie* (2016) begins with coordinates, a location in the Mediterranean between Algeria and Spain. In what follows, we see a short YouTube clip of three minutes and thirty-six seconds created by Terry Diamond and uploaded in September 2012. Traveling on the cruise ship *Adventure of the Seas*, he recorded a meeting on high seas between his ship and a rubber raft filled with thirteen people trying to make a crossing. For ninety minutes the boat waited in the proximity of the raft until a rescue craft could arrive. This event took place before the wars in Syria, Iraq, Kurdistan, Afghanistan, Libya, and other nearby countries sent wave after wave of people toward the borders of the EU looking for a place of refuge. Scheffner had set out to make a documentary about the refugee "crisis." He pursued in documentary fashion the story behind the meeting on high seas. He retrieved the recording of the ship-to-shore and ship-to-ship radio conversation. In the absence of being able to track down the people on the raft, he interviewed other people who had made the crossing as well as the smugglers who set them out on the dangerous voyage. He recorded

Horizon lost to water filling fore and background. *Havarie* (Scheffner 2016). Courtesy of Philip Scheffner, Pong Film GmbH

The Ethics of Visual Alterity • 197

officers of the cruise ship and of a container ship also in the waters. He set out to trace the *Fluchtlinien*, the lines of flight, which the *Flüchtlinge*, the *Geflüchteten*, the refugees, those who fled, travel in a complex documentary archive of images and sounds.

However, when confronted with the "refugee crisis," the flood of images of refugees passing into Greece and through the Balkans, Scheffner decided to undertake a radical transformation of the project. Rather than create a film that edits the recorded images into an informational documentary, he stretched the original short clip out to ninety-three minutes, the time from its first sighting until the boat was rescued. In the original at its normal speed, the occupants of the raft are barely recognizable. We can see a small dot, figures on the water, but not individual faces. The process of slowing the film down, slowing down a moving-image clip already at low-grade YouTube resolution, leads to images that are abstracted.

For ninety-three minutes the spectator watches a dot on the horizon, a zoom into it, its motion on the waves, as it disappears behind the waves, reappears, doubles into afterimages, pixelates, in a fore-, mid-, and background of constantly kaleidoscoping hues of blues and whites. At the end of the three-minute clip, Terry Diamond panned left to the boat. The pan in the film has a strange effect in that the pan is not easily noticeable, and hence the dot of the raft seems simply lost from the frame for a significant portion of the film. The frame is filled only with water, leaving a sense of questioning to arise: what has happened to the boat? But then when the pan actually meets the *Adventure of the Seas*, a sudden localization takes place. Up to then the camera's position was abstract, the omniscient narrative position, located with the unreflected observing eye of god. But as the boat comes into frame, suddenly the camera is located, on a boat, in the hand of a passenger. And suddenly that frame showing passengers leaning over the railing and pointing becomes a self-reflexive image, showing the self as an observer of the other. The soundscape in the abstraction becomes all the more important. The radio contact takes place in real time, and it thus comes to enframe the interviews that are situated in time between the broadcasts. The film takes on something of the quality of a radio broadcast.

Havarie pursues an aesthetic principle somewhere between Harun Farocki's *Nicht löschbares Feuer* (*Inextinguishable Fire*) (1969) and Derek Jarman's *Blue* (1993). Farocki's agitprop film began its investigation of napalm with the question of how to reach the spectator:

> How can we show you the deployment of napalm and the nature of the burns it causes? If we show you pictures of the injuries inflicted by napalm, you will just

Boat at a distance and its flicker from next frame. *Havarie* (Scheffner 2016). Courtesy of Philip Scheffner, Pong Film GmbH

close your eyes. At first you will close your eyes before the pictures, then you will close your eyes before the memory of the pictures, and then you will close your eyes before the realities the pictures represent.

Farocki's question certainly motivated the refusal of the easy documentary image and drew him into experiments with the image. Where Farocki answered this question with a form of Brechtian *Lehrstück*, Scheffner takes up Jarman's strategy of unleashing a film in our heads. It does not give us an image; it does not provide a face. It does give voice to actors in a drama on the high seas. But this strategy forecloses an easy relationship to the other. This film is deeply about a relationship to the other. We can suggest that the pan to the boat ultimately sets up a relationship between the inhabitants of the Northern and Southern Mediterranean rim, between Africa and Europe. Yet for most of the film it is an encounter on the high seas, in a blue frame without easy perspective or position.

For Levinas, the face is, as noted earlier, not the same as the physical visage; rather, the face is the site of the ethical relationship. Scheffner refused to give a face to the people on the raft. In this way, he does not seek to make sense of

The Ethics of Visual Alterity • 199

the people, make them sensible, nor add faces to the already overflowing media stream of migrant faces.

The people on the raft, the black dot in the water, remain unnamed, unidentified. Yet they are not just any other nor the other. The content of the film is about naming, identifying, and narrating the lives of the people involved in this traffic across the waters. Scheffner did track down some of the people on the raft, but no one wanted to be filmed. Yet in those contacts his research opened up contact with people who do and did make the crossings, retrieve stranded refugees from the waters, provide the means of transport, and so on. They are specific people who stand in for others. The lack of visuals actually enhances the sense that they are some other, any others. By deciding not to show those people, he refused to offer us images that stand in for those people on the boat. In viewing we are left on rocky blue seas.

Given that Levinas transformed the matter of alterity into a question of ethics, we can ask, What of ethics in *Havarie*? I suggest that the film does not make an ethical claim on its other, or at least it seeks to avoid the traps that Irigaray, Moten, and Critchley pointed to in Levinas's work where the ethical relationship hides an imposition of a juridical order. The concern of an ethical relationship to the people in the raft derives from a rejection of the juridical order that first transforms them into illegals, people *sans papiers*. If we were to accept that juridical state as just, ethics would pose the question of how to be hospitable to those we have determined to be illegal. In the film, however, the blue screen of the project "shows" this crossing as a crossing of orders. It does not try to integrate the people in the raft into an identity of refugee, migrant, *sans papiers*, or any other such determination of status. In the film they just are on the raft. There is something of a clash of orders played out in the film: the ethical order of the people making the crossing, the ethical order of the cruise ship, and the juridical order of the EU that marks the border and places them in a state of illegality for their actions. We hear motivations, we hear responses, but we do not hear about solutions. We hear about the complex of an encounter without that encounter being framed by voices of authority or explanation. The spectator is not given a privileged position of knowledge, nor are the people undertaking the crossing. The people making the crossing are not imbued with a power to point to our unjust behaviors, nor are they impoverished by the benevolent sympathy of a European subject wanting to help.

The cruise ship is filled with people in a privileged position of watching. The pan reveals the privilege of that ability to spectate. At the premier of the film Scheffner was quick to correct negative audience perceptions of the ship. The ship remains in the waters close to hand until the rescue boat arrives. The ship is not equipped for a rescue at sea. The ship's proximity could have caused the raft to capsize, so its distance is a matter of reasonable safety. The "rescue," which we never see, is a rescue into an order that is different from the life on the cruise ship. Nevertheless, the cruise ship and the cargo ship remained in the area, insisting on a relationship to the raft. The pan may be understood as forcing a face-to-face confrontation but not with the other, rather with the spectator as spectating self. In the image of the passengers leaning over the railing, I sees its self.

But again, the film does not enforce one ethical order over the other, one ethical order onto the other. And the film suggests that in a world of desensitization, facelessness and lack of sensibility should not be treated as equivalent to a lack of intelligibility. It does position the other as incommensurate. There is not a conversation with each other. There is not an explicit challenge to the juridical order that divides the Southern and Northern Mediterranean into Africa and Europe, into North African Arab states contra the EU. The film does not overcome effacement; it shows it: radical visual alterity as monstration of the faceless.

Conclusion

Our brains may not have evolved to watch movies, but our minds have evolved because of what we watch, how we see. Our moving images, our cinemas, our screens have transformed our cognitive capacities. Our cognitive capacities may not have evolved in the sense of improved, but they have changed. Our evolution is not progress in the modernist sense, but it is a sign of our ability to contend with the new around us. Seeing differently does not mean we see better. The rapid inversion of reality TV to televised reality is certainly not without real negative consequences. Nevertheless, in a world where possibilities are ever changing, we need the new seeing.

We have left behind an era of identity and have entered into an era of alterity. We are pulled between common global interests and alterior communities. A sense that the other is incommensurate with my self, a sense that the truth of the other is false, fake, drives a division, a separation that is not necessary and is certainly dangerous. Where nation-states once brought together oppositional parties into a compromise for "the good cause," that attentiveness to universal interests is gone. If in the last instance nationalism once enforced identity on the citizenry, states now divide into opposing camps without compromise in sight. This descent of polities into communities of radical others is a first step toward civil war. When we believe in our incommensurability with the other, when we refuse to hear and we impose on the other a condition of incommunicability, then our condition of alterity sees the other as wrong, unjust. When

202 · *Conclusion*

we do this, the other is no longer a resource for our self. Ethical responsibilities to each other are gone. An all-consuming I arises set to expel, even annihilate, the other, and likely they are so disposed.

There is, of course, a different possibility of alterity. The self recognizes the necessity of the other. *I* requires *You* to be aware of self. But beyond this egocentrism, *I* understands the complexity of its own subjectivity arises in the others encountered. *I* takes on contours, gains facets, becomes multifaceted in encounter with the other. The encounter of others mutually enriches and brings new possibilities. The differences of others, the mutual diversity of others, brings all resources and expands individual potentials. This alterity requires an appreciation of the difference of the other. Why do we have the one and not the other?

There are degrees of alterity, as it were, degrees of difference: there is proximate, intuitive, and radical alterity. The other as bearer of the self takes on particular qualities in these categories. Proximate alterity is a dynamic of repetition of the similar. It is not a matter of geography. Proximity is not a question of miles or light-years but a sense of being in connection, a knowing of the other that is more intense.

But there is also the *other* other as bearer of the more than just this one self. This next other, this neighbor, is a step beyond the relation of the two, *I* and *You*. And this other is not in the dynamic of similarity; rather, they are less or even unknown. Beyond the self and other, *I* can intuit that there are other others, and more than neighbors there are others who have not yet appeared, more different other possibilities. In alterity there may be a dynamic repetition of the similar, but I can also anticipate a different difference that transforms my self further. This other demands new knowledge, which can come at a painful cost to who I am now. I can anticipate this discovery of difference with fear and anxiety. Or I can approach it with anticipation of plenitude and expansion of differentiation, an openness to my self becoming different. Why do some dread while others welcome the distant other? What opens the self to intuitive alterity?

There is also a radical alterity, which I cannot know. Nothing less than the horizon of my world sets the limits of radical alterity. The difference that is unknown to us is beyond our horizons of recognition. I can be aware that I have limits, but as limits I do not know beyond them. Although I can give a name to this radical alterity, I do not know what is beyond those limits. Perhaps in an encounter I could withstand the sublime quality of this radically other. Perhaps this radical knowledge is the surprise that may very well overwhelm me.

The differences of others, the mutual diversity of others, expands individual potentials. Others are diverse; each of us is different from the other. Diversity and difference are not the same. In the opposition of diversity and difference, I worry about diversity and am cautious about difference. Diversity is a community of *differends*, a multicultural side-by-side. Difference is a matter of self and other, differentiation, distinction, comparison, contestation, conflict. In the former there lingers a condition of essentialism, a social categorization, individuality subsumed by groups. Diversity is good. An appreciation of diversity may bring a great step forward out of dangerous differentiations. But there is the possibility that diversity becomes an end and, left embedded in our own diverse proper groups, we become indifferent to each other. With difference it is possible to value how that term, "difference," captures the interdependence of universalization and fragmentation while at the same time aiming for an inherently more equitable flow of power.

I estimate highly the possibility for more equitable negotiations of difference. Equity was never established or recognized without struggle over difference. I will avoid any premature celebration of diversity or difference as political critical directions. Whatever develops among others in the era of alterity, it is certain that at the outset of this new era we confront a tension between the recognition of the equality of political subjects and their alterity and, just as in ages past, regardless of the form of the dynamic, only struggle will accomplish greater equity.

But this project is one of *visual* alterity. Visual alterity—the determination of differences that arise in a field of given circumstances—transforms any thing into some thing. And if we can shift our frames, change our visual fields, we can see an other thing. The changing unfolding of the visual field is history. It is at the heart of story. Visual alterity describes a propensity of the perceiver to become subject in recognition, to see otherness, to detect difference. It is not (only) a matter of individuation, but the relation established in difference to the other is communal. Nevertheless, if seeing difference is recognition of the other, that does not make clear what kind of recognition.

A recurring theme of this study has been that difference is part of perception and that seeing is the seeing of difference. Sight is an apparatus of differentiation. Seeing is not of necessity a negation; quite the opposite, alterity can be an enhancement community, an embellishment of the qualities of interdependence or commonality. It is not a question of *if* we see difference but of how our differentiations arise in the apparatus of seeing.

Difference is visible, seeing is differentiation as such, the other is seen, and yet clearly in our focus on perceiving otherness we may also recognize the same. It might be the case, though, that in the attention to otherness, the same is glossed over in inattentional blindness. To see is in effect to discriminate;

204 · *Conclusion*

nevertheless, to see difference is itself not a determination on how we discriminate. Seeing difference and *techniques of exclusion* are connected but not equivalent. Indeed, the discussion here should not ignore the techne of differentiation. Seeing difference is not voluntaristic; differentiation arises in an apparatus of sight, a techne of seeing this and that. We do not see everything and anything. We perceive in conditions not freely determined by ourselves. Perception is a process of distinction and differentiation within the limits of the body, the technologies, the cultural reading practices, and the environment of any given moment. In this study I have explored how that apparatus produces, for instance, difference to be looked at and difference to be seen, how it makes difference spectacular and how it points and enframes an other as different, how it racializes, calls forward phobia or philia, and so on.

And that leads me to ask, In a period of changing solidarities, how do we recognize these techniques of exclusion? How do we see new differences? How do we go beyond the distinctions that determine our ways of knowing, and seeing, in order to arrive at new ways of knowing, new ways of seeing? How do we come to see difference differently?

How you see is how you know. Your knowledge is defined by your ways of seeing. Cinema has expanded such that screens are ubiquitous, on our subways and planes, decorating our buildings and projected onto our walls, in the black boxes of cinemas and in the pockets of our blue jeans. If the reflections on the photograph gave us to consider the indexicality of the image and its realism, the possibility to walk or drive distractedly because we have a moving image in our hand has augmented reality. There is not an image that represents the real; we move in a reality of images that move. Our world has again changed because of the screens we hold in our hands. There is not an augmented reality distinct from reality; our moving images made mobile now appear intensely in the quotidian of our perception. Seeing differently means to know differently.

If the last century was dominated by cine-cognition, if cinema was the primary technology of sight, it structured that century with a fixed projection surface. The screen in the black box and even the televisual solid-state screen of our console televisions were relatively fixed. We sat in fixed positions in front of them. And we sat in front of them for a duration of time and in particular rhythms: Saturday at the cinema, prime time for family viewers. Now, as once our clunky cameras learned to move and made the moving image more dynamic, our screens have been liberated to move. And they move with us, making our movements more imagistic, more image laden. Cine-cognition is a form of cognition that arose at a particular time in a particular form. It is not a special form of cognition, nor was it inevitable, nor was it permanent. Cine-cognition was one way of knowing, one way of organizing our perceptual systems, but

Conclusion • 205

cine-cognition gives way. As our screens move from the walls, cine-cognition gives way to screen-cognition. It may be a positive development that the populist cry of "fake news" has limited any return of a fantasy of screen-truth as we once contended with the claims of *Kino-Pravda*. Still it seems that many are trapped staring at the screens as if they were more-than-worldly. They are still "only" worldly. They are "only" the way we know our world.

We have the ability to change our perceptions. We have tools to make new images, to take up new positions, to perceive differently. Yet those tools are increasingly dominated by *formatted technologies of representation*. What was once artisanal, requiring lots of time to produce a limited effect, can now be deployed in multiple layers of communication. At the same time, what once demanded understanding of the technology to manipulate it is now a techne prefiguring our communication.

Can a study of visual alterity offer more than critical description? Has it done that? I am confident that understanding historical processes affords insights into the way forward. Nietzsche warned us that too much history was not good for life, and Marx expected revolutions to rupture with the past and its ossified forms, but maybe history is about our present more than our past or our future. We make our own history but not under conditions that we have freely chosen. We enter the world in a field of already determined differentiations. Our subjectivity is in effect predetermined by the conditions of differentiation, into which we grow. For us to be our self, others must appear. Otherness appears but not just any otherness. We emerge recognizing difference but recognizing it in a particular way.

Self-consciousness arises in differentiation, but knowing that the patterns of differentiation that precede us are contingent liberates us to action. Knowing that there have been other differences other differentiations, knowing that they are not natural, fixed, part of a "simple reality," compels attentiveness. We may be "trained" to see difference in a particular way, but we can "learn" to see difference differently. Thus in this study I have advocated anti-essentialism, plasticity, possibility, and diversity and have eschewed determination, limitation, normativization, and standardization.

Postwar negative dialectic placed promise of progress in a critical light, yet current climate conditions set an absolute limit on the existing socioeconomic order. The global challenges call forward positive interventions in human exchange. We must act differently, we must see our world differently, we must differentiate differently.

We move toward a certain conundrum in which the resources necessary to keep the current global organization of exchange in place will confront limits on its patterns of consumption. And as that happens, we can rest assured that

206 · *Conclusion*

the technologies of surveillance and recognition will be deployed to prevent change.

Popular misunderstandings of Rancière's "distribution of the sensible" associate the phrase with capitalism—as if there were some condition in which the sensible was outside of differentiation. The sensible is always "distributed." The question is how.

The distribution of the sensible, as I discussed in chapter 1, sets up an opposition between simple reality and image—for example, the cinematic image. The gesture hopes that producing an awareness of the imageness of the image will allow us to rearrange the way the sensible is distributed. Critical awareness arises here as a form of mindfulness. If we have lost grand narratives like the Marxist narrative of progression toward the revolution of the industrial proletariat, criticality can no longer mean working in the service of that progress against the illusion of ideology. Criticality comes in this moment to mean an awareness of the limiting capacities of the sensible. That is good, but we can push further to a position in which criticality requires us to at least explore, if not understand, the whole regime of imageness, the full apparatus that brings image and spectator together.

In classic apparatus theory the notion of apparatus rested on the theory of representation, with the basic apparatus instituting a situation where the spectator is invited to vest belief in an impression of reality. This impression is caused by the type of representation projected on the screen, following the rules of monocular perspective.

The classic apparatus theory described a unified field in which power largely flowed as ideology in one direction, toward the spectators as a form of entrapment. Foucault's discussion of *dispositif* already challenged the monodirectional deployment of power at work and articulated a complexity of micropower and negotiation. Yet here I have worked against this presumption of a unified *dispositif* or episteme. There is not an apparatus as such. Apparatus is always multiple systems, interlocking arrangements.

François Albéra and Maria Tortajada suggest that the dispositive does not exist:

> The dispositive is a schema, a dynamic play of relations which articulates discourses and practices with one another; a schema which is to be elaborated out of this basis, this apparently modest work tool describing the dispositive in three terms which, in each case, in every research project, have to be entirely redefined and understood in their reciprocal relations: the spectator, the machinery, the representation.[1]

Luhmanian systems theory suggested that as much as one can describe system, no singular unified system exists but rather systems in systems, systems in subsystems. The apparatus is not a closed system but a system of systems. And at any given time in the investigation of a system and its subsystems, the optics can switch such that any subsystem itself can become a system. Thomas Elsaesser has even argued that media technologies, rather than represent a system, are themselves the disruptive force (*Störfaktor*) that "can act as a stabilizing or energizing element in a given system."[2] Cinema thus did not generate a single simple apparatus based on providing an ideological illusion of reality; rather, cinema was a stabilizing and destabilizing factor in various systems.

In his excellent discussion of anarchy, Mohammed Bamyeh has argued against Marx's insistence in *The German Ideology* that the micro-conditions of socialism established by the utopian socialist movements could not count, because they did not achieve the grand social revolution for all.[3] Bamyeh contends that we do not and should not wait for the revolution to transform our social systems; rather, we can find in the present, alongside and within the system of capital, other models, other successful systems organizing relations and behaviors, systems that are noncapitalist.

We must see and be seen differently. Surveillance technology and artificial intelligence reactivated our dreams of plenitude as nightmare. But they are not. They do not see all; they do not know everything; they know a lot of things in a particular way, in a particular frame, certainly in an often dangerous frame of inhumane security and authoritarian anxiety. But that is not everything. It is a frame, a way of seeing, a way of differentiating and only that. The antidote to the technologies of surveillance is not in a fantasy of conscious omniscience but in the experience of the mind as an apparatus of differentiation. Seeing difference and understanding the possibility of our perceptive apparatus to see difference differently means to recognize our consciousness as a destabilizing deterritorializing dis-integrating antidote to the technologies of discrimination that would stabilize and territorialize our perceptions. We will never see only this way or that, this as self and that as other. We will always be able to *kipp*, to see this and then that, to see that as other than same. Each moment of perception is a seeing of the world anew.

Notes

Introduction

1. Halle, *Europeanization of Cinema*; Halle, *German Film after Germany*.
2. Deleuze and Guattari, *What Is Philosophy?*
3. Nietzsche, *Nietzsche*; Nietzsche and Sloterdijk, *Die Geburt der Tragödie aus dem Geiste der Musik*.
4. Vertov, *Kino-Eye*; Vertov, *Schriften Zum Film*.
5. Münsterberg, *Photoplay*, 39.
6. Baranowski and Hecht, "One Hundred Years of Photoplay."
7. Arnheim, *Visual Thinking*.
8. Neisser, *Cognitive Psychology*.
9. Bordwell, *Narration in the Fiction Film*; Plantinga, "Cognitive Film Theory"; Baranowski and Hecht, "One Hundred Years of Photoplay."
10. Bordwell, *Narration in the Fiction Film*, xiii.
11. Ibid.
12. Hoffman, *Visual Intelligence*; Zacks, *Flicker*.
13. Zacks, *Flicker*, 4.
14. Wilmer, Sherman, and Chein, "Smartphones and Cognition"; Montag et al., "Facebook Usage on Smartphones."
15. Kristeva, *Strangers to Ourselves*; Levinas, *Humanism of the Other*; Hegel, *Science of Logic*.
16. Battestini, "Reading Signs of Identity and Alterity"; Petrilli, "Iconicity in Translation"; Ponzio and Petrilli, "Signification and Alterity in Emmanuel Lévinas"; Levinas, "Signification and Sense."

210 · *Notes to Chapter 1*

Chapter 1. The Image of the Some Thing Other

1. Marx and Engels, *Marx and Engels on Literature and Art*.

2. Wertheimer, *Drei Abhandlungen zur Gestalttheorie*; Metzger, *Gesetze des Sehens*; Wertheimer and Metzger, *Produktives Denken*; Zimmer, "Gestaltpsychologische Texte—Lektüre für eine aktuelle Psychologie?"; Thompson and Noë, *Vision and Mind*.

3. Zimmer, "Gestaltpsychologische Texte"; Kosslyn, *Image and Brain*.

4. Kolb, *Brain Plasticity and Behavior*; Kourtzi and DiCarlo, "Learning and Neural Plasticity in Visual Object Recognition"; Merabet et al., "What Blindness Can Tell Us"; Vincent and Jean-Didier, *Custom-Made Brain*.

5. The apparatus theory I am advocating here is distinct from the enactivist "correction" of cognitivism. Enactivism sees the mind and the world as mutually *enacted*. Varela, Thompson, and Rosch, *Embodied Mind*; Thompson, *Mind in Life*; Tikka, "Enactive Cinema."

6. Rancière, *Le Destin des Images*; Rancière, *Future of the Image*.

7. Rancière, *Future of the Image*, 3.

8. Ibid., 4.

9. Ibid., 4–5.

10. Ibid., 6; Rancière, *Le Destin des Images*, 14.

11. Rancière, *Future of the Image*, 7.

12. Rancière, *Le Partage du Sensible*; Rancière, *Film Fables*.

13. Husserl, *Edmund Husserl: Untersuchungen zur Urteilstheorie*; Husserl, *Ideen zu einer reinen phänomenologie und phänomenologischen philosophie*; Husserl, *Zur Phänomenologischen Reduktion*.

14. Rancière, *Le Destin des Images*, 11.

15. Rancière, *Future of the Image*, 8.

16. Gobet et al., "Chunking Mechanisms in Human Learning"; Apps and Tsakiris, "Predictive Codes of Familiarity and Context"; Linhares and Chada, "Nature of the Mind's Pattern-Recognition Process?"

17. Strickland and Scholl, "Visual Perception Involves Event-Type Representations"; Bezdek, "Changes in Attentional Focus"; Findlay and Gilchrist, *Active Vision*.

18. Rancière, *Future of the Image*, 14.

19. Eichenbaum and Cohen, *From Conditioning to Conscious Recollection*; Edelman and Tononi, *Universe of Consciousness*; Hasselmo, *How We Remember*; Rugg and Yonelinas, "Human Recognition Memory"; Assmann, *Cultural Memory and Western Civilization*.

20. Rancière, *Film Fables*, 2.

21. Coulais, *Images Virtuelles et Horizons du Regard*.

22. Richter, *Dada*; Cowan et al., *Hans Richter*.

23. Moholy-Nagy, "Produktion—Reproduktion."

24. Gertz et al., *Bauhaus und die Fotografie*.

25. Adorno and Horkheimer, *Dialectic of Enlightenment*, 120.

26. Stiegler, *Technics and Time*.

27. Ibid., 2, 241.

Notes to Chapters 1 and 2 • 211

28. Ibid., 3, 9.
29. Ibid., 35.
30. Ibid., 11.

Chapter 2. Self/Other Image

1. Hegel, *Science of Logic*, §215; Hegel, *Wissenschaft der Logik*.
2. Hegel et al., *Phenomenology of Spirit*, 111, §179.
3. Hegel and Knox, *Hegel's Philosophy of Right*, §166; Halle, *Queer Social Philosophy*; Benhabib, "Hegel, die Frauen und die Ironie."
4. Hegel, *Lectures on the Philosophy of History*, 95.
5. Ibid., 97.
6. Halle, *Queer Social Philosophy*.
7. Rancière, *Future of the Image*, 4–5.
8. Kittler, *Austreibung des Geistes aus den Geisteswissenschaften*; Kittler, *Optische Medien*; Kittler and Ofak, *Medien vor den Medien*.
9. Coulais, *Images Virtuelles et Horizons du Regard*, 209.
10. Ibid., 235.
11. Jay, *Downcast Eyes*.
12. Bordwell, *Narration in the Fiction Film*; Rosen, *Narrative, Apparatus, Ideology*; Hühn, Schmid, and Schönert, *Point of View, Perspective, and Focalization*; Grant, *Film Genre Reader IV*.
13. Grant, *Film Genre Reader IV*; Altman, *Film / Genre*.
14. Cavell, *Pursuits of Happiness*; Gehring and Bell, *Romantic vs. Screwball Comedy*.
15. Consider Coen brothers films like *Raising Arizona* (1987), *The Hudsucker Proxy* (1994), *Intolerable Cruelty* (2003), *The Ladykillers* (2004), and *Burn after Reading* (2008). Screwball elements to romance appear in films from *The Adventures of Priscilla, Queen of the Desert* (Elliott 1994), through *In & Out* (Oz 1997), *I Think I Do* (Sloane 1998), into the present vehicles for drag stars like Bianca del Rio, *Hurricane Bianca* (Kugelman 2016).
16. Halle, "'Happy Ends' to Crises of Heterosexual Desire."
17. Gaudreault, *From Plato to Lumière*.
18. Cavell, *Pursuits of Happiness*.
19. Adorno, *Authoritarian Personality*; Halle, "Between Marxism and Psychoanalysis."
20. Allport, *Nature of Prejudice*.
21. Ito and Tomelleri, "Seeing Is Not Stereotyping"; Kubota and Ito, "Rapid Race Perception"; Ito and Bartholow, "Neural Correlates of Race"; Mason, Cloutier, and Macrae, "On Construing Others"; Martin and Ruble, "Children's Search for Gender Cues."
22. Hinton, *Stereotypes, Cognition, and Culture*.
23. Hebart and Baker, "Facing Up to Stereotypes"; Stolier and Freeman, "Neural Pattern Similarity."
24. Ito and Tomelleri, "Seeing Is Not Stereotyping."
25. Cohen and Lefebvre, *Handbook of Categorization*.
26. Nicolas and Skinner, "Constructing Race," 608.

212 · *Notes to Chapters 2 and 3*

27. Ibid., 627.

28. Bogle, *Toms, Coons, Mulattoes, Mammies, and Bucks*.

29. Neale, "Same Old Story."

30. Berg, *Latino Images in Film*; Schweinitz, *Film and Stereotype*; Williams, *Black Male Frames*.

31. Dyer, *Matter of Images*.

32. Simmel, *Georg Simmel on Individuality*.

33. Hobbs et al., "How First-Time Viewers Comprehend Editing Conventions"; Schwan and Ildirar, "Watching Film for the First Time"; Ildirar and Schwan, "First-Time Viewers' Comprehension of Films."

34. Tegel, *Jew Süss*; Giesen and Hobsch, *Hitlerjunge Quex, Jud Süss und Kolberg*; Knopp, *NS-Filmpropaganda*; Mannes, *Antisemitismus im Nationalsozialistischen Propagandafilm*; Rentschler, *Ministry of Illusion*; Schulte-Sasse, *Entertaining the Third Reich*. See *Harlan: Im Schatten von Jud Süß* (Moeller 2008) and *Jud Süss: Film ohne Gewissen* (Roehler 2010).

35. Himmler, *Geheimreden 1933 bis 1945 und Andere Ansprachen*.

36. Weinstein, "Dissolving Boundaries."

37. Prager, "Beleaguered under the Sea: Wolfgang Petersen's *Das Boot* (1981) as a German Hollywood Film."

38. Simmel, "Exkurs Über den Fremden"; Simmel, "The Stranger."

39. Heath, "Notes on Suture"; Miller, "Suture: Elements of the Logic of the Signifier"; Silverman, *Subject of Semiotics*.

40. https://www.harunfarocki.de/de/instalationen/2000er/2007/vergleich-ueber -ein-drittes.html.

Chapter 3. Phenomenology and Alterity

1. Jay, *Downcast Eyes*.

2. Husserl, *Ideen zu Einer Reinen Phänomenologie*, 200; Husserl, *Ideas for a Pure Phenomenology*, 192.

3. Halle, "Perceiving the Other"; Koch, "Blindness as Insight."

4. Heidegger, *Nietzsche, Seminare*; Heidegger, *Nietzsche, Vol. 1*.

5. Husserl, *Ideas for a Pure Phenomenology*, 161; Husserl, *Ideen zu Einer Reinen Phänomenologie*, 168ff.

6. Husserl, *Ideas for a Pure Phenomenology*, 105.

7. Husserl, *Ideen zu Einer Reinen Phänomenologie*, 315.

8. Ibid., 200; Husserl, *Ideas for a Pure Phenomenology*, 192.

9. Husserl, *Ideas for a Pure Phenomenology*, 162.

10. Husserl, *Die Krisis der Europäischen Wissenschaften*.

11. Husserl, *Ideen zu Einer Reinen Phänomenologie*, 200; Husserl, *Ideas for a Pure Phenomenology*, 192.

12. "Alas," said the mouse, "the whole world is growing smaller every day. At the beginning it was so big that I was afraid, I kept running and running, and I was glad when I saw walls far away to the right and left, but these long walls have narrowed so

Notes to Chapters 3 and 4 • 213

quickly that I am in the last chamber already, and there in the corner stands the trap that I must run into."

"You only need to change your direction," said the cat, and ate it up.

13. Yacavone, "Film and the Phenomenology of Art."

14. Merleau-Ponty, "Film and the New Psychology," 58.

15. Ibid., 57–58.

16. Merleau-Ponty, *Visible and the Invisible*, 10.

17. Ibid., 155.

18. Ahmed, *Queer Phenomenology*.

19. Ibid., 69.

20. Ahmed, *Differences That Matter*.

21. Merleau-Ponty, *Visible and the Invisible*, 7.

Chapter 4. Apparatus Theory Now More Than Ever!

1. Comolli, "Machines of the Visible," 121.

2. Simons and Chabris, "Gorillas in Our Midst," http://www.theinvisiblegorilla.com/videos.html.

3. De Lauretis and Heath, *Cinematic Apparatus*.

4. Anderson and Anderson, "Motion Perception in Motion Pictures."

5. J. Anderson, *Reality of Illusion*.

6. See Buckland, *Cognitive Semiotics of Film*; Persson, *Understanding Cinema*.

7. Editors, "Launching," v.

8. Ibid., vi.

9. Doane, Mellencamp, and Williams, *Re-Vision*; de Lauretis, *Technologies of Gender*; Mayne, *Cinema and Spectatorship*; Staiger, *Perverse Spectators*.

10. Vaughn, "Political Repression and Capitalist Globalization."

11. Robé, Wolfson, and Funke, "Rewiring the Apparatus."

12. Snead, *White Screens/Black Images*, 23.

13. Reich and Richmond, "Introduction," 11.

14. Gaudreault and Lefebvre, *Techniques et Technologies*; Oever, *Techné/Technology*; Dominique and Lefebvre, "Christian Metz et La Phénoménologie"; Oever, *Ostrannenie*.

15. Flusser, *Kommunikologie*; Weibel, *Time Slot*.

16. Zielinski, *Audiovisionen*; Winkler, *Der Filmische Raum und der Zuschauer*; Kittler, *Grammophon, Film, Typewriter*; Kittler, *Optische Medien*.

17. Casetti, *Lumière Galaxy*; Casetti, "Theory, Post-Theory, Neo-Theories"; Albéra and Tortajada, *Cine-Dispositives*; Albéra and Tortajada, *Cinema beyond Film*; Casetti, Colombo, and Fumagalli, *La Realtà Dell'immaginario*.

18. Gaudreault and Lefebvre, *Techniques et Technologies*; Dulac and Gaudreault, "Dispositifs Optiques et Attraction"; Paci, *La Machine à Voir*; Hagener and Hediger, *Medienkultur und Bildung*; Engell, Fahle, Hediger, and Voss, *Essays zur Film-Philosophie*.

19. Ortel, *Discours, Image, Dispositif*; Loist and de Valck, "Film Festivals/Film Festival Research"; Valcke, "Montage in the Arts."

214 · *Notes to Chapters 4 and 5*

20. Delavaud and Maréchal, *Télévision, Le Moment Expérimental*; Tinsobin, *Das Kino als Apparat*; Rebentisch, *Ästhetik der Installation*.

21. Agamben, "Che cos'è un dispositivo?"; Agamben, *"What Is an Apparatus?"*

22. Wollen, "Cinema and Technology"; Allen, "Industrial Context of Film and Technology."

23. Allen, "Industrial Context of Film and Technology," 29.

24. Musser, "Stereopticon and Cinema," 131.

25. Germer et al., "Apparate."

26. Kittler, *Gramophone, Film, Typewriter*, xxxix.

27. Kittler, *Austreibung des Geistes aus den Geisteswissenschaften*.

28. Foucault, *Power/Knowledge*.

29. Albéra and Tortajada, *Cine-Dispositives*,

30. Comolli, "Machines of the Visible," 121.

31. Musser, "Stereopticon and Cinema," 157.

32. Albéra and Tortajada, *Cine-Dispositives*, 43.

33. Kafka, *Metamorphosis, In the Penal Colony, and Other Stories*.

34. Agamben, *"What Is an Apparatus?"*, 14.

35. Muckli et al., "Integration of Multiple Motion Vectors"; Treuting, "Eye Tracking and the Cinema"; Hasson et al., "Neurocinematics"; Bezdek, "Changes in Attentional Focus."

36. Tikka et al., "Enactive Cinema Paves Way"; Tikka, "Enactive Cinema."

37. Plantinga, "Cognitive Film Theory," 20.

38. Hasson et al., "Neurocinematics," 1.

39. Ibid.

40. Ibid., 6.

41. Zacks, *Flicker*.

42. Bordwell, "Case for Cognitivism," 29.

43. Plantinga, "Cognitive Film Theory," 20–21.

44. Bordwell, "Case for Cognitivism," 16.

45. Nagel and Christensen, *Cognitive Vision Systems*.

46. Montag et al., "Facebook Usage on Smartphones."

47. Grodal, "High on Crime Fiction and Detection"; Grodal and Kramer, "Empathy, Film, and the Brain"; Grodal, *Embodied Visions*; Grodal, *Moving Pictures*; Bordwell, "Case for Cognitivism."

48. Messaris, *Visual Literacy*; Gibson, *Ecological Approach to Visual Perception*.

Chapter 5. Cine-Cognition: Montage

1. Ellenbogen, *Reasoned and Unreasoned Images*.

2. Clegg, *Man Who Stopped Time*.

3. Prince and Hensley, "Kuleshov Effect."

4. Bruni, "Re-Examining the Kuleshov Effect."

5. Mobbs et al., "Kuleshov Effect."

6. Ibid., 95.

Notes to Chapter 5 • 215

7. Ibid.

8. Ibid., 103.

9. Laham et al., "Elaborated Contextual Framing."

10. Magliano and Zacks, "Impact of Continuity Editing"; Heimann et al., "'Cuts in Action.'"

11. Sahakyan and Kelley, "Contextual Change Account"; Delaney and Sahakyan, "Unexpected Costs"; Spillers and Unsworth, "Costs of Directed Forgetting."

12. Grodal, *Embodied Visions*.

13. Grodal, "How Film Genres Are a Product," 1; Grodal, *Embodied Visions*.

14. Grodal, "*Die Hard* as an Emotion Symphony."

15. Hurtrez, "Torben Grodal: Embodied Visions"; Pierson, "Embodied Visions"; Smith, "Reviews."

16. Jordan-Young and Rumiati, "Hardwired for Sexism?"

17. Grossi, "Hardwiring"; Lilienfeld et al., "Fifty Psychological and Psychiatric Terms to Avoid"; Jordan-Young and Rumiati, "Hardwired for Sexism?"; Churchland, *Touching a Nerve*; Churchland, *Brain-Wise*; Churchland, Ramachandran, and Sejnowski, "A Critique of Pure Vision."

18. See the special issue of *Evolutionary Applications* and its report on the Evolution and Biodiversity summit. Mergeay and Santamaria, "Evolution and Biodiversity."

19. Girodana Grossi identified eleven general ways in which "hardwired" and "innate" have been deployed in behavior and cognitive literature in the past forty-five years. Grossi, "Hardwiring."

20. Grodal, "How Film Genres Are a Product."

21. Grabowski, *Neuroscience and Media*.

22. Lambert et al., "Optimizing Brain Performance"; Lappe et al., "Cortical Plasticity"; Kourtzi and DiCarlo, "Learning and Neural Plasticity"; Balaban, "Cognitive Developmental Biology"; Merabet et al., "What Blindness Can Tell Us about Seeing Again"; Pascual-Leone et al., "Plastic Human Brain Cortex"; Röder and Rösler, "Principles of Brain Plasticity."

23. Kuleshov, *Kuleshov on Film*.

24. For an excerpt, see "*Walking from Munich to Berlin* (excerpt) by Oskar Fischinger," Center for Visual Music, Los Angeles, Vimeo, https://vimeo.com/54587466.

25. Hass-Cohen and Findlay, *Art Therapy and the Neuroscience of Relationships*; Underwood, *Cognitive Processes in Eye Guidance*; Wurtz and Goldberg, *Neurobiology of Saccadic Eye Movements*.

26. Eisenstein, "Dramaturgy of Film Form," 95.

27. Eisenstein, "Dickens, Griffith, and the Film Today."

28. Magliano and Zacks, "Impact of Continuity Editing."

29. Smith, Levin, and Cutting, "Window on Reality," 107.

30. Ildirar and Schwan, "First-Time Viewers' Comprehension of Films."

31. Shimamura, *Psychocinematics*; Shimamura et al., "How Attention Is Driven by Film Edits"; Heimann et al., "'Cuts in Action.'"

32. Eisenstein, "Dramaturgy of Film Form," 95.

216 · *Notes to Chapters 5, 6, and 7*

33. Coward, "Understanding Complex Cognitive Phenomena," 11.6.1.

34. Barnes-Holmes and Barnes-Holmes, "Naming, Story-Telling, and Problem-Solving."

Chapter 6. Cine-Cognition: Collage, Fragmentation, Integration

1. Frick, "Laurie Frick"; Banks, "Michelebanksartworks."

2. Hass-Cohen and Findlay, *Art Therapy and the Neuroscience of Relationships*; Stewart, "Art Therapy and Neuroscience Blend."

3. Stafford, *Echo Objects*; Stafford, *Field Guide to a New Meta-Field*.

4. Kuenzli, *Dada and Surrealist Film*, 7.

5. Settele and Hausheer, *Found Footage Film*.

6. Bann, "Collage."

7. Manovich, "Database as a Symbolic Form."

8. "Lev Manovich: Soft Cinema."

9. http://www.julienpatry.com/portfolio/berlin-classified/.

10. politicalremix, "Read My Lips—by A Thousand Points of Night (1992)," YouTube, https://www.youtube.com/watch?v=gvmrLuw4log. I am especially grateful to Steve Sloto, Luke Bergenthal, and Daniel Malinowski in my 2014 Avant-garde Film seminar for their introduction of poop into the discussion.

11. SuperYoshi, "I'd Say He's Hot on Our Tail," YouTube, https://www.youtube.com/watch?v=suSSdHr8sog&t=90s.

12. madanonymous, "jonathan swift returns from the dead to eat a cheese sandwich," YouTube, https://www.youtube.com/watch?v=8hC3H-wv7SU&t=4s.

13. cs188, "(YTP) Omaba's New World Order Acid Trip," YouTube, https://www.youtube.com/watch?v=xMHANUJD5NQ. This video relied on this practice for political commentary.

14. Enitniralc, "(YTP) I'm-beaming-up.pproj," YouTube, https://www.youtube.com/watch?v=eugynX4Z-Qo&list=UUXVu-SqMUOL2SXtCqFZUsWQ. "I'm_beaming _up.pproj" is part of a game of "tennis" between Peskeh and Butcher.

15. Yoshimaniac, "YTP—Mickey Mouse's Clubhouse Catastrophe (MMC Collab)," YouTube, https://www.youtube.com/watch?v=PsXgZHouJio.

16. Henderson, "Toward a Non-Bourgeois Camera Style," 5.

17. Pessoa, *Cognitive-Emotional Brain*; Boals and Rubin, "Integration of Emotions in Memories"; Giesbrecht et al., "Cognitive Processes in Dissociation"; Alvarez, "Some Questions Concerning States of Fragmentation"; Wildgoose, Clarke, and Waller, "Treating Personality Fragmentation and Dissociation."

18. Bakouie and Gharibzadeh, "Toward a Unifying Hypothesis," E25.

Chapter 7. Cine-Cognition: The *Kippbild*, Dis/Ambiguation

1. Metzger, *Gesetze des Sehens*; Weintraub and Cowan, *Vision/Visual Perception*; Findlay and Gilchrist, *Active Vision*.

2. Jastrow, *Studies from the Laboratory*.

3. Metzger, *Gesetze des Sehens*; Arnheim, *Visual Thinking*.

4. Ihde, *Experimental Phenomenology*.

5. Ibid., 128.

6. Leitner and Schobert, *German Avant-Garde Film*, 102.

7. *Rhythmus 21,* https://vimeo.com/227255950; *Rhythmus 23,* https://vimeo.com/265731430.

8. Azoulai, "Rotation Reversals."

9. Leitner and Schobert, *German Avant-Garde Film*, 106.

10. Ibid., 108.

11. Ibid.

12. Cowan et al., *Hans Richter*.

13. Zauner et al., "Alpha Entrainment"; Wimber et al., "Rapid Memory Reactivation"; Thut et al., "Rhythmic TMS Causes Local Entrainment"; McCairn and Turner, "Deep Brain Stimulation."

14. Biederman and Ju, "Surface versus Edge-Based Determinants"; Deco and Schürmann, "Neuro-Cognitive Visual System"; Bar, "Cortical Mechanism for Triggering."

15. Ullman, *High-Level Vision*.

16. Ni, Braunstein, and Andersen, "Scene Layout from Ground Contact."

17. Kochukhova and Gredebäck, "Learning about Occlusion."

18. Strickland and Scholl, "Visual Perception," 579.

19. Gobet et al., "Chunking Mechanisms in Human Learning," 236.

20. Ibid.

21. Di Ieva et al., "Fractals in the Neurosciences, Part I"; Di Ieva et al., "Fractals in the Neurosciences, Part II."

22. Omelchenko et al., "Loss of Coherence in Dynamical Networks"; Omelchenko et al., "Transition from Spatial Coherence to Incoherence"; Omelchenko et al., "When Nonlocal Coupling between Oscillators Becomes Stronger"; Hövel and Omelchenko, "Multi-Chimera States"; Omelchenko et al., "Tweezers for Chimeras in Small Networks."

23. Omelchenko et al., "Loss of Coherence in Dynamical Networks."

24. Ibid.

25. Kornmeier and Bach, "Ambiguous Figures."

26. Ibid., 17.

27. Ibid., 20.

28. Curiger et al., "Glitzern im Tunnel."

29. Ibid., 303.

30. Ibid., 304.

31. Schneider and Korot, *Video Art*; Huffman, *Video*; Herzogenrath, *Videokunst in Deutschland 1963–1982*.

32. Marshall, "Video"; Krauss, "Video."

33. Krapp, *Noise Channels*.

34. Betancourt, *Glitch Art in Theory and Practice*.

35. Phelan et al., *Pipilotti Rist*, 10.

36. http://www.vdb.org/titles/i-want-see-how-you-see.

218 · *Notes to Chapters 7, 8, and 9*

37. http://www.coryarcangel.com/ and https://www.youtube.com/watch?v=XHyr FoUr3iQ.

38. https://www.youtube.com/watch?v=fCmADoTwGcQ.

39. https://www.youtube.com/watch?v=Ad9zdlaRvdM.

40. Owi Mahn, *Pastell Kompressor*, Vimeo, https://vimeo.com/4215189.

41. Betancourt, *Glitch Art in Theory and Practice*, 36.

42. Menkman, "Resolution Studies: Beyond Resolution."

43. https://www.youtube.com/watch?v=wMHoe8kIZtE.

44. https://vimeo.com/17765488.

45. Davis, "Define Your Terms (or Kanye West Fucked Up My Show)."

46. Ihde, "Multistability and Cyberspace."

47. Press kit, http://www.pillowcastlegames.com.

48. Marchiafava, "Antichamber Review—A Lesson in Originality."

49. Gonzalez-Franco and Lanier, "Model of Illusions and Virtual Reality."

50. Men et al., "Impact of Transitions on User Experience in Virtual Reality."

Chapter 8. The Apparatus of Difference

1. Cieślik and Hagemejer, "Assessing the Impact of the EU-Sponsored Trade Liberalization."

2. European Commission, "Television without Frontiers" (TVWF) directive.

3. Halle, *German Film after Germany*.

4. "Profile: RTL Group."

5. Toth, "Right-Wing Extremists in Hungary."

Chapter 9. The Cinematic Face

1. Calder and Young, "Understanding the Recognition of Facial Identity."

2. Mandal and Awasthi, *Understanding Facial Expressions*; Apps and Tsakiris, "Predictive Codes of Familiarity and Context"; Kret and de Gelder, "Social Context Influences Recognition."

3. Nicolas and Skinner, "Constructing Race," 608.

4. Ho and Pezdek, "Postencoding Cognitive Processes"; Crisp and Turner, "Cognitive Adaptation."

5. Rodger et al., "Mapping the Development"; Thomas et al., "Development of Emotional Facial Recognition"; Batty and Taylor, "Development of Emotional Face Processing"; Nelson and De Haan, "Neurobehavioral Approach to the Recognition of Facial Expressions."

6. Assogna et al., "Intensity-Dependent Facial Emotion Recognition"; Kanwisher and Moscovitch, *Cognitive Neuroscience of Face Processing*.

7. Gonzalez-Gadea et al., "Emotion Recognition and Cognitive Empathy Deficits"; Gelder and Kret, "When a Smile Becomes a Fist"; Carr and Lutjemeier, "Relation of Facial Affect Recognition and Empathy."

8. Gunning, *D. W. Griffith and the Origins*.

Notes to Chapters 9 and 10 • 219

9. Cacioppo, Visser, and Pickett, *Social Neuroscience*; Wimmer and Perner, "Beliefs about Beliefs."

10. Apperly, *Mindreaders*.

11. Gallagher and Frith, "Functional Imaging of 'Theory of Mind.'"

12. Zacks, *Flicker*; Hasson et al., "Neurocinematics."

13. Grodal, *Embodied Visions*, 90.

14. Wyeth, *Matter of Vision*.

15. Grodal and Kramer, "Empathy, Film, and the Brain," 19.

16. Birzache, *Holy Fool in European Cinema*; Klinger, "Die Modernisierte Ikone"; Schrader, *Transcendental Style in Film*.

17. Dyer, *Now You See It*; Dyer, *Matter of Images*.

18. Baume, *About Face*.

19. Ibid., 82.

20. Angell, *Andy Warhol Screen Tests*.

21. Warhol, *Andy Warhol Photobooth Pictures*.

22. Boxer, "Critic's Notebook; Andy Warhol's 'Screen Tests.'"

23. James, *Allegories of Cinema*, 69.

24. Wolf, "Collaboration as Social Exchange."

25. Dyer, *Now You See It*, 209.

26. Ibid., 210.

27. Crimp, *"Our Kind of Movie,"* 7.

28. Flatley, "Warhol Gives Good Face."

29. Crimp, *"Our Kind of Movie,"* 8.

30. Dyer and Pidduck, *Now You See It*, 288.

31. Crimp, *"Our Kind of Movie,"* 12.

32. Flatley, *Like Andy Warhol*, 85.

33. Feldmann, *Werner Schroeter*; Corrigan, "Werner Schroeter's Operatic Cinema"; Corrigan, "On the Edge of History"; Seiderer, *Film Als Psychogramm*; Sieglohr, "Imaginary Identities."

34. Grundmann, *Werner Schroeter*; Langford, *Allegorical Images*.

35. Herdt, *Third Sex, Third Gender*.

36. Schroeter and Foucault, "Conversation."

37. Ibid., 39.

38. Ibid., 40.

39. Ibid., 39.

40. Ibid., 44.

41. Ibid., 44.

42. Halle, *Queer Social Philosophy*.

Chapter 10. The Ethics of Visual Alterity

1. Bledsoe, *Facial Recognition Project Report*.

2. Stanley and Steinhardt, "Drawing a Blank."

3. Calder and Young, "Understanding the Recognition of Facial Identity."

220 · *Notes to Chapter 10 and Conclusion*

4. Deleuze, "Postscript on the Societies of Control."

5. Atterton and Calarco, *Radicalizing Levinas*, ix.

6. Cooper, "Introduction," i.

7. Levinas, "Ethics as First Philosophy," 84.

8. Levinas, "Signification and Sense," 15.

9. Ibid., 16.

10. Ibid., 33.

11. Ibid., 18.

12. Mroué, "Bilder bis zum Sieg?"

13. Ibid.

14. Ruchel-Stockmans, "Revolution Will Be Performed," 7.

15. Critchley, "Five Problems in Levinas's View," 41.

16. Levinas, *Time and the Other*.

17. Halle, *Queer Social Philosophy*.

18. The notion of mystery reappears throughout his writing.

19. Levinas, *Totality and Infinity*.

20. Irigaray, "What Other Are We Talking About?"; Sandford, *Metaphysics of Love*; Chanter, *Feminist Interpretations*; Irigaray, "Question of the Other."

21. Critchley, "Five Problems in Levinas's View," 43.

22. Robbins, *Is It Righteous to Be?*, 149.

23. Blond, "Levinas, Europe, and Others"; Dabashi, "Slavoj Zizek and Harum Scarum"; Eaglestone, "Postcolonial Thought and Levinas's Double Vision"; Moten, "There Is No Racism Intended."

24. Eaglestone, "Postcolonial Thought and Levinas's Double Vision," 58.

25. Levinas, "Prayer without Demand," 230.

26. Levinas, *Levinas Reader*, 292.

27. Ibid., 294.

28. Butler, *Parting Ways*.

29. Perpich, "Levinas, Feminism, and Identity Politics."

Conclusion

1. Albéra and Tortajada, *Cine-Dispositives*, 44.

2. Elsaesser, "Between Knowing and Believing," 51.

3. Bamyeh, *Anarchy as Order*.

Bibliography

Adorno, Theodor W., ed. *The Authoritarian Personality*. 1st ed. Studies in Prejudice Series. New York: Harper, 1950.

Adorno, Theodor W., and Max Horkheimer. *Dialectic of Enlightenment*. London: Verso Editions, 1979.

Agamben, Giorgio. *Che cos'è un dispositivo?* Milano: Nottetempo, 2006.

———. *"What Is an Apparatus?" and Other Essays*. Stanford, CA: Stanford University Press, 2009.

Ahmed, Sara. *Differences That Matter: Feminist Theory and Postmodernism*. Cambridge: Cambridge University Press, 1998.

———. *Queer Phenomenology: Orientations, Objects, Others*. Durham, NC: Duke University Press, 2006.

Albéra, François, and Maria Tortajada, eds. *Cine-Dispositives: Essays in Epistemology across Media*. Amsterdam: Amsterdam University Press, 2015.

———. *Cinema beyond Film: Media Epistemology in the Modern Era*. Film Culture in Transition. Amsterdam: Amsterdam University Press, 2010.

Allen, Jeanne Thomas. "The Industrial Context of Film and Technology: Standardisation and Patents." In *The Cinematic Apparatus*, edited by Teresa de Lauretis and Stephen Heath, 26–37. New York: St. Martin's Press, 1980.

Allport, Gordon W. *The Nature of Prejudice*. Cambridge, MA: Addison-Wesley, 1954.

Altman, Rick. *Film / Genre*. London: British Film Institute, 1999.

Alvarez, Anne. "Some Questions Concerning States of Fragmentation: Unintegration, Under-Integration, Disintegration, and the Nature of Early Integrations." *Journal of Child Psychotherapy* 32, no. 2 (2006): 158–80.

222 · Bibliography

Anderson, Barbara, and Joseph Anderson. "Motion Perception in Motion Pictures." In *The Cinematic Apparatus*, edited by Teresa de Lauretis and Stephen Heath, 76–95. New York: St. Martin's Press, 1980.

Anderson, Joseph. *The Reality of Illusion: An Ecological Approach to Cognitive Film Theory*. Carbondale: Southern Illinois University Press, 1996.

Angell, Callie. *Andy Warhol Screen Tests: The Films of Andy Warhol: Catalogue Raisonné*. New York: H. N. Abrams, 2006.

Apperly, Ian. *Mindreaders: The Cognitive Basis of "Theory of Mind."* Hove, UK: Psychology Press, 2011.

Apps, Matthew A. J., and Manos Tsakiris. "Predictive Codes of Familiarity and Context during the Perceptual Learning of Facial Identities." *Nature Communications* 4 (2013): 2698.

Arnheim, Rudolf. *Visual Thinking*. Berkeley: University of California Press, 1969.

Assmann, Aleida. *Cultural Memory and Western Civilization*. New York: Cambridge University Press, 2011.

Assogna, Francesca, Francesco Pontieri, Luca Cravello, Antonella Peppe, Mariangela Pierantozzi, Alessandro Stefani, Paolo Stanzione, Clelia Pellicano, Carlo Caltagirone, and Gianfranco Spalletta. "Intensity-Dependent Facial Emotion Recognition and Cognitive Functions in Parkinson's Disease." *Journal of the International Neuropsychological Society* 16, no. 5 (2010): 867–76.

Atterton, Peter, and Matthew Calarco, eds. *Radicalizing Levinas*. Albany: SUNY Press, 2010.

Azoulai, Shai David. "Rotation Reversals in the Kinetic Depth Effect." PhD diss., University of California, San Diego, 2014.

Bakouie, Fatemeh, and Shahriar Gharibzadeh. "Toward a Unifying Hypothesis for Schizophrenia and Autism Visual Fragmentation." *Journal of Neuropsychiatry and Clinical Neurosciences* 23, no. 3 (2011): E25.

Balaban, Evan. "Cognitive Developmental Biology: History, Process and Fortune's Wheel." *Cognition* 101, no. 2 (2006): 298–332.

Balázs, Béla. *Béla Balázs: Early Film Theory: Visible Man and the Spirit of Film*. Edited by Erica Carter. Translated by Rodney Livingstone. New York: Berghahn, 2014.

Bamyeh, Mohammed A. *Anarchy as Order: The History and Future of Civic Humanity*. Lanham, MD: Rowman and Littlefield, 2009.

Banks, Michele. "Michelebanksartworks." https://www.artologica.net/.

Bann, Stephen. "Collage: The Poetics of Discontinuity?" *Word & Image* 4, no. 1 (1988): 353–63.

Bar, Moshe. "A Cortical Mechanism for Triggering Top-Down Facilitation in Visual Object Recognition." *Journal of Cognitive Neuroscience* 15, no. 4 (2003): 600–609.

Baranowski, Andreas, and Heiko Hecht. "One Hundred Years of Photoplay: Hugo Münsterberg's Lasting Contribution to Cognitive Movie Psychology." *Projections* 11, no. 2 (2017): 1–21.

Barnes-Holmes, Yvonne, and Dermot Barnes-Holmes. "Naming, Story-Telling, and Problem-Solving: Critical Elements in the Development of Language and Cognition." *Behavioral Development Bulletin* 11, no. 1 (2002): 34–38.

Battestini, Simon. "Reading Signs of Identity and Alterity: History, Semiotics, and a Nigerian Case." *African Studies Review* 34, no. 1 (1991): 99.

Batty, Magali, and Margot J. Taylor. "The Development of Emotional Face Processing during Childhood." *Developmental Science* 9, no. 2 (2006): 207–220.

Baume, Nicholas, ed. *About Face: Andy Warhol Portraits*. Hartford, CT: Wadsworth Atheneum, 1999.

Benhabib, Seyla. "Hegel, die Frauen und die Ironie." In *Denken der Geschlechterdifferenz. Neue Fragen und Perspektiven der feministischen Philosophie*, 19–39. Denken der Geschlechterdifferenz. Wien: Wiener Frauenverlag, 1990.

Berg, Charles Ramírez. *Latino Images in Film: Stereotypes, Subversion, and Resistance*. Austin: University of Texas Press, 2002.

Betancourt, Michael. *Glitch Art in Theory and Practice: Critical Failures and Post-Digital Aesthetics*. New York: Routledge, 2017.

Bezdek, Matthew A. "Changes in Attentional Focus During Suspenseful Film Viewing." PhD diss., State University of New York at Stony Brook, 2012.

Biederman, Irving, and Ginny Ju. "Surface versus Edge-Based Determinants of Visual Recognition." *Cognitive Psychology* 20, no. 1 (1988): 38–64.

Birzache, Alina G. *The Holy Fool in European Cinema*. New York: Routledge, 2016.

Bledsoe, Woodrow Wilson. *A Facial Recognition Project Report*, 1963. http://archive.org/details/firstfacialrecognitionresearch.

Blond, Louis. "Levinas, Europe, and Others: The Postcolonial Challenge to Alterity." *Journal of the British Society for Phenomenology* 47, no. 3 (2016): 260–75.

Boals, Adriel, and David C Rubin. "The Integration of Emotions in Memories: Cognitive Emotional Distinctiveness and Posttraumatic Stress Disorder." *Applied Cognitive Psychology* 25, no. 5 (2011): 811–16.

Bogle, Donald. *Toms, Coons, Mulattoes, Mammies, and Bucks: An Interpretive History of Blacks in American Films*. New York: Viking Press, 1973.

Bordwell, David. "A Case for Cognitivism." *Iris* 9, no. 1989 (1989): 11–40.

———. *Narration in the Fiction Film*. Madison: University of Wisconsin Press, 1985.

Boxer, Sarah. "Critic's Notebook; Andy Warhol's 'Screen Tests' Were 3-Minute Eternities." *New York Times*. May 23, 2003, National edition, sec. E.

Bruni, Pietra T. "Re-Examining the Kuleshov Effect." April 2015. BPhil thesis, University of Pittsburgh, 2015.

Buckland, Warren. *The Cognitive Semiotics of Film*. Cambridge: Cambridge University Press, 2000.

Butler, Judith. *Parting Ways: Jewishness and the Critique of Zionism*. New York: Columbia University Press, 2013.

Cacioppo, John T., Penny S. Visser, and Cynthia L. Pickett. *Social Neuroscience: People Thinking about Thinking People*. Social Neuroscience Series. Cambridge: MIT Press, 2006.

Calder, Andrew J., and Andrew W. Young. "Understanding the Recognition of Facial Identity and Facial Expression." *Nature Reviews Neuroscience* 6, no. 8 (2005): 641–51.

Carr, M., and J. Lutjemeier. "The Relation of Facial Affect Recognition and Empathy to Delinquency in Youth Offenders." *Adolescence* 40, no. 159 (2005): 601–19.

224 · *Bibliography*

Casetti, Francesco. *The Lumière Galaxy: Seven Key Words for the Cinema to Come*. New York: Columbia University Press, 2015.

———. "Theory, Post-Theory, Neo-Theories: Changes in Discourses, Changes in Objects." *Cinémas* 17, no. 2 (2007): 33–45.

Casetti, Francesco, Fausto Colombo, and Armando Fumagalli, eds. *La Realtà Dell'immaginario: I Media Tra Semiotica e Sociologia: Studi in Onore di Gianfranco Bettetini*. Ricerche. Media, Spettacolo, Processi Culturali. Milano: V&P università, 2003.

Cavell, Stanley. *Pursuits of Happiness: The Hollywood Comedy of Remarriage*. Rev. ed. Cambridge, MA: Harvard University Press, 1981.

Chanter, Tina, ed. *Feminist Interpretations of Emmanuel Levinas: Re-Reading the Canon*. University Park: Pennsylvania State University Press, 2001.

Churchland, Patricia S. *Brain-Wise: Studies in Neurophilosophy*. Cambridge: MIT Press, 2002.

Churchland, Patricia S., V. S. Ramachandran, and Terrence J. Sejnowski. "A Critique of Pure Vision." In *Large-Scale Neuronal Theories of the Brain*, edited by Christof Koch and Joel L. David, 23. Cambridge: MIT Press, 1993.

Churchland, Patricia Smith. *Touching a Nerve: The Self as Brain*. 1st ed. New York: W. W. Norton, 2013.

Cieślik, Andrzej, and Jan Hagemejer. "Assessing the Impact of the EU-Sponsored Trade Liberalization in the MENA Countries." *Journal of Economic Integration* 24, no. 2 (2009): 343–68.

Clegg, Brian. *The Man Who Stopped Time: The Illuminating Story of Eadweard Muybridge— Pioneer Photographer, Father of the Motion Picture, Murderer*. Washington, DC: Joseph Henry Press, 2007.

Cohen, Henri, and Claire Lefebvre, eds. *Handbook of Categorization in Cognitive Science*. Oxford, UK: Elsevier Science & Technology, 2017.

Comolli, Jean-Louis. "Machines of the Visible." In *The Cinematic Apparatus*, edited by Teresa de Lauretis and Stephen Heath, 121–43. New York: St. Martin's Press, 1980.

Cooper, Sarah. "Introduction: Levinas and Cinema." *Film-Philosophy* 11, no. 2 (2009).

Corrigan, Timothy. "On the Edge of History: The Radiant Spectacle of Werner Schroeter." *Film Quarterly* 37, no. 4 (1984): 6–18.

———. "Werner Schroeter's Operatic Cinema." *Discourse* 3 (1981): 46–59.

Coulais, Jean-François. *Images Virtuelles et Horizons du Regard*. Paris: Metis Press, 2015.

Cowan, Michael, Christoph Bareither, Kurt Baels, Paul Dobryden, Karin Fest, Klaus Müller-Richter, and Birgit Nemec, eds. *Hans Richter: "Rhythmus 21": Schlüsselfilm der Moderne*. Würzburg: Königshausen u. Neumann, 2013.

Coward, L. Andrew. "Understanding Complex Cognitive Phenomena." In *Towards a Theoretical Neuroscience: From Cell Chemistry to Cognition*, 349–88. Springer Series in Cognitive and Neural Systems. Vol. 8. Springer, Dordrecht, 2013.

Crimp, Douglas. *"Our Kind of Movie": The Films of Andy Warhol*. Cambridge: MIT Press, 2012.

Crisp, Richard J., and Rhiannon N. Turner. "Cognitive Adaptation to the Experience of Social and Cultural Diversity." *Psychological Bulletin* 137, no. 2 (2011): 242–66.

Critchley, Simon. "Five Problems in Levinas's View of Politics and the Sketch of a Solution to Them." In *Radicalizing Levinas*, edited by Peter Atterton and Matthew Calarco, 41–53. Albany: SUNY Press, 2010.

Curiger, Bice, Peter Fischli, David Weiss, and Valentin Groebner, eds. "Glitzern im Tunnel." In *Fischli/Weiss: Fragen & Blumen: Eine Retrospektive*, 301–304. Zürich: Kunsthaus, 2006.

Dabashi, Hamid. "Slavoj Zizek and Harum Scarum." *Al Jazeera*. November 11, 2011, English ed., sec. Opinion.

Davis, Paul B. "Define Your Terms (or Kanye West Fucked Up My Show)." Artist's Statement. *Seventeen Gallery*. http://www.seventeengallery.com/exhibitions/paul-b -davis-define-your-terms-or-kanye-west-fucked-up-my-show.

Deco, G., and B. Schürmann. "A Neuro-Cognitive Visual System for Object Recognition Based on Testing of Interactive Attentional Top-Down Hypotheses." *Perception* 29, no. 10 (2000): 1249–64.

de Gelder, B., and M. E. Kret. "When a Smile Becomes a Fist: The Perception of Facial and Bodily Expressions of Emotion in Violent Offenders." *Experimental Brain Research* 228, no. 4 (2013): 399–410.

Delaney, Peter, and Lili Sahakyan. "Unexpected Costs of High Working Memory Capacity Following Directed Forgetting and Contextual Change Manipulations." *Memory & Cognition* 35, no. 5 (2007): 1074–82.

De Lauretis, Teresa. *Technologies of Gender: Essays on Theory, Film, and Fiction*. Bloomington: Indiana University Press, 1987.

De Lauretis, Teresa, and Stephen Heath, eds. *The Cinematic Apparatus*. New York: St. Martin's Press, 1980.

Delavaud, Gilles, and Denis Maréchal, eds. *Télévision, Le Moment Expérimental: De l'invention à l'institution (1935–1955)*. Médias et Nouvelles Technologies. Rennes: Éditions Apogée, 2011.

Deleuze, Gilles. "Postscript on the Societies of Control." *October* 59 (Winter 1992): 3–7.

Deleuze, Gilles, and Felix Guattari. *What Is Philosophy?* Translated by Hugh Tomlinson and Graham Burchell. New York: Columbia University Press, 1996.

Di Ieva, Antonio, Francisco Esteban, Fabio Grizzi, Wlodzimierz Klonowski, and Miguel Martín-Landrove. "Fractals in the Neurosciences, Part II: Clinical Applications and Future Perspectives." *The Neuroscientist* 21, no. 1 (2015): 30–43.

Di Ieva, Antonio, Fabio Grizzi, Herbert Jelinek, Andras Pellionisz, and Gabriele Losa. "Fractals in the Neurosciences, Part I: General Principles and Basic Neurosciences." *The Neuroscientist* 20, no. 4 (2014): 403–17.

Doane, Mary Anne, Patricia Mellencamp, and Linda Williams, eds. *Re-Vision: Essays in Feminist Film Criticism*. Frederick, MD: University Publications of America, 1984.

Dominique, Chateau, and Martin Lefebvre. "Christian Metz et La Phénoménologie." *1895. Mille Huit Cent Quatre-Vingt-Quinze* (June 1, 2013): 82–119.

226 · *Bibliography*

Dulac, Nicolas, and André Gaudreault. "Dispositifs Optiques et Attraction." *Cahier Louis-Lumière (Les Dispositifs)* 4 (June 2007): 91–108.

Dyer, Richard. *The Matter of Images: Essays on Representations*. 2nd ed. New York: Routledge, 2002.

———. *Now You See It: Studies in Lesbian and Gay Film*. 2nd ed. New York: Routledge: 2002.

Eaglestone, Robert. "Postcolonial Thought and Levinas's Double Vision." In *Radicalizing Levinas*, edited by Peter Atterton and Matthew Calarco, 57–69. Albany: SUNY Press, 2010.

Edelman, Gerald M., and Giulio Tononi. *A Universe of Consciousness: How Matter Becomes Imagination*. New York: Basic Books, 2000.

Editors, The. "Launching." *Projections* 1, no. 1 (2007): v–vii.

Eichenbaum, Howard, and Neal J. Cohen. *From Conditioning to Conscious Recollection: Memory Systems of the Brain*. Vol. 35. Oxford Psychology Series. Upper Saddle River, NJ: Oxford University Press, 2001.

Eisenstein, Sergei. "Dickens, Griffith, and the Film Today." In *Film Form: Essays in Film Theory*, translated by Jay Leyda, 195–256. New York: Harcourt, 1969.

———. "The Dramaturgy of Film Form (The Dialectical Approach to Film Form)." In *The Eisenstein Reader*, edited by Richard Taylor, 93–110. London: BFI Publishers, 1998.

Ellenbogen, Josh. *Reasoned and Unreasoned Images: The Photography of Bertillon, Galton, and Marey*. University Park: Pennsylvania State University Press, 2012.

Elsaesser, Thomas. "Between Knowing and Believing: The Cinematic Dispositive after Cinema." In *Cine-Dispositives: Essays in Epistemology across Media*, edited by François Albéra and Maria Tortajada, 45–72. Amsterdam: University of Amsterdam Press.

Engell, Lorenz, Oliver Fahle, Vinzenz Hediger, and Christiane Voss. *Essays zur Film-Philosophie*. Paderborn, Germany: Wilhelm Fink, 2015.

European Commission. Television broadcasting activities: "Television without Frontiers" (TVWF) Directive, Pub. L. No. Council Directive 89/552/EEC, OJ L 298 of 17.10.1989 Brussels: 1991.

Feldmann, Sebastian. *Werner Schroeter*. Vol. 20. München, Wien: Hanser, 1980.

Findlay, John M., and Iain D. Gilchrist. *Active Vision: The Psychology of Looking and Seeing*. Oxford Psychology Series 37. Oxford: Oxford University Press, 2003.

Flatley, Jonathan. *Like Andy Warhol*. Chicago: University of Chicago Press, 2017.

———. "Warhol Gives Good Face: Publicity and the Politics of Prosopopoeia." In *Pop Out*, edited by Jennifer Doyle, Jonathan Flatley, and José Esteban Muñoz, 101–133. Durham, NC: Duke University Press, 1996.

Flusser, Vilém. *Kommunikologie*. Frankfurt am Main: Fischer, 1998.

Foucault, Michel. *Power/Knowledge: Selected Interviews and Other Writings, 1972–1977*. Edited by Colin Gordon. 1st American ed. New York: Pantheon Books, 1980.

Freitas-Ferrari, Maria Cecilia, Jaime E. C. Hallak, Clarissa Trzesniak, Alaor Santos Filho, João Paulo Machado-de-Sousa, Marcos Hortes N. Chagas, Antonio E. Nardi, and José Alexandre S. Crippa. "Neuroimaging in Social Anxiety Disorder: A Systematic Review of the Literature." *Progress in Neuro-Psychopharmacology and Biological Psychiatry* 34, no. 4 (2010): 565–80.

Frick, Laurie. "Laurie Frick." http://www.lauriefrick.com.

Gallagher, Helen L., and Christopher D. Frith. "Functional Imaging of 'Theory of Mind.'" *Trends in Cognitive Sciences* 7, no. 2 (2003): 77–83.

Gaudreault, André. *From Plato to Lumière: Narration and Monstration in Literature and Cinema*. Translated by Tim Barnard. Toronto: University of Toronto Press, 2009.

Gaudreault, André, and Martin Lefebvre, eds. *Techniques et Technologies du Cinéma Modalités, Usages et Pratiques des Dispositifs Cinématographiques à Travers l'histoire*. Rennes: Presses Universitaires de Rennes, 2015.

Gehring, Wes D., and Steve Bell. *Romantic vs. Screwball Comedy: Charting the Difference*. Lanham, MD: Scarecrow Press, 2002.

Germer, Stefan, Isabelle Graw, Tom Holert, and Astrid Wege, eds. "Apparate." *Texte Zur Kunst* 21 (March 1996).

Gertz, Corina, Christoph Schaden, Kris Scholz, Ute Famulla, and Kai-Uwe Hemken. *Bauhaus und die Fotografie: Zum Neuen Sehen in der Gegenwartskunst*. 1st ed. Bielefeld: Kerber Verlag, 2019.

Gibson, James J. *The Ecological Approach to Visual Perception*. 1st ed. New York: Psychology Press, 1979.

Giesbrecht, Timo, Steven Jay Lynn, Scott O. Lilienfeld, and Harald Merckelbach. "Cognitive Processes in Dissociation: An Analysis of Core Theoretical Assumptions." *Psychological Bulletin* 134, no. 5 (2008): 617–47.

Giesen, Rolf, and Manfred Hobsch. *Hitlerjunge Quex, Jud Süss und Kolberg*. Berlin: Schwarzkopf & Schwarzkopf, 2005.

Gobet, Fernand, Peter C. R. Lane, Steve Croker, Peter C-H. Cheng, Gary Jones, Iain Oliver, and Julian M. Pine. "Chunking Mechanisms in Human Learning." *Trends in Cognitive Sciences* 5, no. 6 (2001): 236–43.

Gonzalez-Franco, Mar, and Jaron Lanier. "Model of Illusions and Virtual Reality." *Frontiers in Psychology* 8 (2017): 1125.

Gonzalez-Gadea, Maria Luz, Eduar Herrera, Mario Parra, Pedro Gomez Mendez, Sandra Baez, Facundo Manes, and Agustin Ibanez. "Emotion Recognition and Cognitive Empathy Deficits in Adolescent Offenders Revealed by Context-Sensitive Tasks." *Frontiers in Human Neuroscience* 8 (2014): 850.

Grabowski, Michael. *Neuroscience and Media: New Understandings and Representations*. New York: Routledge, 2014.

Grant, Barry Keith. *Film Genre Reader IV*. Austin: University of Texas Press, 2012.

Grodal, Torben. "*Die Hard* as an Emotion Symphony: How Reptilian Scenarios Meet Mammalian Emotions in the Flow of an Action Film." *Projections: The Journal for Movies and Mind* 11, no. 2 (2017): 87.

———. *Embodied Visions: Evolution, Emotion, Culture, and Film*. Oxford: Oxford University Press, 2009.

———. "High on Crime Fiction and Detection." *Projections: The Journal of Movies and Mind* 4, no. 2 (2010): 64–85.

———. "How Film Genres Are a Product of Biology, Evolution and Culture—An Embodied Approach." *Palgrave Communications* 3, no. 1 (2017): 1–8.

228 · Bibliography

———. *Moving Pictures: A New Theory of Film Genres, Feelings and Cognition*. Oxford: Clarendon Press, 2002.

Grodal, Torben, and Mette Kramer. "Empathy, Film, and the Brain." *Recherches sémiotiques* 30, nos. 1–3 (2010): 19–35.

Grossi, Giordana. "Hardwiring: Innateness in the Age of the Brain." *Biology & Philosophy* 32, no. 6 (2017): 1047–82.

Grundmann, Roy, ed. *Werner Schroeter*. [Vienna]: Österreichisches Filmmuseum; Vienna: SYNEMA—Gesellschaft für Film und Medien [2018].

Gunning, Tom. *D. W. Griffith and the Origins of American Narrative Film: The Early Years at Biograph*. Urbana: University of Illinois Press, 1994.

Hagener, Malte, and Vinzenz Hediger, eds. *Medienkultur und Bildung: Ästhetische Erziehung Im Zeitalter Digitaler Netzwerke*. Frankfurt am Main: New York Campus Verlag, 2015.

Halle, Randall N. "Between Marxism and Psychoanalysis: Antifascism and Antihomosexuality in the Frankfurt School." *Journal of Homosexuality* 29, no. 4 (1995): 295–317.

———. *The Europeanization of Cinema: Interzones and Imaginative Communities*. Urbana: University of Illinois Press, 2014.

———. *German Film after Germany: Toward a Transnational Aesthetic*. Urbana: University of Illinois Press, 2008.

———. "'Happy Ends' to Crises of Heterosexual Desire: Toward a Social Psychology of Recent German Comedies." *Camera Obscura* 15, no. 2 (2000): 1–39.

———. "Perceiving the Other in the Land of Silence and Darkness." In *A Companion to Werner Herzog*, edited by Brad Prager, 1st ed., 487–509. Oxford: Wiley-Blackwell, 2012.

———. *Queer Social Philosophy: Critical Readings from Kant to Adorno*. Urbana: University of Illinois Press, 2004.

Hass-Cohen, Noah, and Joanna Clyde Findlay. *Art Therapy and the Neuroscience of Relationships, Creativity, and Resiliency: Skills and Practices*. Norton Series on Interpersonal Neurobiology. New York: W. W. Norton, 2015.

Hasselmo, Michael E. *How We Remember: Brain Mechanisms of Episodic Memory*. Cambridge: MIT Press, 2011.

Hasson, Uri, Ohad Landesman, Barbara Knappmeyer, Ignacio Vallines, Nava Rubin, and David J. Heeger. "Neurocinematics: The Neuroscience of Film." *Projections* 2, no. 1 (2008): 1–26.

Heath, Stephen. "Notes on Suture." *Screen* 18, no. 4 (1977): 48–76.

Hebart, Martin N., and Chris I. Baker. "Facing Up to Stereotypes." *Nature Neuroscience* 19, no. 6 (2016): 763–64.

Hegel, Georg Wilhelm Friedrich. *Lectures on the Philosophy of History*. Translated by John Sibree. London: G. Bell and Sons, 1878.

———. *The Science of Logic*. Translated and edited by George Di Giovanni. Cambridge: Cambridge University Press, 2010.

———. *Wissenschaft der Logik*. 7., Aufl. Vol. 5. 20 vols. Frankfurt am Main: Suhrkamp, 2007.

Hegel, Georg Wilhelm Friedrich, and T. M. Knox. *Hegel's Philosophy of Right.* Legal Classics Library. Oxford: Clarendon Press, 1942.

Hegel, Georg Wilhelm Friedrich, Arnold V. Miller, J. N. Findlay, and Johannes Hoffmeister. *Phenomenology of Spirit.* Oxford: Clarendon Press, 1979.

Heidegger, Martin. *Nietzsche, Seminare 1937 und 1944.* Edited by Peter von Ruckteschell. Vol. 4. Abteilung, Hinweise und Aufzeichnungen. Gesamtausgabe. Frankfurt am Main: Vittorio Klostermann, 2004.

———. *Nietzsche,* Vol. 1: *The Will to Power as Art;* Vol. 2: *The Eternal Recurrence of the Same.* Translated by David Farrrrell Krell. Reprint ed. San Francisco: HarperOne, 1991.

Heimann, Katrin S., Sebo Uithol, Marta Calbi, and Maria A. Umiltà. "'Cuts in Action': A High-Density EEG Study Investigating the Neural Correlates of Different Editing Techniques in Film." *Cognitive Science* 41, no. 6 (2017): 1555–88.

Henderson, Brian. "Toward a Non-Bourgeois Camera Style." *Film Quarterly* 24, no. 2 (1970–1971): 2–14.

Herdt, Gilbert H., ed. *Third Sex, Third Gender: Beyond Sexual Dimorphism in Culture and History.* New York: Zone Books, 1996.

Herzogenrath, Wulf, ed. *Videokunst in Deutschland 1963–1982.* Stuttgart: Hatje Cantz Verlag, 1987.

Himmler, Heinrich. *Geheimreden 1933 bis 1945 und Andere Ansprachen.* Edited by Agnes F. Peterson and Bradley F. Smith. Frankfurt am Main: Propyläen Verlag, 1974.

Hinton, Perry R. *Stereotypes, Cognition, and Culture.* Psychology Focus Series. Philadelphia: Psychology Press, 2000.

Ho, Michael R., and Kathy Pezdek. "Postencoding Cognitive Processes in the Cross-Race Effect: Categorization and Individuation during Face Recognition." *Psychonomic Bulletin & Review* 23, no. 3 (2016): 771–80.

Hobbs, Renée, Richard Frost, Arthur Davis, and John Stauffer. "How First-Time Viewers Comprehend Editing Conventions." *Journal of Communication* 38, no. 4 (1988): 50–60.

Hoffman, Donald D. *Visual Intelligence: How We Create What We See.* New York: W. W. Norton, 1998.

Hövel, Philipp, and Iryna Omelchenko. "Multi-Chimera States in FitzHugh-Nagumo Oscillators." *BMC Neuroscience* 14, Suppl 1 (2013). http://dx.doi.org/10.1186/1471 -2202-14-S1-P303.

Huffman, Kathy Rae. *Video: A Retrospective 1974–1984.* Long Beach, CA: Long Beach Museum of Art, 1984.

Hühn, Peter, Wolf Schmid, and Jörg Schönert, eds. *Point of View, Perspective, and Focalization: Modeling Mediation in Narrative.* 1st ed. Berlin: Walter de Gruyter, 2009.

Hurtrez, Lionel. "Torben Grodal: Embodied Visions: Evolution, Emotion, Culture, and Film." *Mise au Point,* June 2, 2014. http://journals.openedition.org/map/1661.

Husserl, Edmund. *Die Krisis der Europäischen Wissenschaften und die Transzendentale Phänomenologie.* Edited by Reinhold Smid. Vol. ErgänzungsBd, Texte aus dem Nachlaß 1934–1937. Dordrecht: Kluwer, 1993.

230 · Bibliography

———. *Ideas for a Pure Phenomenology and Phenomenological Philosophy.* Translated by Daniel O. Dahlstrom. Indianapolis: Hackett, 2014.

———. *Ideen zu Einer Reinen Phänomenologie und Phänomenologischen Philosophie.* 3. Unveränderter Abdruck. Halle a. d. S: M. Niemeyer, 1929.

———. *Untersuchungen zur Urteilstheorie: Texte aus dem Nachlass (1893–1918).* Dordrecht: Springer-Verlag, 2009.

———. *Zur Phänomenologischen Reduktion: Texte aus dem Nachlass (1926–1935).* Edited by Sebastian Luft. Vol. 34. Dordrecht: Kluwer Academic Publishers, 2002.

Ihde, Don. *Experimental Phenomenology: Multistabilities.* Albany: State University of New York Press, 2012.

———. "Multistability and Cyberspace." In *Experimental Phenomenology: Multistabilities,* 145–54. Albany: State University of New York Press, 2012.

Ildirar, Sermin, and Stephan Schwan. "First-Time Viewers' Comprehension of Films: Bridging Shot Transitions." *British Journal of Psychology* 106, no. 1 (2015): 133–51.

Irigaray, Luce. "The Question of the Other." Translated by Noah Guynn. *Yale French Studies* 87 (1995): 7–19.

———. "What Other Are We Talking About?" Translated by Esther Marion. *Yale French Studies,* no. 104 (2004): 67–81.

Ito, Tiffany A., and Bruce D. Bartholow. "The Neural Correlates of Race." *Trends in Cognitive Sciences* 13, no. 12 (2009): 524–31.

Ito, Tiffany A., and Silvia Tomelleri. "Seeing Is Not Stereotyping: The Functional Independence of Categorization and Stereotype Activation." *Social Cognitive and Affective Neuroscience* 12, no. 5 (2017): 758–64.

James, David E. *Allegories of Cinema: American Film in the Sixties.* Princeton, NJ: Princeton University Press, 1989.

Jastrow, Joseph. *Studies from the Laboratory of Experimental Psychology of the University of Wisconsin, 1889–93.* Madison, WI: 1893.

Jay, Martin. *Downcast Eyes: The Denigration of Vision in Twentieth-Century French Thought.* Berkeley: University of California Press, 1994.

Jordan-Young, Rebecca, and Raffaella I. Rumiati. "Hardwired for Sexism? Approaches to Sex/Gender in Neuroscience." *Neuroethics* 5, no. 3 (2012): 305–15.

Jung, Bernd, ed. *Der "Wille zur Macht": Kein Buch von Friedrich Nietzsche.* Auf Der Grundlage der Digitalen Kritischen Gesamtausgabe. nietzschesource.org, 2009.

Kafka, Franz. *The Metamorphosis, In the Penal Colony, and Other Stories.* New York: Schocken Books, 2000.

Kanwisher, Nancy, and Morris Moscovitch, eds. *The Cognitive Neuroscience of Face Processing: A Special Issue of Cognitive Neuropsychology.* Hove, East Sussex [England]: Psychology Press, 2000.

Kittler, Friedrich A., ed. *Austreibung des Geistes aus den Geisteswissenschaften: Programme des Poststrukturalismus.* Paderborn, Germany: Schöningh, 1980.

———. *Grammophon, Film, Typewriter.* Berlin: Brinkmann und Bose, 1986.

———. *Gramophone, Film, Typewriter.* Translated by Geoffrey Winthrop-Young and Michael Wutz. 1st ed. Stanford, CA: Stanford University Press, 1999.

———. *Optische Medien: Berliner Vorlesung 1999*. Berlin: Merve-Verlag, 2002.

Kittler, Friedrich A., and Ana Ofak, eds. *Medien vor den Medien*. Munich: Wilhelm Fink, 2007.

Klinger, Judith. "Die Modernisierte Ikone. Mittelalter-Mythen und Inszenierungen von 'Weiblichkeit' in Jeanne d'Arc-Filmen." *Zeitschrift Für Germanistik* 13, no. 2 (2003): 263–85.

Knopp, Daniel. *NS-Filmpropaganda:* Wunschbild und Feindbild in Leni Riefenstahls "Triumph des Willens" und Veit Harlans "Jud Süss." Marburg, Germany: Tectum, 2004.

Koch, Gertrud. "Blindness as Insight: Visions of the Unseen in Land of Silence and Darkness." In *The Films of Werner Herzog: Between Mirage and History*, edited by Timothy Corrigan, 73–86. New York: Methuen, 1987.

Kochukhova, Olga, and Gustaf Gredebäck. "Learning about Occlusion: Initial Assumptions and Rapid Adjustments." *Cognition* 105, no. 1 (2007): 26–46.

Kolb, Bryan. *Brain Plasticity and Behavior*. Mahwah, NJ: Lawrence Erlbaum Associates, 1995.

Kornmeier, Jürgen, and Michael Bach. "Ambiguous Figures—What Happens in the Brain When Perception Changes but Not the Stimulus." *Frontiers in Human Neuroscience* 6 (2012): 51.

Kosslyn, Stephen Michael. *Image and Brain: The Resolution of the Imagery Debate*. Cambridge: MIT Press, 1994.

Kourtzi, Zoe, and James J. DiCarlo. "Learning and Neural Plasticity in Visual Object Recognition." *Current Opinion in Neurobiology* 16, no. 2 (2006): 152–58.

Krapp, Peter. *Noise Channels: Glitch and Error in Digital Culture*. Minneapolis: University of Minnesota Press, 2011.

Krauss, Rosalind. "Video: The Aesthetics of Narcissism." *October* 1 (1976): 50–64.

Kret, Mariska, and Beatrice de Gelder. "Social Context Influences Recognition of Bodily Expressions." *Experimental Brain Research* 203, no. 1 (2010): 169–80.

Kristeva, Julia. *Strangers to Ourselves*. European Perspectives Series. New York: Columbia University Press, 1991.

Kubota, Jennifer T., and Tiffany Ito. "Rapid Race Perception Despite Individuation and Accuracy Goals." *Social Neuroscience* 12, no. 4 (2017): 468–78.

Kuenzli, Rudolf E. *Dada and Surrealist Film*. New York: Locker and Owens, 1987.

Kuleshov, Lev Vladimirovich. *Kuleshov on Film: Writings by Lev Kuleshov*. Edited by Ronald Levaco. Berkeley: University of California Press, 1975.

Laham, Simon M., Yoshihisa Kashima, Jennifer Dix, Melissa Wheeler, and Bianca Levis. "Elaborated Contextual Framing Is Necessary for Action-Based Attitude Acquisition." *Cognition and Emotion* 28, no. 6 (2014): 1119–26.

Lambert, Kelly, Amelia J. Eisch, Liisa A. M. Galea, Gerd Kempermann, and Michael Merzenich. "Optimizing Brain Performance: Identifying Mechanisms of Adaptive Neurobiological Plasticity." *Neuroscience & Biobehavioral Reviews* 105 (2019): 60–71.

Langford, Michelle. *Allegorical Images: Tableau, Time, and Gesture in the Cinema of Werner Schroeter*. Lanham, MD: Intellect Books, 2006.

232 · Bibliography

Lappe, C., S. C. Herholz, L. J. Trainor, and C. Pantev. "Cortical Plasticity Induced by Short-Term Unimodal and Multimodal Musical Training." *Journal of Neuroscience* 28, no. 39 (2008): 9632–39.

Leitner, Angelika, and Walter Schobert, eds. *The German Avant-Garde Film of the 1920's*. Munich: Goethe-Institut, 1989.

"Lev Manovich: Soft Cinema." http://manovich.net/index.php/projects/soft-cinema.

Levinas, Emmanuel. "Ethics as First Philosophy." In *The Levinas Reader*, edited by Sean Hand, 75–88. Cambridge, MA: Blackwell Publishers, 1989.

———. *Humanism of the Other*. Edited by Richard A. Cohen. Translated by Nidra Poller. Urbana: University of Illinois Press, 2005.

———. *The Levinas Reader*. Edited by Sean Hand. Cambridge, MA: Blackwell Publishers, 1989.

———. "Prayer without Demand." In *The Levinas Reader*, edited by Sean Hand, 227–34. Cambridge, MA: Blackwell Publishers, 1989.

———. "Signification and Sense." In *Humanism of the Other*, edited by Richard A. Cohen, translated by Nidra Poller, 9–44. Urbana: University of Illinois Press, 2005.

———. *Time and the Other and Additional Essays*. Pittsburgh: Duquesne University Press, 1987.

———. *Totality and Infinity: An Essay on Exteriority*. Translated by Alphonso Lingis. Pittsburgh: Duquesne University Press, 1969.

Lilienfeld, Scott O., Katheryn C. Sauvigné, Steven Jay Lynn, Robin L. Cautin, Robert D. Latzman, and Irwin D. Waldman. "Fifty Psychological and Psychiatric Terms to Avoid: A List of Inaccurate, Misleading, Misused, Ambiguous, and Logically Confused Words and Phrases." *Frontiers in Psychology* 6 (August 3, 2015): 1100.

Linhares, Alexandre, and Daniel M Chada. "What Is the Nature of the Mind's Pattern-Recognition Process?" *New Ideas in Psychology* 31, no. 2 (2013): 108–121.

Loist, Skadi, and Marijke de Valck. "Film Festivals/Film Festival Research: Thematic, Annotated Bibliography." 2nd ed. January 22, 2010. Compiled for the Film Festival Research Network. http://berichte.derwulff.de/0091_08.pdf.

Magliano, Joseph P., and Jeffrey M. Zacks. "The Impact of Continuity Editing in Narrative Film on Event Segmentation." *Cognitive Science* 35, no. 8 (2011): 1489–1517.

Mandal, Manas K., and Avinash Awasthi, eds. *Understanding Facial Expressions in Communication: Cross-Cultural and Multidisciplinary Perspectives*. New Delhi: Springer India, 2015.

Mannes, Stefan. *Antisemitismus im Nationalsozialistischen Propagandafilm*. Vol. 5. Filmwissenschaft. Köln: Teiresias, 1999.

Manovich, Lev. "Database as a Symbolic Form." *Millennium Film Journal* 34 (Fall 1999): 24–43.

Marchiafava, Jeff. "Antichamber—A Lesson in Originality." *Game Informer*. https://www.gameinformer.com/games/antichamber/b/pc/archive/2013/01/31/antichamber-review-a-lesson-in-originality.aspx.

Marshall, Stuart. "Video: Technology and Practice." *Screen* 20, no. 1 (1979): 109–19.

Martin, Carol Lynn, and Diane Ruble. "Children's Search for Gender Cues: Cognitive Perspectives on Gender Development." *Current Directions in Psychological Science* 13, no. 2 (2004): 67–70.

Marx, Karl, and Friedrich Engels. *Marx and Engels on Literature and Art*. Edited by Lee Baxandall and Stefan Morawski. Vol. 1. *Documents on Marxist Aesthetics*. Milwaukee: Telos, 1973.

Mason, Malia F., Jasmin Cloutier, and C. Neil Macrae. "On Construing Others: Category and Stereotype Activation from Facial Cues." *Social Cognition* 24, no. 5 (2006): 540–62.

Mayne, Judith. *Cinema and Spectatorship*. New York: Routledge, 1993.

McCairn, Kevin W., and Robert S. Turner. "Deep Brain Stimulation of the Globus Pallidus Internus in the Parkinsonian Primate: Local Entrainment and Suppression of Low-Frequency Oscillations." *Journal of Neurophysiology* 101, no. 4 (2009): 1941–60.

Men, L., N. Bryan-Kinns, A. S. Hassard, and Z. Ma. "The Impact of Transitions on User Experience in Virtual Reality." In *2017 IEEE Virtual Reality (VR)* (2017): 285–86.

Menkman, Rosa. "Resolution Studies: Beyond Resolution." *Refuse to Let the Syntaxes of (a) History Direct Our Futures*. An Introduction to Resolution/Presentations and Class Materials, *Beyond Resolution*. https://beyondresolution.info/Resolution-Studies.

Merabet, Lotfi B., Joseph F. Rizzo, Amir Amedi, David C. Somers, and Alvaro Pascual-Leone. "What Blindness Can Tell Us about Seeing Again: Merging Neuroplasticity and Neuroprostheses." *Nature Reviews Neuroscience* 6, no. 1 (2005): 71–77.

Mergeay, Joachim, and Luis Santamaria. "Evolution and Biodiversity: The Evolutionary Basis of Biodiversity and Its Potential for Adaptation to Global Change." *Evolutionary Applications* 5, no. 2 (2012): 103–6.

Merleau-Ponty, Maurice. "The Film and the New Psychology." In *Sense and Non-Sense*, translated by Hubert L. Dreyfus and Patricia Allen Dreyfus, 48–59. Evanston, IL: Northwestern University Press, 1964.

———. *The Visible and the Invisible*. Edited by Claude Lefort. Translated by Alphonso Lingis. Evanston, IL: Northwestern University Press, 1968.

Messaris, Paul. *Visual Literacy: Image, Mind, and Reality*. 1st ed. Boulder, CO: Westview Press, 1994.

Metzger, Wolfgang. *Gesetze des Sehens*. Frankfurt am Main: Kramer, 1936.

Miller, Jacques Alain. "Suture: Elements of the Logic of the Signifier." *Screen* 18, no. 4 (1977): 25–26.

Mobbs, Dean, Nikolaus Weiskopf, Hakwan C. Lau, Eric Featherstone, Ray J. Dolan, and Chris D. Frith. "The Kuleshov Effect: The Influence of Contextual Framing on Emotional Attributions." *Social Cognitive and Affective Neuroscience* 1, no. 2 (2006): 95–106.

Moholy-Nagy, László. "Produktion-Reproduktion." *de Stijl* 7, no. 5 (1922): 98–101.

Montag, Christian, Alexander Markowetz, Konrad Blaszkiewicz, Ionut Andone, Bernd Lachmann, Rayna Sariyska, Boris Trendafilov, et al. "Facebook Usage on Smartphones and Gray Matter Volume of the Nucleus Accumbens." *Behavioural Brain Research* 329 (June 2017): 221–28.

234 · Bibliography

Moten, Fred. "There Is No Racism Intended." Lecture presented at the InTransit Lectures, Haus der Kulturen der Welt, Berlin, June 12, 2009.

Mroué, Rabih. "Bilder bis zum Sieg?" ein Interview mit Rahib Mroué. Interview by Katrarina Vladiva Bruch. Goethe Institut, August 2016. https://www.goethe.de/de/kul/tut/gen/tup/20812525.html.

Muckli, Lars, Wolf Singer, Friedhelm E. Zanella, and Rainer Goebel. "Integration of Multiple Motion Vectors over Space: An FMRI Study of Transparent Motion Perception." *NeuroImage* 16, no. 4 (2002): 843–56.

Münsterberg, Hugo. *The Photoplay: A Psychological Study*. New York: D. Appleton, 1916.

Musser, Charles. "The Stereopticon and Cinema: Media Form or Platform?" In *Cine-Dispositives: Essays in Epistemology across Media*, edited by François Albéra and Maria Tortajada, 129–60. Amsterdam: Amsterdam University Press, 2015.

Nagel, Hans-Helmut, and Henrik I. Christensen. *Cognitive Vision Systems: Sampling the Spectrum of Approaches*. New York: Springer, 2006.

Neale, Steve. "The Same Old Story: Stereotypes and Difference." In *The Screen Education Reader: Cinema, Television, Culture*, edited by Manuel Alvarado, Edward Buscombe, and Richard Collins, 41–47. London: Macmillan Education UK, 1993.

Neisser, Ulric. *Cognitive Psychology*. Englewood Cliffs, NJ: Prentice-Hall, 1967.

Nelson, Charles A., and Michelle De Haan. "A Neurobehavioral Approach to the Recognition of Facial Expressions in Infancy." In *The Psychology of Facial Expression*, edited by James A. Russell and José Miguel Fernández-Dols, 176–204. Studies in Emotion and Social Interaction. Cambridge: Cambridge University Press, 1997.

Ni, Rui, Myron L. Braunstein, and George J. Andersen. "Scene Layout from Ground Contact, Occlusion, and Motion Parallax." *Visual Cognition* 15, no. 1 (2007): 48–68.

Nicolas, Gandalf, and Allison L. Skinner. "Constructing Race: How People Categorize Others and Themselves in Racial Terms." In *Handbook of Categorization in Cognitive Science*, edited by Henri Cohen and Claire Lefebvre, 607–36. Oxford, UK: Elsevier Science & Technology, 2017.

Nietzsche, Friedrich. *Nietzsche: The Birth of Tragedy and Other Writings*. Edited by Raymond Geuss and Ronald Speirs. 1st ed. Cambridge: Cambridge University Press, 1999.

Nietzsche, Friedrich, and Peter Sloterdijk. *Die Geburt der Tragödie aus dem Geiste der Musik*. 4th ed. Frankfurt am Main: Insel Verlag, 2000.

Nietzsche, Friedrich Wilhelm. *The Will to Power*. Edited by Walter Arnold Kaufmann. Translated by R. J. Hollingdale. New York: Random House, 1967.

Oever, Annie van den. *Ostrannenie : On "Strangeness" and the Moving Image : The History, Reception, and Relevance of a Concept*. Amsterdam: Amsterdam University Press, 2010.

———, ed. *Techné/Technology: Researching Cinema and Media Technologies, Their Development, Use and Impact*. Amsterdam: Amsterdam University Press, 2014.

Omelchenko, Iryna, Yuri Maistrenko, Philipp Hövel, and Eckehard Schöll. "Loss of Coherence in Dynamical Networks: Spatial Chaos and Chimera States." *Physical Review Letters* 106, no. 23 (2011): 234102.

Omelchenko, Iryna, Oleh E. Omel'chenko, Philipp Hövel, and Eckehard Schöll. "When Nonlocal Coupling between Oscillators Becomes Stronger: Patched Synchrony or Multichimera States." *Physical Review Letters* 110, no. 22 (2013): 224101.

Omelchenko, Iryna, Oleh E Omel'chenko, Anna Zakharova, Matthias Wolfrum, and Eckehard Schöll. "Tweezers for Chimeras in Small Networks." *Physical Review Letters* 116, no. 11 (2016): 114101.

Omelchenko, Iryna, Bruno Riemenschneider, Philipp Hövel, Yuri Maistrenko, and Eckehard Schöll. "Transition from Spatial Coherence to Incoherence in Coupled Chaotic Systems." *Physical Review E* 85, no. 2 (2012): 026212.

Ortel, Philippe, ed. *Discours, Image, Dispositif*. Paris: L'Harmattan, 2008.

Paci, Viva. *La Machine à Voir: À Propos de Cinéma, Attraction, Exhibition*. Arts du Spectacle. Images et Sons. Villeneuve-d'Ascq, France: Presses universitaires du Septentrion, 2012.

Pascual-Leone, Alvaro, Amir Amedi, Felipe Fregni, and Lotfi B. Merabet. "The Plastic Human Brain Cortex." *Annual Review of Neuroscience* 28, no. 1 (2005): 377–401.

Perpich, Diane. "Levinas, Feminism, and Identity Politics." In *Radicalizing Levinas*, edited by Peter Atterton and Matthew Calarco, 21–37. Albany: SUNY Press, 2010.

Persson, Per. *Understanding Cinema: A Psychological Theory of Moving Imagery*. Cambridge: University of Cambridge Press, 2003.

Pessoa, Luiz. *The Cognitive-Emotional Brain: From Interactions to Integration*. Cambridge: MIT Press, 2013.

Petrilli, Susan. "Iconicity in Translation: On Similarity, Alterity, and Dialogism in the Relation among Signs." *American Journal of Semiotics* 24, no. 4 (2008): 237.

Pierson, Ryan. "Embodied Visions: Evolution, Emotion, Culture, and Film by Torben Grodal." *Critical Quarterly* 52, no. 2 (2010): 93.

Phelan, Peggy, Hans-Ulrich Obrist, Elisabeth Bronfen, and Pipilotti Rist. *Pipilotti Rist*. Contemporary Artists. London : Phaidon, 2001.

Plantinga, Carl. "Cognitive Film Theory: An Insider's Appraisal." *Cinémas: Revue d'études Cinématographiques* 12, no. 2 (2002): 15.

Ponzio, Augusto, and Susan Petrilli. "Signification and Alterity in Emmanuel Lévinas." *Semiotica: Journal of the International Association for Semiotic Studies/Revue de l'Association Internationale de Sémiotique* 171, nos. 1–4 (2008): 115.

Prager, Brad. "Beleaguered under the Sea: Wolfgang Petersen's *Das Boot* (1981) as a German Hollywood Film." In *Light Motives: German Popular Film in Perspective*, edited by Randall Halle and Margaret McCarthy, 237–58. Contemporary Film and Television Series. Detroit: Wayne State University Press, 2003.

Prince, Stephen, and Wayne E. Hensley. "The Kuleshov Effect: Recreating the Classic Experiment." *Cinema Journal* 31, no. 2 (1992): 59–75.

"Profile: RTL Group." http://www.rtlgroup.com/en/about_us/the_group/profile.cfm.

Rancière, Jacques. *Film Fables*. Translated by Emiliano Battista. New York: Berg, 2006.

———. *Le Destin des Images*. Paris: La Fabrique Éd., 2005.

———. *Le Partage du Sensible: Esthétique et Politique*. Paris: Fabrique : Diffusion Les Belles Lettres, 2000.

236 · Bibliography

———. *The Future of the Image*. Translated by Gregory Elliott. Reprint. London: Verso, 2009.

Rebentisch, Juliane. *Ästhetik der Installation*. Frankfurt am Main: Suhrkamp Verlag, 2003.

Reich, Elizabeth, and Scott C. Richmond. "Introduction: Cinematic Identifications." *Film Criticism* 39, no. 2 (2014): 3–24.

Rentschler, Eric. *The Ministry of Illusion: Nazi Cinema and Its Afterlife*. Cambridge, MA: Harvard University Press, 1996.

Richter, Hans. *Dada: Art and Anti-Art*. Reprint. New York: Thames & Hudson, 1997.

Robbins, Jill, ed. *Is It Righteous to Be? Interviews with Emmanuel Levinas*. Stanford, CA: Stanford University Press, 2002.

Robé, Chris, Todd Wolfson, and Peter N. Funke. "Rewiring the Apparatus: Screen Theory, Media Activism, and Working-Class Subjectivities." *Rethinking Marxism* 28, no. 1 (2016): 57–72.

Röder, Brigitte, and Frank Rösler. "The Principles of Brain Plasticity." In *Principles of Learning and Memory*, edited by Rainer H. Kluwe, Gerd Lüer, and Frank Rösler, 27–49. Basel: Birkhäuser Basel, 2003.

Rodger, Helen, Luca Vizioli, Xinyi Ouyang, and Roberto Caldara. "Mapping the Development of Facial Expression Recognition." *Developmental Science* 18, no. 6 (2015): 926–39.

Rosen, Philip. *Narrative, Apparatus, Ideology*. New York: Columbia University Press, 1986.

Ruchel-Stockmans, Katarzyna. "The Revolution Will Be Performed: Cameras and Mass Protests in the Perspective of Contemporary Art." *Acta Universitatis Sapientiae, Film and Media Studies* 10, no. 1 (2015): 7–23.

Rugg, Michael D., and Andrew P. Yonelinas. "Human Recognition Memory: A Cognitive Neuroscience Perspective." *Trends in Cognitive Sciences* 7, no. 7 (2003): 313–19.

Sahakyan, Lili, and Colleen M. Kelley. "A Contextual Change Account of the Directed Forgetting Effect." *Journal of Experimental Psychology: Learning, Memory, and Cognition* 28, no. 6 (2002): 1064–72.

Sandford, Stella. *The Metaphysics of Love: Gender and Transcendence in Levinas*. London: Bloomsbury Academic, 2001.

Schneider, Ira, and Beryl Korot, eds. *Video Art: An Anthology*. New York: Harcourt Brace Jovanovich, 1976.

Schrader, Paul. *Transcendental Style in Film: Ozu, Bresson, Dreyer*. Berkeley: University of California Press, 1972.

Schroeter, Werner, and Michel Foucault. "Conversation." In *Werner Schroeter*, edited by Gérard Courant, 39–44. Éditions La Cinémathèque Française et Goethe Institut. Paris: Goethe Institut, 1982.

Schulte-Sasse, Linda. *Entertaining the Third Reich: Illusions of Wholeness in Nazi Cinema*. Post-Contemporary Interventions Series. Durham, NC: Duke University Press, 1996.

Schwan, Stephan, and Sermin Ildirar. "Watching Film for the First Time: How Adult Viewers Interpret Perceptual Discontinuities in Film." *Psychological Science* 21, no. 7 (2010): 970–76.

Schweinitz, Jörg. *Film and Stereotype: A Challenge for Cinema and Theory*. Film and Culture Series. New York: Columbia University Press, 2011.

Seiderer, Ute. *Film Als Psychogramm: Bewußtseinsräume und Vorstellungsbilder in Werner Schroeters Malina (Deutschland, 1991)*. München: Diskurs-Film-Verlag, 1994.

Settele, Christoph, and Cecilia Hausheer, eds. *Found Footage Film*. Lucerne: VIPER/Zuklopverlog, 1992.

Shimamura, Arthur P., ed. *Psychocinematics: Exploring Cognition at the Movies*. Oxford : Oxford University Press, 2013.

Shimamura, Arthur P., Brendan I. Cohn-Sheehy, Brianna L. Pogue, and Thomas A. Shimamura. "How Attention Is Driven by Film Edits: A Multimodal Experience." *Psychology of Aesthetics, Creativity, and the Arts* 9, no. 4 (2015): 417–22.

Sieglohr, Ulrike. "Imaginary Identities in Werner Schroeter's Cinema : An Institutional, Theoretical, and Cultural Investigation." PhD thesis, University of East Anglia, 1994.

Silverman, Kaja. *The Subject of Semiotics*. New York: Oxford University Press, 1984.

Simmel, Georg. "Exkurs Über den Fremden." In *Soziologie: Untersuchungen Über die Formen der Vergesellschaftung*, 509–512. Berlin: Duncker & Humblot, 1908.

———. *Georg Simmel on Individuality and Social Forms*. Edited by Donald N. Levine. New ed. Chicago: University of Chicago Press, 1972.

———. "The Stranger." In *Georg Simmel on Individuality and Social Forms: Selected Writings*, edited by Donald N. Levine, 143–49. Chicago: University of Chicago Press, 1971.

Simons, D. J., and C. F. Chabris. "Gorillas in Our Midst: Sustained Inattentional Blindness for Dynamic Events." *Perception* 28, no. 9 (1999): 1059–74.

Smith, Tim J. "Reviews: 'Moving Viewers: American Film and the Spectator's Experience'; 'Embodie Visions: Evolution, Emotion, Culture and Film.'" *Screen* 51, no. 4 (2010): 433–37.

Smith, Tim J., Daniel Levin, and James E. Cutting. "A Window on Reality: Perceiving Edited Moving Images." *Current Directions in Psychological Science* 21, no. 2 (2012): 107.

Snead, James. *White Screens/Black Images: Hollywood from the Dark Side*. New York: Routledge, 1994.

Spillers, Gregory, and Nash Unsworth. "Are the Costs of Directed Forgetting Due to Failures of Sampling or Recovery? Exploring the Dynamics of Recall in List-Method Directed Forgetting." *Memory & Cognition* 39, no. 3 (April 2011): 403–411.

Stafford, Barbara Maria. *A Field Guide to a New Meta-Field: Bridging the Humanities–Neurosciences Divide*. Chicago: University of Chicago Press, 2011.

———. *Echo Objects: The Cognitive Work of Images*. Chicago: University of Chicago Press, 2007.

Staiger, Janet. *Perverse Spectators: The Practices of Film Reception*. New York: NYU Press, 2000.

Stanley, Jay, and Barry Steinhardt. "Drawing a Blank: Report on Tampa Police Records Reveals Poor Performance of Face-Recognition Technology." An ACLU Special Report. ACLU, January 3, 2002. https://www.aclu.org/report/drawing-blank-report -tampa-police-records-reveals-poor-performance-face-recognition.

238 · Bibliography

Steakley, James D. "Cinema and Censorship in the Weimar Republic: The Case of *Anders als die Andern.*" *Film History* 11, no. 2 (1999): 181–203.

Stewart, Ellen Greene. "Art Therapy and Neuroscience Blend: Working with Patients Who Have Dementia." *Art Therapy* 21, no. 3 (2004): 148–55.

Stiegler, Bernard. *Technics and Time.* Vol. 3. Stanford, CA: Stanford University Press, 2010.

———. *Technics and Time, 2: Disorientation.* Translated by Stephen Barker. Stanford, CA: Stanford University Press, 2008.

———. *Technics and Time, 3: Cinematic Time and the Question of Malaise.* Translated by Stephen Barker. Stanford, CA: Stanford University Press, 2010.

Stolier, Ryan M., and Jonathan B. Freeman. "Neural Pattern Similarity Reveals the Inherent Intersection of Social Categories." *Nature Neuroscience* 19, no. 6 (2016): 795–97.

Strickland, Brent, and Brian J. Scholl. "Visual Perception Involves Event-Type Representations: The Case of Containment versus Occlusion." *Journal of Experimental Psychology: General* 144, no. 3 (2015): 570–80.

Tegel, Susan. *Jew Süss.* New York: Continuum, 2011.

Thomas, Laura A., Michael D. De Bellis, Reiko Graham, and Kevin S. LaBar. "Development of Emotional Facial Recognition in Late Childhood and Adolescence." *Developmental Science* 10, no. 5 (2007): 547–58.

Thompson, Evan. *Mind in Life: Biology, Phenomenology, and the Sciences of Mind.* Cambridge, MA: Belknap Press, 2007.

Thompson, Evan, and Alva Noë. *Vision and Mind : Selected Readings in the Philosophy of Perception.* Cambridge: MIT Press, 2002.

Thut, Gregor, Domenica Veniero, Vincenzo Romei, Carlo Miniussi, Philippe Schyns, and Joachim Gross. "Rhythmic TMS Causes Local Entrainment of Natural Oscillatory Signatures." *Current Biology* 21, no. 14 (2011): 1176–85.

Tikka, Pia. *Enactive Cinema: Simulatorium Eisensteinense.* Helsinki: University of Art and Design, 2008.

Tikka, Pia, Aleksander Väljamäe, Aline W. de Borst, Roberto Pugliese, Niklas Ravaja, Mauri Kaipainen, and Tapio Takala. "Enactive Cinema Paves Way for Understanding Complex Real-Time Social Interaction in Neuroimaging Experiments." *Frontiers in Human Neuroscience* 6, no. 1 (2012).

Tinsobin, Eva. *Das Kino als Apparat: Medientheorie und Medientechnik im Spiegel der Apparatusdebatte.* 1st ed. Boizenburg, Germany: Verlag Werner Hülsbusch, 2007.

Toth, Borbala. "Right-Wing Extremists in Hungary Build Their Own Media. And Businesses. And Popularity." *MediaPowerMonitor*, September 24, 2015. http://mediapower monitor.com/content/right-wing-extremists-hungary-build-their-own-media -and-businesses-and-popularity.

Treuting, Jennifer. "Eye Tracking and the Cinema: A Study of Film Theory and Visual Perception." *SMPTE Motion Imaging Journal* 115 (January 1, 2006): 31–40.

Ullman, Shimon. *High-Level Vision: Object Recognition and Visual Cognition*. Cambridge: MIT Press, 1996.

Underwood, Geoffrey, ed. *Cognitive Processes in Eye Guidance*. Oxford: Oxford University Press, 2005.

Valcke, Jennifer. "Montage in the Arts: A Reassessment." *Avant-Garde Critical Studies* 17, no. 1 (2005): 299–310.

Varela, Francisco J., Evan T. Thompson, and Eleanor Rosch. *The Embodied Mind: Cognitive Science and Human Experience*. Rev. ed. Cambridge: MIT Press, 1992.

Vaughn, Paul Anthony. "Political Repression and Capitalist Globalization: A Theory of a Transnational Repressive Apparatus." PhD diss., Northern Arizona University, 2008.

Vertov, Dziga. *Kino-Eye: The Writings of Dziga Vertov*. Edited by Annette Michelson. Translated by Kevin O'Brien. Berkeley: University of California Press, 1985.

———. *Schriften zum Film*. München: Hanser, Carl GmbH + Co., 1985.

Vincent, Jean-Didier, and Pierre-Marie Lledo. *The Custom-Made Brain: Cerebral Plasticity, Regeneration, and Enhancement*. New York: Columbia University Press, 2014.

Warhol, Andy. *Andy Warhol Photobooth Pictures*. New York: Robert Miller Gallery, 1989.

Weibel, Peter. *Time Slot: Geschichte und Zukunft der Apparativen Wahrnehmung von Phenakistiskop Bis Zum Quantenkino*. Köln: König, 2006.

Weinstein, Valerie. "Dissolving Boundaries: Assimilation and Allosemitism in E. A. Dupont's 'Das Alte Gesetz' (1923) and Veit Harlan's 'Jud Süss' (1940)." *German Quarterly* 78, no. 4 (2005): 496.

Weintraub, Samuel, and Robert J. Cowan, eds. *Vision/Visual Perception*. Newark, NJ: International Reading Association, 1982.

Wertheimer, Max. *Drei Abhandlungen zur Gestalttheorie*. Neuherausgabe. Erlangen: Verl. der Philos. Akademie, 1925.

Wertheimer, Max, and Wolfgang Metzger. *Produktives Denken*. Frankfurt am Main: Kramer, 1957.

Wildgoose, Amanda, Sue Clarke, and Glenn Waller. "Treating Personality Fragmentation and Dissociation in Borderline Personality Disorder: A Pilot Study of the Impact of Cognitive Analytic Therapy." *British Journal of Medical Psychology* 74 (March 2001): 47.

Williams, Roland Leander. *Black Male Frames: African Americans in a Century of Hollywood Cinema, 1903–2003*. 1st ed. Television and Popular Culture Series. Syracuse, NY: Syracuse University Press, 2015.

Wilmer, Henry H., Lauren E. Sherman, and Jason M. Chein. "Smartphones and Cognition: A Review of Research Exploring the Links between Mobile Technology Habits and Cognitive Functioning." *Frontiers in Psychology* 8 (April 25, 2017): 605.

Wimber, Maria, Anne Maaß, Tobias Staudigl, Alan Richardson-Klavehn, and Simon Hanslmayr. "Rapid Memory Reactivation Revealed by Oscillatory Entrainment." *Current Biology* 22, no. 16 (2012): 1482–86.

Wimmer, Heinz, and Josef Perner. "Beliefs about Beliefs: Representation and Constraining Function of Wrong Beliefs in Young Children's Understanding of Deception." *Cognition* 13, no. 1 (1983): 103–128.

Winkler, Hartmut. *Der Filmische Raum und der Zuschauer: "Apparatus," Semantik, "Ideology."* Heidelberg: Carl Winter, 1992.

Wolf, Reva. "Collaboration as Social Exchange: Screen Tests/A Diary by Gerard Malanga and Andy Warhol." *Art Journal* 52, no. 4 (1993): 59–66.

Wollen, Peter. "Cinema and Technology: A Historical Overview." In *The Cinematic Apparatus*, edited by Teresa de Lauretis and Stephen Heath, 14–23. New York: St. Martin's Press, 1980.

Wurtz, Robert H., and Michael E. Goldberg, eds. *The Neurobiology of Saccadic Eye Movements*. Reviews of Oculomotor Research Series, v. 3. Amsterdam: Elsevier, 1989.

Wyeth, Peter. *The Matter of Vision: Affective Neurobiology and Cinema*. New Barnet, Herts, UK: John Libbey Publishing, 2015.

Yacavone, Daniel. "Film and the Phenomenology of Art: Reappraising Merleau-Ponty on Cinema as Form, Medium, and Expression." *New Literary History* 47, no. 1 (2016): 159–85.

Zacks, Jeffrey. *Flicker: Your Brain on Movies*. 1st ed. Oxford: Oxford University Press, 2014.

Zauner, Andrea, Robert Fellinger, Joachim Gross, Simon Hanslmayr, Kimron Shapiro, Walter Gruber, Sebastian Müller, and Wolfgang Klimesch. "Alpha Entrainment Is Responsible for the Attentional Blink Phenomenon." *NeuroImage* 63, no. 2 (2012): 674–86.

Zielinski, Siegfried. *Audiovisionen: Kino und Fernsehen als Zwischenspiele in der Geschichte*. Reinbek bei Hamburg: Rowohlt, 1994.

Zimmer, Alf C. "Gestaltpsychologische Texte—Lektüre für eine aktuelle Psychologie?" *Gestalt Theory* 11, no. 2 (1989): 95–121.

Index

Absolute Film, 116–17, 121, 130, 142

abstraction, 22, 32, 61, 92, 116–19, 125–32, 137, 138, 142, 197; image, 121, 134, 185–88, 195

Abstrakter Film (*Abstract Film*) (Hein 2013), 185–87

actualités, 157

Adorno, Theodor, 23–25, 138

affect, 11, 71, 77, 86, 91, 93, 123, 145, 166. *See also* emotion

Africa, 28–29, 148, 190, 198, 200

Agamben, Giorgio, 72–73, 75, 76

Ahmed, Sara, 62–65

Aimee & Jaguar (Färberböck 1998), 48

Albera, François, 72, 75

aliud, 9, 51, 52

Allen, Jeanne Thomas, 73, 74

Alles wird gut (*Everything will be Fine*) (Maccarone 1998), 36, 47

allosemitism, 43

alterity, 2–3, 8–11, 177; dialectical, 85; diegetic, 35–36, 46–47; dynamic, 25, 40; eros and, 188; intuitive, 10, 202; montage as, 85; politics, 194; proximate, 144, 145, 147, 148, 157, 202; Rancière on, 15–16; visual, 2, 11–12, 15, 18, 20, 24–27, 34–37, 53, 69, 153, 154, 170, 181, 182, 187, 200,

203. *See also* face; Hegel; otherness; radical alterity; subjectivity

Althusser, Louis, 50, 70, 71, 74, 76

ambiguity-disambiguation, 127–28

Anders als die Andern (*Different from the Others*) (Oswald 1919), 161

Anderson, Barbara and Joseph, 68–69

Antichamber (Demruth 2013), 141

anti-Semitism 35, 38, 43, 46, 48, 68, 157, 194, 195; technology, 50; versus allosemitism, 43

apparat, 71, 72

apparatus, 12, 15–16, 79, 83, 148, 206, 207; abjecting, 147–49; Althusserian, 70, 71, 74, 76; apparatuses, 68, 206, 207; cinematic, 94, 100, 161, 175, 207; cognitive science, 83; historical development, 68; of knowledge, 75; media, 149–53; perceptual, 14, 21, 27, 30–32, 62, 64–69, 83, 89, 93, 95, 105, 114, 115, 118, 120, 123, 127, 128, 153, 204, 207; and politics, 76; productive, 66, 69, 71, 75, 76, 77; of sight, 84, 166, 203–4; state, 2, 43, 51, 71, 72, 73, 76, 150, 180, 184, 185, 201; surveillance, 6, 37, 51, 54, 73, 138, 178, 180; technological determinism, 73. *See also* apparatus theory; classic apparatus theory; regime

242 · *Index*

apparatus theory, 69, 75; and cognitive science, 70, 78, 82; revising, 71, 73–77, 82. *See also* classic apparatus theory
appearance, 5, 10–15, 18–20, 27, 37, 41, 44, 46–49, 64, 127, 181; and otherness, 27
apperception, 3, 64
apprehension, 10, 50–51, 64, 69–70, 84, 105, 170
Arcangel, Cory, 135–36
Arnheim, Rudolf, 7
attentiveness, 19, 55, 67, 201, 205
avant-garde, 5, 74, 92, 99, 118, 130; classical, 22, 85, 100, 101, 158; neo-, 133, 138; Soviet, 22, 84, 85, 91; of sight, 2, 12, 61, 68
Azoulai, Shai, 118

Bach, Michael, 127
Baginski, Laura, 137
Balázs, Béla, 7, 154, 158, 171, 174
Banks, Michele, 98
Barbara (Petzold 2013), 37
Barnes-Holmes, Yvonne and Dermot, 96
Bellenbaum, Rainer, 104–7
Benjamin, Walter, 7
Bergson, Henri, 59
Berlin (Classified) (Patry 2016), 105–7
Betancourt, Michael, 130, 136, 137–39
Bewegte Mann, Der (Maybe, Maybe Not) (Wortmann 1994), 34–35
bioculturalism, 78, 81, 83, 88
Birth of a Nation (Griffith 1915), 42–43
BlacKkKlansman (Lee 2018), 36
Black Lives Matter, 73, 77
Blow Job (Warhol 1964), 163, 164, 176
Blue (Jarman 1993), 197
body, 11, 48, 55, 59, 63, 64, 89, 205. *See also* embodiment
Bordwell, David, 7, 33, 69–70, 80, 82
brain, 6, 8, 14, 59, 68, 91, 94, 125, 153, 155, 156, 186, 201; active, 98, 115; 123, 127 ; architecture, 155; cognitive science and, 69, 78–79, 81–82; experience of, 115; entrainment, 119; formative, 14, 19; fragmentation, 110; hardwired, 89, 90, 91; higher and lower functions, 67, 68, 96, 120; memory, 155; plastic, 28, 81, 90, 93, 110, 111; recognition, 155; versus mind, 15, 19, 79, 83
Brakhage, Stan, 101, 111

Bringing up Baby (Hawks 1938), 33–35
Bruni, Pietra, 87–88
Buckland, Warren, 69
bundling, 19, 59, 90, 110–11
Butler, Judith, 172, 192–93, 195

Calder, Andrew, 155, 179
camera, 5, 6, 25, 44, 46, 67, 85, 103–5, 129, 131, 138, 142, 158, 163, 166, 174, 179–80, 197, 204; as apparatus, 70, 73, 75; cellphone, 72, 77, 183–86; cognitive science and, 79, 80; in-camera editing, 92–94; phenomenology and, 56–59; and sight, 59
camera obscura, 14, 32, 56, 115
Campus, Peter, 129
Carroll, Noël, 69–70
Casetti, Francesco, 72
categorization, 14–15, 38, 40, 42, 46, 48, 162, 175, 202; gender; 39; racial, 39, 43, 156; social, 41, 42, 46–47, 165, 203; versus typicality 40–41; visual, 40–41
Cavell, Stanley, 34
change blindness, 67, 81
chimera, 126
chunking, 19, 122–23, 129
cine-cognition, 5–8, 24, 80–82, 85, 91, 97, 136, 204–5
cinema, 3, 4, 8, 11, 17, 19, 22, 23, 30, 41, 49, 53, 64–66, 87, 93, 113, 120, 181; apparatus of, 70, 72–74, 94, 207; avant-garde of sight, 2, 12, 21, 61–62, 68, 85, 116, 204; cognition and, 68–69, 80–82, 158, 201; consciousness and, 6, 8, 22, 24, 96; defamiliarization and, 100–101, 103; expanded, 108, 117, 184, 204; experimental, 116; and the face, 157, 158, 159; frame and, 28–30; Kuleshov effect and, 86–87, 161, 175; montage and, 93–94, 95; narrative, 86, 88, 96, 111, 160; perception and, 21, 42, 62, 91; special case of viewing, 20–21, 60, 95, 119; technology of differentiation, 157, 160, 161, 162, 204; underground, 163–64; Vertov on, 5, 22
cinematography, 62, 154, 158; and language, 61, 158
classic apparatus theory, 50, 66–76, 79, 83, 149, 182, 206. *See also* apparatus theory
cliché, 9

Clouds (Arcangel 2002), 135

coevality, 89, 90

cognitive film studies, 7, 68–69, 77, 88–90, 159–60; and cognitive science, 78–79, 80–82; and embodiment, 89. *See also* bioculturalism

cognitive science, 6, 8, 37–39, 67, 77–78, 80–81; and apparatus theory, 68–69, 77–78; chimera and 126–27; collage, 98–99; efficiency, 39; entrainment and, 119; evolution and, 82; and film history, 79–80; fragmentation, 110–12; history of, 154–55; imagery debates, 14; kinetic depth effect, 118; naming, 96; race and, 156; Soviet avant-garde, 84–85; on stereotyping, 37–39; and storytelling, 94–95, 96–97, 111, 160, 175. *See also* emotions; face; neuroscience

collage, 21, 52; atactic/heterotactic, 101, 102; emotions and, 99–100, 103, 109; de/fragmentation, 103, 109–12; paratactic, 101, 107; versus *Kippbild*, 120; versus montage, 98

Comolli, Jean-Louis, 66, 75

con films, 50–51

Conner, Bruce, 100, 111

consciousness, 2, 14, 19, 22, 56–57, 153; active, 24, 56, 59, 65; always consciousness of something, 54, 55, 57–58, 60; and/of the other, 26, 49, 155, 185; cinematic, 22, 24, 70, 85, 96; in cognitive theory, 38, 77, 78, 83, 110, 119; differentiated, 29–30; efficiency, 39, 41–42; experience of, 3, 55, 120, 123; expository desire, 175; higher level processing, 38, 67, 68, 96, 102; history and, 28, 30; perception and, 3, 7, 11, 12, 30, 55–56, 61, 68, 93, 96, 207; recognition and, 15; self-, 2, 9–10, 28, 38, 47, 50, 97, 182, 205; secondary, 96; technology and, 23–24, 71, 85; unhappy, 188

Cooper, Sarah, 181

Coulais, Jean-François, 21, 31–32, 54

Cowan, Michael, 119

Crichtley, Simon, 181, 187, 189, 199

Crimp, Douglas, 164–65

cueing, 42, 87, 99, 123

Dada, 85, 99, 100, 106, 111, 117, 118, 121

Das Boot (Petersen 1981), 46

datamoshing, 137–39, 142

Davis, Paul, 139

defamiliarization, 17, 19, 61, 62, 100, 103, 136

deformation, 109, 119, 137, 142

defragmentation, 115, 142

Deleuze, Gilles, 4, 59

desire, 47, 157, 161, 167, 170–77, 182, 183, 188–89; same-sex, 83, 161, 174; with/as, 100, 175

detective films, 51

determination, 3, 4, 27, 30, 33, 83, 176, 180, 188, 203–5; cognitive, 90; and differentiation, 28, 30, 40; embodied, 63–64; Hegel on, 26–27, 40; Husserl on, 57; ideological, 74–75; and phenomenology, 55, 57

determinism, 31, 75, 82, 89–90, 123, 156; 172; alterability, 157; genetic, 83; technological, 68, 74–75

dialectic, 27, 84–85

diegetic/extra-diegetic, 16, 33, 35–36, 46–47, 175

difference, 2, 6, 89, 90, 173; and cinema, 31, 66; and determination, 27, 204; differently, 6, 30, 36, 37, 49, 91, 166, 202, 204, 205, 207; essential, 40, 43, 48; history of, 28–30; and narrative, 33–34; and otherness, 188, 202; overcoming of, 194–95; perception and, 153, 154, 165–66; and power, 3; race and, 40–41; recognition of, 51–52, 101, 157, 162, 165, 205; and stereotype, 9; subject formation, 18, 20, 27, 49; technologies of, 67; versus diversity, 203. *See also* difference-to-be-looked-at; differentiation; gender; homosexuality; perception; race; seeing; sight

difference-to-be-looked-at/difference-to-be-seen, 35–36, 46, 47, 48, 160, 161, 204; did you see it coming, 50; homosexuality, 161, 164

differentiation, 2, 10, 11–12, 21, 26–30, 34, 36, 37, 187; anti-Semitism and, 43–44, 46; apparatus of, 6, 166, 203–4, 207; changing, 162, 173, 202, 205; cognition and, 89; community formation (sociation), 109, 143, 144, 180; gender and, 171;

244 · *Index*

differentiation (*continued*): homosexuality and, 161–62; perceiving as, 50, 53, 90, 165, 203–4; refusal of 43; sex-gender, 176; subject formation, 18, 20, 27, 49, 50, 143, 203, 205; technology of, 157, 204, 207; versus difference, 157, 166; viewing as, 52

Digital TV Dinner (Fenton, Zaritsky, and Ainsworth 1979), 136

disambiguatiion, 127–28

discrimination, 2–3, 64, 157, 203–4; stereotyping, 8; technologies of, 6, 207

dispositive (*dispositif*), 69–70, 71–72, 73, 75–76, 77, 206; versus *appareil*, 69

distortion, 108, 109, 126, 128–29, 130–31, 136, 137, 141

distribution of the sensible, 17, 206

dis/union 27

domination, 72–73, 75, 76, 77. *See also* Agamben, Giorgio; power

Dryer, Carl Theodor, 160–61, 162, 169

Dyer, Richard, 41, 161, 163, 164, 165; on typicality and stereotypicality, 42

dynamic core hypothesis (DCH), 110–12

Edelman, Gerald, 110–11

edge recognition, 117–19, 121

effacement, 193, 195, 200. *See also* face; faceless

Eggeling, Viking, 116–18, 130,

Eisenstein, Sergei, 5, 22, 84, 85, 94–96, 101, 103, 119, 158

embodiment, 2, 88, 89, 90, 182 185–86; disembodied, 63, 134

emotion, 6, 7, 28, 47, 65, 82, 123, 131, 162, 169, 171, 174, 187; and collage, 99–100, 103, 109; and face, 24, 87–88, 91, 94, 99, 154–58, 159–60; and montage, 88, 91–92, 93; system, 77, 88–89

empathy, 99, 156, 159, 160–61, 187

entrainment, 119

epistemology/episteme, 4, 5, 11, 23, 26, 72, 75, 206

Escher, M. C., 121, 140, 141

essentialism, 9, 28–29, 36, 40, 43, 48, 155, 176, 189

Eternal Jew, The (*Der ewige Jude*) (Hippler 1940), 46

ethics, 153, 164, 181, 184; and difference, 165; otherness and, 181–82, 184, 187, 200

Europa Europa (*Hilterjunge Salomon*) (Holland 1990), 48

Europe (EU), 29, 46, 68, 134, 182, 193, 194, 198, 199; Eurocentrism, 189–90; and migration, 146, 147, 148, 150, 153

European media apparatus, 150–51

evolution, 68, 78, 159, 201; determinism, 80, 83, 89, 155; diversity, 90; hardwiring, 81, 82, 89; state of nature, 83, 88

expressionist film, 116

eye, 13, 21, 22, 24, 32, 42, 43, 153; absolute film and, 117, 118; being for the eye, 55; and collage, 105, 106; embodied vision, 182, 186; Kino-Eye, 22 85; movement, 93, 186; naked, 20, 84

eye tracking, 77, 78, 81

face, 24, 27–28; cinema and, 157–59; cognitive theory and, 155; and emotions, 24, 87–88, 99, 154–58, 159–60; and evolution, 159; homosexuality, 161–62; neuroscience and, 155; not *for us*, 164; *photogénie*, 16, 158–59; surface and, 163–64; theory of mind and, 159, 174. *See also* effacement; faceless

faceless, 187, 192, 195–96, 200

facial recognition, 64, 155–57, 164, 170–71, 173, 178–79, 194; cybernetic model, 154–55; Levinas and, 192; racialized, 156

Fantasia (1940), 121

Färblein (*Colourette*) (Bellenbaum and Freund 1991), 104–5, 106–7

Farocki, Harun, 52, 111, 197–98

Fez (Polytron 2012), 140

film philosophy, 3–5, 54, 173, 181

filtering, 12, 38, 67, 102, 137, 142

Finkielkraut, Alain, 190–91

Fischinger, Oskar, 92–93, 97, 99, 116–17, 121, 130

Flatley, Jonathan, 164, 166

foreignness, 50, 144

Foucault, Michel, 27, 52, 72, 74–76, 173–76, 206; on passion, 173–74; queer opacity, 174; and Werner Schroeter, 173, 176

found footage, 100, 107, 111

fovea, 64, 67

fragmentation, 103, 109–12, 130 142; and integration, 110, 118, 120, 131; and universalization, 203

Index · 245

frame, 28, 30, 67, 121, 134, 146, 149, 163, 166, 171; and camera, 5; contextual, 87–88, 91, 94; and difference, 48; and fragmentation, 111–12; key, 131, 142; relational, 96

Freund, Bärbel, 104–7

Frick, Laurie, 98

functional magnetic resonance imaging (fMRI), 6, 78, 79, 81, 87, 94–95, 125

Le Gai Savoir (1969), 101–2, 106,

Garden of Earthly Delights, The (Brakhage 1981), 101

Gaudreault, André, 34–35, 72

gay, 34–35, 47, 161, 163–66, 176

gaze, 22, 23, 40, 61, 63, 65, 81, 83, 94, 166, 174, 177, 187; shoegaze, 142; tracking, 120

gender, 3, 28–30, 34–41, 63, 64, 89, 156, 157, 164, 171–73, 176, 188, 189; cognitive and neuroscientific approaches, 37–39; dimorphic, 177; performance, 176

genre, 33, 36, 46, 62, 172; biological basis, 89, 90; patterns, 151; Rancière, 16

Gestalt, 7, 14, 15, 20, 60, 113, 115, 117

glitch, 108, 109, 130, 136–39

globalization, 1, 52, 144–45, 151

Gobet, Fernand, 122

Godard, Jean-Luc, 93, 101–2, 104, 106

Good, the Bad, and the Ugly, The (Leone 1966)

gorilla experiment, 67

Grabowski, Michael, 90

Griffith, David Wark, 42, 94, 158–59

Grodal, Torben, 82, 88, 89, 90, 159–60, 171

Groebner, Valentin, 128

Guattari, Félix, 4

Gunning, Tom, 158

Handbook of Categorization in Cognitive Science, The, 39, 156

hardwired, 8, 14, 31, 156, 159; brain, 89, 90, 91; evolution, 78, 81, 82, 89

Havarie (Scheffner 2016), 196–98

Hegel, Georg Wilhelm Friedrich, 9–10, 26–28, 33, 37, 182; on Africa 28–29, 190; defining of otherness, 26, 143; and determination, 26–27, 40, 57, 91; in error, 30; and Levinas, 185, 188–89; stereotyping and, 40; subjectivity, 27, 49; the third, 50, 51

Heidegger, Martin, 4, 11, 23, 55, 58; being in front of the eyes (*Voraugensein*), 55

Hein, Birgit, 185–87

Henderson, Brian, 109–10

Hensley, Wayne, 86–88

heteronormativity, 26, 33

heterotaxia, 101, 102, 107–9

Hirschfeld, Magnus, 161–63

Histoire(s) du Cinéma (Godard 1998), 102

Holocaust, 46, 192, 193

homosexuality, 47–48, 161; differentiation and, 161–62; otherness and, and, 161, 162

Horkheimer, Max, 23–25

Husserl, Edmund, 4, 65; camera, 56–58, 63; *Einstellung* as shot, 56–57; *epoché*, 57, 58

identification, 71, 162, 171–72, 179

identity, 2, 9–10, 27, 37, 164, 165, 172, 190, 199, 201; and alterity, 27, 41, 201; national, 46; politics, 194

Ihde, Don, 115, 140

image, 6–8, 13, 18–19, 69, 165, 171, 173; abstract, 121, 134, 185, 186, 187, 188, 195; apparatus, 150, 153; as artificial, 14, 21, 111; cinematic, 157, 158, 159; code of, 161, 176, cognitive theory and, 78–79, 81–83, 186; collage and, 99, 100, 101, 102, 103–4, 106; digital, 32, 105, 129, 130, 131, 137; flood of, 150, 184, 185, 186, 187, 197; gender and, 176; material world as, 30, 57, 74–75, 77, 85, 186; montage and, 85–86, 92–95, 175; pixelated, 184, 186, 187, 197; poop and, 107–9; Rancière on 15–16, 18; subjectivity and, 163, 170, 194; theory of mind and, 174; virtual, 32. *See also* face; *Kippbild*; moving

imaginative communities, 2, 75–76

Imitation of Life (Sirk 1959), 35–36

in/coherence, 127–28, 131

information integration theory (IIT), 110–12

integration, 6, 10, 73, 88, 110, 112, 118, 120, 131, 144, 189, 199

intersubject correlation analysis (ISC), 78

interzone, 147

Irigaray, Luce, 189, 199

I Want To See How You See (Rist 2003), 134–35

246 · *Index*

Jarman, Derek, 197, 198
Jastrow, Joseph, 113, 114, 131
Jay, Martin, 33, 54
jonathan swift returns from the dead to eat a cheese sandwich (madanonymous 2010), 108
Jud Süß (*Jew Süss*) (Harlan 1940), 43–46, 50
Just in Time (Winter 1999), 131–32

Kafka, Franz, 59, 76
Kant, Immanuel, 14, 96, 102, 111, 115
Kentridge, William, 111
Kino-Pravda, 5–6, 22
Kippbild, 113–16; absolute film and, 118–19; datamoshing as, 137–39, 142; as moving image, 116; versus collage, 120. *See also* multistable image; Wittgenstein
Kittler, Friedrich, 31, 72, 74
Kluge, Alexander, 102–3
knowledge, 4–5, 10, 11, 21, 22, 50, 54, 63, 74–75, 80, 88, 110, 144–45, 159, 174, 182, 202, 204; anti-Semitism and, 43, 46, 48; photoknowledge, 6, 8; technology and, 6, 81, 84
Kornmeier, Jürgen, 127
Krapp, Peter, 129
Kratky, Andreas, 103
Kraus, Werner 43, 44
Kristeva, Julia, 10
Kuenzli, Rudolf, 100
Kuleshov, Lev, 84, 91, 94–95, 96, 161
Kuleshov effect, 86–88, 91, 96, 161, 171, 175; about narrative, 94–95

Lacan, Jacques, 3, 50, 71, 77
László, Petra, 149–50, 152, 153
Lefebvre, Martin, 72
lesbian, 36, 47, 164, 176
Levinas, Emmanuel, 4, 10, 164; racism and, 189–90, 195. *See also* Black Lives Matter
linguistics of heterosexuality, 176
looking, 23, 55, 70, 83, 139, 166; history of, 31; theory as, 4; voyeuristic, 164

Mahn, Owi, 137
Manovich, Lev, 103
Mat (*Mother*) (Pudovkin 1926), 92
Mekas, Jonas, 93, 100, 111
Melhus, Bjørn, 131
melodrama, 94, 160, 170, 173

memory, 6, 7, 81, 92, 95, 96, 119, 120, 132, 155; cognitive mechanisms, 64, 81, 94, 122–23; and emotion, 65, 155; and recognition, 126, 132
Menkman, Rosa, 138–40
Mensch im Ding, Der (*The Person in the Thing*) (Tykwer 2008), 103
Merleau-Ponty, Maurice, 4, 13, 60–62, 63, 65; on film, 60–61; sight as seeing something, 60, 62
Metz, Christian, 71, 72
mind, 5–6, 8, 14; formative, 14, 19, 28, 128; neurocinematics and, 78–79; versus brain, 15, 19, 79
mirror, 12, 13, 23, 64, 67, 154, 194
mirroring, 78, 81, 154, 159, 160, 164
mirror neurons, 78, 81, 159
Mission to Earth (Kratky and Manovich 2005), 103–4
Mobbs, Dean, 87–88, 94
Moholy-Nagy, László, 22
monstration, 34–35, 37
montage, 21; emotions and, 88, 91–92, 93, 131; narration and, 86, 87, 94–96, 98, 101, 102, 110, 116, 123, 142, 175; Soviet, 84
Montezuma, Magdalena, 171, 176
Monument Valley (Ustwo 2014), 141
More Sweetly Play the Dance (Kentridge, 2015), 111
Moten, Fred, 190, 199
Mothlight (1963), 101
moving image, 3–8, 12, 13, 16, 18, 24, 31, 34, 53, 61–64, 95, 99, 103, 106, 109–13, 158, 183, 197, 201, 204; apparatus and, 70, 71, 72, 75, 77; cognitive theory and, 67–69, 78, 79, 82–85, 119, 120, 127, 159; face and, 160–62, 167; *Kippbild*, 116–18, 130, 131, 136
Mroué, Rabih, 182–85, 187
multistability, 113, 115, 116, 120, 127, 129, 140; datamoshing as, 137–39, 142; in music, 114; in virtual reality, 141
Mulvey, Laura 35, 70, 71, 164
München-Berlin Wanderung (*Walking from Munich to Berlin*) (Fischinger, 1927), 92, 99
Münsterberg, Hugo, 6–7, 84
Museum of Simulation Technology (Pillow Castle Games 2013–15), 141
Musser, Charles, 74, 76
Muybridge, Eadweard, 84

My Hustler (Warhol 1967), 165–66

Nachrichten aus der ideologischen Antike—Marx/Eisenstein/Das Kapital (*News from Ideological Antiquity—Marx/Eisenstein/Capital*) (Kluge 2008), 103

narrative, 7, 11, 22, 25, 30–33, 62, 80, 103–4, 107, 109, 170, 206; absolute film and, 117–19; and cognition, 94; cognitive propensity, 94–95, 96–97, 111, 160, 175; collage and, 101–2, 109; Dada and, 100–102; and differentiation, 30–31, 50–51; face and, 159, 160; and film, 33, 52, 53, 80, 86, 88, 93, 96, 99, 100, 111, 116, 160, 199; icon and, 170–71, 175; *Kippbild* and, 122, 123, 128, 132; and montage, 86, 87, 94–95, 98, 101, 102, 110, 116, 142, 175

nation (nationalism), 1, 2, 7, 35, 46, 147, 152, 153, 201; markets, 150. *See also* transnationalism

Necker cube, 115, 140. See also *Kippbild*; multistability; optical illusion

Neisser, Ulric, 7, 178

neurocinematics, 78–80

neurons, 78, 81, 128, 159; bundling, 110–11. *See also* mirror neurons

neuroscience, 6, 8, 19, 67; critique of cognitive science, 155; facial recognition, 155, 159, 179–80; fragmentation, 110–12; imagery debates, 14; on *Kippbild*, 115, 125, 126; on stereotyping, 37–39; Soviet avant-garde, 84–85

New American Cinema, 100, 111

New Seeing, 20–21, 22, 129, 142, 201; FiFo (Film and Photo 1929), 22

Ni, Rui, 120

Nicht der Homosexuelle ist pervers sonder die Situation in der er lebt (*It Is Not the Homosexual Who is Perverse, But the Society in Which He Lives*) (von Praunheim 1971), 47, 166

Nicht löschbares Feuer (*Inextinguishable Fire*) (Farocki 1969), 197

Nietzsche, Friedrich, 4, 11, 13, 15, 24, 68, 205; *The Birth of Tragedy*, 56

normativity, 26, 63, 89–90, 157, 172, 205; gender, 173; heteronormativity, 34–36; homonormativity, 165

occlusion, 15, 117, 120, 140, 142,

Oever, Annie van den, 72

Omelchenko, Iryna, 126–27, 128

opacity, 174. *See also* theory of mind

optical Illusion, 78, 101, 113–14, 120, 121, 140–41

optics, 32

ostranenie, 19, 62; Viktor Shklovsky, 17

otherness, 27–28, 50, 91, 101, 143, 170, 199; being-for-the, 188; cinema and, 161, 204; essential, 43, 176; ethics and, 181–82, 184, 187, 200; face and, 154–55, 156, 164, 166, 171, 180–82, 187, 195; film and, 85, 86, 96; gendered, 29, 188–89; group formation (sociation), 40, 46, 143, 147; Hegel and, 26, 28, 33, 37, 50, 143, 185; homosexuality and, 161, 162; interiority of, 159, 174, 191; and knowledge, 144–45, 148, 182, 183, 200–201; narration and, 34; perception and, 68; other others, 91, 143, 202; power and, 36; racialized, 29, 39, 156, 190; seeing, 30, 35, 37, 41, 43, 67, 166; self and, 37–41, 67, 177, 185, 194, 201–3, 205, 207; static, 43; technology of, 149. *See also* third, the

Paik, Nam Jun, 129

Palestinians, 190–91, 192–93

parataxis (visual), 100–101, 107

Paris, Texas (1984), 21

Parrhasius of Ephesus, 18–19

Passion de Jeanne d'Arc, La (*The Passion of Joan of Arc*), 160–61, 162, 169

Pastell Kompressor (Mahn and Baginski 2003), 137

Patry, Julien, 105, 107

perception, 2, 11, 14–15, 20, 22, 55, 58, 62, 67, 82, 83, 93, 102, 153; apparatus of, 153, 207; cinema and, 61–62, 116–17, 118; cognitive theory and, 90–91, 118, 120, 154, 155; dissonance, 140; dynamic, 93, 94, 96, 97, 173, 183, 186, 205; embodied, 89, 90; face and, 159; and film, 88; gender normative, 173; Gestalt and, 113, 115; as the history of thinking perception, 32; Husserl on, 56; *Kippbild* and, 114, 115, 116; Nietzsche on, 56; of difference, 165–66, 203–4; perfection of, 22; racialized, 156; reversals, 127; sight as special form, 57–59, 182; threshold, 68; as translation, 15, 56; VR and, 141

248 · *Index*

Perpich, Diane, 194
perspective, 2, 11, 90, 115, 118; monocular, 206; multistability and, 132, 133, 140, 141; Renaissance, 118; subjectivity and, 177
Persson, Per, 69
phenomenal world, 14–15, 55, 57, 61, 181; versus cinematic 62
phenomenology, 3, 31–32, 54–56, 115, 182; and natural seeing, 13, 32, 61, 64
Pixelated Revolution, The (Mroué 2012), 183–85
Plantinga, Carl, 78, 80
Portal (Valve Corporation 2007), 140
power, 27, 30, 49, 66, 72–73, 77. *See also* Agamben, Giorgio; domination
priming, 19, 38, 88, 102
priming mechanisms, 19, 38, 96
Praunheim, Rosa von, 47, 166
Prince, Stephen, 86–88
production and reproduction, 16–18, 22, 23, 31, 32, 37, 40, 41, 52, 64, 103, 131, 144–45; apparatus and, 66, 69, 71, 75, 76, 77
Projections: The Journals for Movies and Mind, 69, 70
prospettiva artificiale, 13, 17, 18, 140
prospettiva naturalis, 13, 17, 140
psyche, 73, 77–79, 83, 119
psychoanalysis, 7, 77, 83; Freudian, 11, 70, 71, 189; Lacanian, 3, 50, 71, 77

queer, 161, 165, 172; opacity, 174–76; visual language, 174

race, 8, 28–29, 34–36, 40, 63, 89, 157, 189–90, 195; cognitive and neuroscientific approaches, 37–39, 156; film studies approaches, 39–41
radical alterity, 10, 20, 101, 173, 187, 193–94, 200, 201, 202. *See also* alterity
Radio Television Luxembourg (RTL), 149, 150–53
Rancière, Jacques, 5, 15, 18, 20, 33; the alterity of images; 15–16; the imageness of the image, 31
realism, 7, 16, 74, 115, 160, 186, 204
reality, 13, 14, 16, 73; cognitive construction of, 115; and cyberspace, 140; radical,

19–20; simple, 17–19, 20, 30; virtual, 73, 140, 141–42
recognition, 10, 12, 15, 22, 27–28, 30, 37, 117, 141, 153, 158; of difference, 48, 161–62, 177, 181, 182, 202, 203, 205; edge, 117–19, 121; experiencing, 19, 111, 113, 116, 141, 207; facial, 64, 155–57, 164, 170–71, 173, 178–79, 192; and memory, 123; nonrecognition, 116, 120, 125–37, 186; priming mechanisms, 38; stable, 115; technologies of, 206
regime, 14, 16–20, 25, 39, 153, 206
repetition, 9–10; dynamic, 202; Warhol and, 165
representation, 4, 20, 32–35, 39, 66, 75, 117, 137, 138, 164, 184, 205, 206; codes of, 153, 157, 163, 172; mimetic, 18, 73, 204; society and, 66; stereotypical, 39–40, 41–43
reproduction, 7, 9, 21, 22, 32, 37, 76–77, 83, 100, 121–22, 144–45, 151
retina, 56, 59, 64, 69
Rhythmus 21 (Rhythm 21) (Richter 1921), 117, 120
Rhythmus 23 (Rhythm 23) (Richter 1923), 117
Richter, Hans, 22, 99, 116–21, 130
Richter, Stephan, 149, 153
Rist, Pipilotti, 131, 132–34, 137
Riva, Manuela, 171, 176
romantic comedies, 33–34
Ruchel-Stockmans, Katarzyna, 184–85
Ruttmann, Walter, 116–17, 121

Sabra and Shatila, 190–91, 192–93
saccades, 64, 65, 93, 186
scanning, 19, 93, 96
Scheffner, Philip, 196–99
Scholl, Brian, 120
Schroeter, Werner, 168, 182, and *Gestus* 168; and Foucault, 173; and opera, 168–69
"Screen Tests" (Warhol 1964–6), 163–64, 166, 172, 174
seeing, 11–15, 65, 114, 165, 201, 203–4; any thing other, 24; apparatus of, 65; dynamic, 96, 153; *idein,* 54; natural, 12, 13, 57, 60, 62–65, 67, 114, 134; the other, 182; phenomenologically, 115; the new seeing, 20–21, 129, 142, 201; of something 11, 13–14, 61, 62, 67, 89; technologies

of, 153; ways of, 21, 84, 207. *See also* differentiation
self/other, 9–11, 26–28, 37, 50, 143, 144, 154, 155, 197, 205, 207; complexity of, 177, 202–3; racism and, 40; static, 40–41
semiotics 7, 102, 177; film studies, 69, 80
Shklovsky, Viktor, 17
sight, 7, 8, 10, 11, 21–22, 23, 31; active, 59–60; apparatus of, 11–12, 59, 65, 68, 84, 114, 129, 203, 204; camera, 59; natural, 13, 64, 67; and perception, 57–59; as seeing something, 60, 62, 64; technologies of, 68, 129, 205; thinking sight, 32, 54–56
signification, 11, 15–16, 20; non-signifying presence, 19–20
Simmel, Georg, 41, 50, 119
situational awareness, 19, 81; change blindness, 67, 81
Situationist International. 100, 108
Sleep (Warhol 1963), 163
Sobchack, Vivian, 60, 65
social categorization, 38, 39, 41, 42, 46–47
social relations, 25, 31, 41, 50, 66, 74, 75, 76, 77; bodies and, 63; configuration, 66; seeing in, 54
societies of alterity, 180
Society for Cognitive Studies of the Moving Image, 69
spectacle, 76
spectator, 4, 7, 15–17, 18, 19, 49; and apparatus theory, 72; and awareness, 22; cognitive film studies, 77, 79, 82; Lacanian, 50; object relations, 71; and position, 4
Stafford, Barbara, 98
stereopticon, 76
stereoscopy, 9, 37, 117–18
stereotyping, 8–9, 37–39, 47; film studies approaches, 39–41; Georg Simmel on, 41; priming mechanisms, 38; Richard Dyer on, 41; Stephen Neale on, 40
Stiegler, Bernard, 23–25, 31
Strickland, Brent, 120
structural/material film movement, 100, 111, 186
subjectivity, 8, 9–11, 19–20, 27, 57, 70; and differentiation, 29, 49; and power, 76–77; subjectivization versus subjugation, 77

sublimation, 63, 161
sublime, 21, 102, 111, 115, 125, 161, 202
Sudden Wealth of the Poor People of Krombach,The (*Der plötzliche Reichtum der armen Leute von Krombach*) (Schlöndorff 1971), 51
Super 8, 108, 138
superimposition, 104, 121, 123, 124–25, 128, 132
SuperYoshi, 108
Surrealism, 85, 100, 111, 141,
surveillance, 6, 37, 51, 54, 73, 138
Suture (McGehee and Siegel, 1993), 48
suture, 21, 50–51, 65, 123
Symphonie Diagonal (*Diagonal Symphony*) (Eggeling 1924) 117

techne, 2, 11, 23, 35, 73, 75, 82, 113, 129, 144, 180, 204, 205; metavision, 8; power and, 76–77
technological determinism, 73–74
technology, 2, 12, 41, 65, 103, 149, 179, 207; apparatus theory and, 73; cinema, 23, 62, 65, 66, 157, 160, 161, 162; cognitive theory and, 77–79, 91; and consciousness, 24; of difference, 160, 161, 166, 204, 207; formatted technologies of representation, 205; as frame, 5–6; innovation, 103, 130, 138–39, 207; and knowledge (see also *techne*), 74, 75, 129; popularization, 135–36; repurposed, 138, 184; of sight, 7, 21, 22–23, 67, 129, 153, 204; visual, 23, 42–43, 53, 62, 64, 102, 129, 138, 142, 163, 178, 180, 184. *See also* facial recognition; surveillance
Television without Frontiers (TVWF), 150
theater, 4, 11, 12, 55, 56, 62, 65, 168
theorein, 4, 55, 56
theory of mind, 159, 174; versus surface, 163–64. *See also* face; opacity
third, the, 26, 27, 48, 49, 50, 51–52
Thomas, Mickalene, 2
Tikka, Pia, 78
Tinsobin, Eva 72
Tod der Maria Malibran, Der (*The Death of Maria Malibran*) (Schroeter 1971), 167–68, 169–73, 174, 176
Toms, Coons, Mulattoes, Mammies, and Bucks, 39

250 · *Index*

Tortajada, Maria, 72, 76
T,O,U,C,H,I,N,G (Sharits 1968), 121
Transformation Scenario (Wedemeyer 2018), 49
transnationalism, 1, 144–45, 151, 153; transnational repressive apparatus, 71
Twitty, Conway, 2
Tykwer, Tom, 103
typification, 8, 41–42

underground, 100, 163–64, 166
universalism, 2, 29, 203; of consciousness, 30, 50, 185; difference as, 27–28; Husserl and, 57–58; Irigary on, 189; Levinas on, 188, 191; Merleau-Ponty and, 61, 63
Unsettled Work/Eine unerledigte Arbeit (Fischli and Weiss 2000–2006), 125–26, 128
Untitled (Flowers) and *Untitled (Mushrooms)* (Fischli and Weiss 1998) 125–26
Urbandale (Arcangel 2001), 135

Verfremdung, 19; Bertolt Brecht, 17
Vergleich über ein Drittes (Comparisons via a Third) (Farocki 2007), 52
Vertov, Dziga, 2, 5–6, 22, 24, 84, 85, 101, 104, 158,
video, 18, 78, 102, 107–9, 121, 129–31, 133, 134, 137–39, 152, 179, 180; cell phone, 183–86; video in video (ViV) 108. *See also* YouTube
video game, 107, 135, 136, 138, 140
viewer, 18, 27, 36, 42, 43, 46–49, 51, 52, 109, 174, 175, 186; in cognitive film studies, 69, 70, 78, 79, 81, 82, 159, 160; of collage, 102; experience of viewing, 113, 115, 122, 125, 137 ; formatting and, 151; freedom of viewing, 102, 109; in phenomenology, 62; virtual reality, 141, 142
Visible World/Sichtbare Welt (Fischli and Weiss 1997), 121–22, 123–25

vision, 1, 31, 63–64; monocular, 64, 206; ocular, 31, 33, 54, 60–64, 166, 181; outside of history, 33; persistence of, 69
visual field, 30, 41, 203
visual intelligence, 8, 15, 98, 99, 112, 115, 153,
visual language, 100, 102, 117, 158, 159, 173; queer, 174
Vormittagsspuk (Ghosts before Breakfast) (1928), 99
Vostell, Wolf, 129

Warhol, Andy, 100, 129, 130, 162–66, 169, 171, 172, 175–77, 182
ways of knowing, 3, 11, 12, 21, 22–23, 140, 204
ways of seeing, 3–6, 12, 19, 21, 22, 41, 81, 84, 162, 204
Weibel, Peter, 72
West, Kanye, 140
will, 11, 55, 56, 59, 182
Willow Springs (Schroeter 1973), 173
Winter, Kirsten, 131–32, 134, 137
Witness, The (Thekla 2016), 141
Wittgenstein, Ludwig, 114–15
Women on the Edge of a Nervous Breakdown (Almodóvar 1988), 34–35
Wyeth, Peter, 160

xenophobia, 1, 144–45

Young, Andrew, 155, 179
YouTube, 107, 108, 131, 135, 152, 162, 179, 180, 196, 197; and Arab Spring, 183–84
YouTube Poop (YTP), 108–9, 135, 136, 139, 140; heterotactic, 109

Zacks, Jeffrey, 8
Zeuxis of Hereclea, 18–19
Zielinski, Siegfried, 72

RANDALL HALLE is the Director of the Film and Media Studies Program and the Klaus W. Jonas Professor of German Film and Cultural Studies at the University of Pittsburgh. His books include *The Europeanization of Cinema: Interzones and Imaginative Communities* and *Queer Social Philosophy: Critical Readings from Kant to Adorno*.

The University of Illinois Press
is a founding member of the
Association of University Presses.

University of Illinois Press
1325 South Oak Street
Champaign, IL 61820-6903
www.press.uillinois.edu

Printed by Printforce, United Kingdom